"The great message ... ... is take responsibility for your life, tell the truth, turn in your library books on time, respect your country, respect your parents, respect those who have gone on before you, don't whine, don't carp, don't cavil. To me, those are good checkpoints to live by. I see Limbaugh as the kind of guy who stands out there and rings the fire bell in the night. He rings that bell vey loudly. And I think there's good reason to ring it."

—Phil Gioia, San Francisco, California

"I think Rush has received a bad rap from women . . . As a woman, I don't find him offensive. I am an intelligent human being and Rush talks to me like an intelligent human being."

—Joyce Adams, Bellaire, Florida

"I don't agree with everything Limbaugh says, but I think he's right most of the time. He makes conservatives feel good about themselves. No one else is voicing these opinions on the radio every day and saying so many things that people agree with. That's why people are so attracted to him . . . It's good for America—whether you're liberal or conservative—because he opens up discussion and debate."

—Kurt Busboom, Lafayette, California

RUSH
TO US

D. HOWARD KING AND
GEOFFREY MORRIS

PINNACLE BOOKS
WINDSOR PUBLISHING CORP.

PINNACLE BOOKS are published by

Windsor Publishing Corp.
850 Third Avenue
New York, NY 10022

First Printing: September, 1994

Printed in the United States of America

Acknowledgments

The authors would like to thank the many people who helped out on the book, especially Jessica King, who worked tirelessly, except the day she took off to have her baby, Hazel. Also, for their contributions: Walter Abbott, George Anhang, Thomas Auth, Norris Carden, Bonnie Cobb, Paul Dinas, Rich Lowry, Deroy Murdock, Teenage Republicans, Scott Waxman, and Bob and Pat Worn. Special thanks to Dan Quayle and Charlton Heston for their insightful contributions.

TABLE OF CONTENTS

Foreword

Americans Answer the Call

by Dan Quayle

I will never forget my first real experience with Rush Limbaugh's fans. In the fall of 1992, I made a campaign stop in Cape Girardeau, Missouri—Rush's hometown. I had prepared a rather simple bipartisan speech for what I thought would be a typical Midwestern bipartisan audience. I soon learned otherwise, and in hindsight, given Rush's powerful influence there, I should have known better. When I said, "Well, I'm not here to give a partisan speech," the crowd loudly showed their disapproval. I quickly changed gears, threw aside my speech, and served up some feisty conservative partisanship. They were strong in number, focused in their conviction, and unanimous in their approval.

In *Rush to Us,* Americans of all kinds, from every state in the nation, go on record. They speak out about the man who speaks out for them. Rush Limbaugh promotes the values passed down by their parents and grandparents. The common refrain heard over and over here is, "He says what I have always thought." The ways in which he has touched America, as told here by hundreds of his listeners, are truly astounding.

To take a close look at Rush Hudson Limbaugh and his twenty million fans is to have one's hope in America's future restored. The Limbaugh phenomenon has achieved what Republican politicians have been trying to accomplish for years. He has motivated and mobilized the American people to work toward their own futures and not let government control their lives and their destinies.

It is no coincidence that as the Republican leadership has grown more timid, Rush Limbaugh has grown more popular. Doubtless, the breadth of his reach is owed in part to the era of technology in which we live. We hear a lot of talk about global town halls and the "Information Super Highway" from today's leaders. But the one who has brought these closest to reality is not a politician. More than any other media figure, Rush Limbaugh has harnessed modern communication to become the day's moderator for the American conversation. He is helping mainstream Americans rediscover and reaffirm the traditional principles they share, to celebrate them and to ensure that they survive as the backbone of our culture.

We can also thank him for restoring something that had been missing from our political culture—a sense of humor. In the summer of 1992, Rush invited me on his show. I am one of the few ever to have that pleasure. He was gracious, engaging, and extremely funny. I will always remember the enormous response George Bush and I received from that appearance. By encouraging a steady dialogue with Congress and the White House, he ensures that the voices of all Americans are heard. With his can-do attitude, he restores our sense of determination.

Rush Limbaugh's success has been a classic American tale of hard work, second chances, a certain genius, and a gratitude to the country that gave him his opportunity. No government programs have caused so many Americans to tune in and talk back—by phone and by mail, on computer terminals and person-to-person. Unlike the staged town-hall meetings run by current politicians, Rush is spontaneous. He has helped families talk about important moral and ethical issues, to rise above generation gaps and celebrate all that is so good and right in America.

But the most telling measure of his success is the extent to which the liberal media have discounted him—like the newspapers that ignored his books until they reached the top of their own best-seller lists. He is a man who cannot be ignored. His success is so far-reaching at this point that it has taken on a life of its own—and that life force is his fans. I am proud to consider myself a part of this group.

Here are hundreds of stories—many new to Limbaugh himself—on the rejuvenation and excitement inspired by the commentator's message. Like me, you may be thrilled when you read about the two hundred members of the Rush Limbaugh Supper Club in Shreveport, Louisiana, who meet each month for Cajun cooking and conservative talk. These folks gather to discuss the crime bill Limbaugh spoke about that week or the way he explained the Clintons' troubles in the White House. They also converse about their lives, their kids and grandchildren, their joys and tribulations.

And how about the College Republicans at West Virginia's Marshall University? Inspired by Limbaugh, they started their own newspaper as a challenge to their campus's liberal orthodoxy. In South Bend, Indiana—not far from where I grew up—a pizza-delivery man takes his own political poll, hits the library for some serious research, and becomes one of the area's top-rated radio talk-show hosts. Who else could have inspired him but Rush Limbaugh?

Limbaugh has struck a common chord in all regions of the country. From upstate New York, we hear of Sue Hollar, an audiologist and mother of two, and of Stu Buchalter, the owner of a bagel bakery. They successfully fight to put Limbaugh's television show on the air in their community. In Lafayette, California, Kurt Busboom battles his high-school administration for the right of his Rush Limbaugh Club to meet on campus. In my home state, the Burggraf family turns a biker bar into a family restaurant that serves as a community gathering place. It also has a Rush Room, where Limbaugh himself has stopped for a slice of prime rib and where neighbors gather to watch him each night on television.

Reading these accounts, you can see why I say in my book, *Standing Firm,* that Rush Limbaugh is the most influential conservative in America. He is also among the most courageous and indisputably the most entertaining. You will be inspired by the many sincere efforts to bolster America's traditional values that are recounted in *Rush to Us.* I read them with admiration. I am greatly encouraged that in 1996, the conservative voice will be heard loud and clear, not in millions of individual cries— but in one united chorus.

Introduction

Words Mean Things

The first time I heard Rush, I was varnishing my sailboat. It was a beautiful day, and I was wearing a Walkman. I was tuning around, and I heard this guy doing a commentary. The first word that I heard was 'Femi-Nazi.' I couldn't believe it. It was a word that went right to the inner lobe of my brain.
—Phil Gioia, San Francisco, California

In terms of memorable moments, it might not rank up there with the day that John F. Kennedy was assassinated or the day that astronaut Neil Armstrong took man's first walk on the moon. . . . But then again, it might. For many fans, the first time they heard Rush Limbaugh is a moment locked in their minds for life. Limbaugh spoke to them in the way that great literature does. He put things they had always thought and accepted as truth into plain and simple English. He provided honest, positive and convincing arguments for these beliefs.

Or he made them mad, sometimes really mad.

But that was okay. When Limbaugh hit the national airwaves in the summer of 1988, he asked listeners to do him just one favor—give him a chance. It might take a few weeks or a couple of months to understand where he was coming from, but if he could just keep you listening, he was sure that his reasoning—and sense of humor—would prevail.

For most people, it didn't take long. A ritual quickly evolved on *The Rush Limbaugh Show.* In order to save time, callers refrained from heaping lengthy praise on the commentator. Instead, they followed the example of a woman in Lancaster, Pennsylvania, who simply said, "Ditto what the last guy said."

Limbaugh's devout fans began to refer to themselves as "Dittoheads."

With his motto "Words mean things," Limbaugh challenged and continues to challenge listeners to think about what they value in life and to stand up for that. And if you say you feel one way about a subject, your actions and your reasoning better be consistent with that pronouncement. Remember, words mean things.

Reared in a traditional Missouri family, Limbaugh's solutions to problems call for such old-fashioned concepts as hard work, responsibility, abstinence, sacrifice, respect, and duty. And the people who listen to, read, and watch Limbaugh—Dittoheads—believe in these things, too. It's a message that cuts across race, sex, religion, age—and often even political party lines. Grandparents and grandkids are listening to the same station for the first time. In *Rush to Us,* they speak out about Limbaugh and their common beliefs.

Richard Hood, a Louisiana college professor, first heard about Limbaugh from a friend. "A couple days later I listened," says Hood. "Rush is right when he says you have to listen for a while because you might tune in in the middle of something and think, 'My goodness, who is this guy and what is he doing?' But the thing that impressed me was his graciousness to a caller. He treats callers with respect. In the South we have an expression, 'He comes from good stock.' Rush loves his mother, he loved his dad. He talks about his grandfather. That means something to me. I love my parents. I love what they taught me. I love what they stood for. I respect Rush for having that kind of sensitivity."

"At first I was just amused by him, but the more I listened, the more he made sense," says Paul Westphal, coach of the NBA's Phoenix Suns. "He never pushes his point beyond what he can defend. That's an outstanding quality. He has many messages that America needs, but one of his best is for people to stop blaming others for their troubles and to roll up their sleeves and get to work."

"When Charles Barkley came here," recalls Westphal, "people said, 'How's this guy going to make it in a conservative state like Arizona?' I said, 'The guy's pursued success relentlessly by hard work and enjoying himself along the way. He didn't make it by handouts and kissing anybody's butt. He'll be the most popular guy in the state.' I used Rush's thought process to explain why he would be wildly well received here, and he was."

"I think most people in our country are satisfied with just doing whatever they're doing," Barkley later tells *The Limbaugh Letter.* "I don't think they really want to be the best. I never want to take my God-given talent for granted. . . . To me, if you're going to do something, you might as well do it 110 percent. . . . You know what? I really appreciate some of the things you say," he tells Limbaugh. "And I'm going to be watching and listening. So you keep up the good work."

"Charles gets a kick out of Rush," says Westphal. "Several of the guys have read his books. Lionel Hollins, an assistant coach, and a stewardess on our charter plane subscribe to *The Limbaugh Letter,* and it gets passed around on flights. Joe Klein and Danny Ainge like Rush a lot. Kevin Johnson's on the fence—he went to Berkeley—but he can't really argue with too much of Rush's stuff. Besides, we're the official team of EIB." EIB stands for Excellence in Broadcasting, Limbaugh's national network.

With his ebullient *joie de vivre*—something many conservatives have lacked—Limbaugh has also redefined the word "conservative" for a younger generation. "I have a 25-year-old brother who until recently was a confessed liberal," says Kennedy, a twenty-one-year-old female MTV video jockey, who goes by her middle name only. "We used to butt heads politically all the time. Then I got him to listen to Rush. All of a sudden, he has changed parties. Rush changed his political beliefs. Rush puts strong ideas into layman's terms and draws every argument out to its natural conclusion, rather than just passing judgment—and he's really funny. Rush rocks!"

Limbaugh's show has even attracted more than a few liberals. "Every morning, I listen when I'm taking a shower and getting dressed. I listen in the car," says

Markie Post, the brainy blonde star of *Hearts Afire,* on which Limbaugh guest-starred in the spring of 1994, setting ratings records. "Although I like him very much personally, sometimes I just want to go, 'Oh, Rush, come on! Please don't do that!' Bill and Hillary Clinton are friends of mine. I feel like I know the true nature of these people and he doesn't. When he's not talking about the Clintons, I can really enjoy it. Rush is a great showman, and there are some things I agree with. Liberals tend to equivocate too much."

And then there are the other radio guys. "I started doing radio in 1992 during the presidential campaign," says Charles Sykes, the Milwaukee, Wisconsin, author of *A Nation of Victims.* "Limbaugh paved the way. He created the modern radio listener. My show wouldn't exist if it weren't for him. And this is probably the case in cities across the country. Rush somehow demythologizes the issues. If an opinion journal writes about a certain policy, it may reach 100,000 people. He takes that article, reads it on the air and gives it resonance. Welfare reform, school choice, discharge petitions can be dense and daunting, but he makes them accessible. His listeners are intelligent and want to get involved. You could not find articulate conservatives 15 years ago. Now many of the problems Clinton faces have a great deal to do with talk radio. He is the first Democratic president to face talk radio."

Limbaugh has also inspired a boom in black conservative talk radio. "I speak to the arrogance of people who think we're too dumb to get it," says Denver's Ken Hamblin, also known as the "Black Avenger."

"The Limbaugh haters and bashers are the ones who

have fallen asleep behind the microphone and are now in trouble. Rush Limbaugh has transformed the medium. He has made it a communications medium reaching down, reaching back and spreading to every American who is fed up. It's obvious that if there are no statesmen among the politicians, one will arise from the ranks of the people. I think Rush Limbaugh is that person," Hamblin observes.

"I am impressed with his audience," declares Walter Williams, a George Mason University economics professor, who sometimes guest-hosts for Limbaugh. "They're great Americans, several notches above average in terms of their interest in political matters. Rush has done wonders for our country. His major contribution is a departure from the normal way that conservatives have been acting: moaning and groaning about the liberal agenda. He just holds it up for ridicule, and that's very effective. He has a lot of influence. I think that talk radio in general, in which he provides leadership, is not letting politicians get away with the crap they usually get away with. People are getting involved, calling and writing letters. A lot of that has to do with Rush."

How else are they getting involved? *Rush to Us* takes a look around the nation, where Limbaugh fans are talking, gathering, voicing their opinions—often in the face of opposition from the liberal establishment. But above all they are informing themselves so that they can win where the real battle takes place, in, as Limbaugh likes to call it, "the arena of ideas."

"When you're in northern Indiana, you just don't have access to some things," states John Hiler, a former Indiana congressman and Bush Administration official. "Rush digs into stories that are not played up in the mainstream press—like the events of the Whitewater deal. Unless you follow these stories on a regular basis from many news sources, you can't learn a lot about them—a budget, a tax bill, health care you can. But some issues the mainstream media choose not to talk about much. So when Rush talks about it, that's fresh information. And because of his access to information that pours in through listeners and his staff, he is very accurate."

In Indiana, as in the rest of the nation, Hiler was certainly not alone in his admiration for Limbaugh and his discussion of current events. In fact, before the congressman ever began listening, some of his fellow Hoosiers started a trend that swept the nation. When the River Bank Restaurant & Lounge opened its "Rush Room," dedicating its lunch hours to listening to Limbaugh, the unprecedented enthusiasm sent a thundering message from coast to coast. The Limbaugh phenomenon was under way.

Part One

The Rise of Rushdom:
Dittoheads Unite

One

Live at the River Bank:
The Nation's First Rush Room

*I wanted to impress him. I came around the bar,
and I grabbed a big tumbler. I filled that baby full
of Crown Royal, and I walked over and said, "Here
you go, Rush, EIB, Excellence in Bartending," and
I dropped it right in his lap. I was just mortified.*
—Norm Burggraf, Jr.

In July 1988 while visiting his daughter in Sacramento,
Dick Van Mele, co-owner of radio station WAMJ 1580-
AM in South Bend, Indiana, tuned in to Rush Limbaugh.
Van Mele had been tipped off about the show by a politically astute friend in Washington, D.C. The station
owner quickly recognized a surefire winner for the South
Bend area—home to both the University of Notre Dame,
the Catholic higher-education bastion, and much of the
recreational-vehicle industry. Before South Bend's larger
stations even had a chance, Van Mele called New York
and snapped up the show for WAMJ, which became one

of the fifty-six charter stations to carry *The Rush Limbaugh Show.*

A former assistant to Indiana Governor Otis Bowen and the first director of the Indiana Legislative Council, Van Mele prided himself on knowing the people of his state and their political leanings. Targeting sponsors in the "Michiana" area (South Bend stations reach into southern Michigan) for Limbaugh's opinionated show came almost naturally to him. It was no coincidence that he was seated at the lunch counter of the River Bank Restaurant & Lounge eating one of the establishment's famed Hickory Burgers on the first of August when *The Rush Limbaugh Show* premiered nationally.

"I told Norm Jr., owner Norm Burggraf Sr.'s son, he had to listen to this man," says Van Mele. So Norm turned on the radio. But unknown to the two of them, Norm Sr. was listening on another radio in the back room. "Suddenly, he hustled through the door during a commercial and said, 'You ought to listen to this guy,'" recalls Van Mele. "Norm Jr. said, 'Dad, we were just talking about him.' And Norm Sr. said, 'Let's go for it.' He wanted to start advertising."

As Van Mele had predicted, the show was a perfect fit for this down-home family-owned neighborhood restaurant in Mishawaka (a small town contiguous to South Bend), across the St. Joseph's River from the U.S. Rubber Factory and just a few miles from the Notre Dame campus. Divided in half like an English country pub—one side for the bar, the other for family meals—the River Bank exhibited traditional values even in its architecture.

It was a perfect match for Rush Limbaugh, a traditionalist above all.

But back at the station, Van Mele had an unexpected problem. "That first day, we had a hundred calls saying, 'Get this damn guy off,' " recalls the South Bend businessman.

"Limbaugh couldn't have been more of a 180-degree change in what we were doing," points out Mark Murray, then general manager and morning talk-show host for the station, whose standbys included ABC Talk Radio softies like Owen Span, the ever-polite Michael Jackson, and friendly radio psychologist Dr. Joy Brown. "Span was the nice Everyman talk-show host who would spend two hours doing the origins of the fruitcake. It was mostly lightweight, and then one day Span said good-bye, and the next day Rush Limbaugh was on," explains Murray. "It was quite a shock. And for the first few days, we were concerned about it." They both called Ed McLaughlin, the former ABC executive who masterminded Limbaugh's launch onto the national airwaves.

"Ed told us to hang loose," reports Murray. "He told us the guy was a big hit in Sacramento and this was going to be wonderful. Just give it a while." Van Mele also called Limbaugh directly to report the trouble. The next thing they knew, Limbaugh mentioned the incident live on national radio. The results were instant. Murray recounts, "The day after we complained, Rush said, 'Some people just don't get it in South Bend. So if you really want my show, let the people at WAMJ know you want this program on the air.' And people did call. That made us feel a lot better."

"Someone from a station in Madison, Wisconsin, called and said, 'Please, don't take him off. After two or three weeks, your ratings go straight up in the air,' " says Van Mele. And that's exactly what happened, along with plenty of media attention.

"We were not a major station. We were a thousand watts from sunrise to sunset. Outside of that, we were only 500 watts," discloses Murray. "We were not one of the top-rated stations either. But my morning show took many calls on what people thought of Rush. We were getting attention from it. At that point I was about ready to hire some protesters and get the TV stations to come over," he jokes. "But seriously, it was easy to sell Rush's show, and it certainly helped out the station a great deal."

Van Mele quickly found more advertisers, like Bud Zolman, owner of Zolman Tire. "When I asked him to listen to Rush, he said he'd give the show a try," notes Van Mele. "About a month later, he says, 'You know, I'm getting tired of Rush Limbaugh. I said, 'What do you mean?' Laughing now, he says, 'Every radio in my house—I can't go from the bathroom to the kitchen—every place has Rush Limbaugh on.' "

Zolman and his wife, Diane, who works in the company's accounting office, were converts in a big way. "From noon to 3 o'clock, every one of our trucks, all the offices, have radios tuned to Rush," states Zolman. "When people come in to wait, they'll hear Rush. There's a switch there, and they can change the button, but that rarely happens. Back in the commercial office, back in the wholesale office, he's on." The Zolmans decided to advertise. "To start with, it was a little controversial, but

I knew people were listening to him," maintains Zolman. "And then it seemed to pyramid. It had a very positive effect on our business. One lady said she wasn't going to bring her car back for work because we supported Limbaugh. But as a whole, it was far more positive. We are in a very conservative area."

Nonetheless, Zolman, a nuts-and-bolts businessman who bought a failing garage in 1978 and turned it into one of the state's larger tire companies, decided to conduct his own test of the show's popularity, and he was in a unique position to do it. "We service over 100 cars a day. For a 90-day period, we checked car dials," he reveals. "Dick didn't know until I had it done." The results? "Over 56 percent of those we checked were tuned to 1580, Limbaugh's station," reports Zolman.

Considering that it was the show's first year and WAMJ was a small station, it was a major coup for both Van Mele and Rush Limbaugh. With Zolman's permission, Van Mele used the data to help convince other businesses to advertise, too.

Meanwhile in early September, Norm Sr., the fifty-seven-year-old owner of the River Bank, cranked up the volume on *The Rush Limbaugh Show* in the bar area at lunchtime. It was a hit with his customers. Burggraf decided to broadcast Limbaugh every day during lunch. Almost immediately the show started bringing in customers—regulars and new ones. "And I liked the new clientele better too," chuckles Burggraf. "Rush fans are neat people, from all walks of life. Friendships developed over the fact that we were all fans."

Soon Van Mele started promoting the lunch hour on

the air. He and Murray called it the "Rush Room," and
Van Mele told Limbaugh what was going on. "Rush said,
'Great, do it,' and then he started talking about it on the
air," says Van Mele. Although it was too early for anyone
to know, the seed for the nationwide Rush Room phenomenon had been planted.

But the energetic Van Mele, who was also operating
the insurance agency he had bought in 1975 as well as
hosting WAMJ's eight A.M. talk show, was just getting
started. He mailed fliers to potential listeners. At first,
the target was upper-income thirty-five- to fifty-five-
year-olds. But Van Mele made an important discovery
one day while a crew from Indiana & Michigan Power
was working on the power lines in back of the radio
station. "I'll never forget," he says. "The radio in their
truck was tuned to Rush, and the fellow up on the pole
was listening to Rush on headphones. He told me that
all the I & M linemen listened to Rush." It didn't take
long for Van Mele to realize that Indiana & Michigan
Power's giant fleet represented a huge segment of the
Limbaugh market he had overlooked.

The station owner decided to dig deeper during his
morning talk hour. When he brought up the subject on
the air, the phone board lit up. "Sure enough," he relates,
"I found out that the gas company people and the bread
company people were also listening. So then we started
promoting Rush to the masses." By the end of 1989,
WAMJ was beating its much larger competitor stations
during midday.

When Van Mele had the opportunity to bring Limbaugh to town in June 1990, he jumped on it. For a nomi-

nal fee and expenses, the station sponsored a South Bend stop on the "Rush to Excellence" tour, which took the tireless commentator to forty-five cities in both 1989 and 1990 for speaking engagements. Not only did the $10 admission charge recoup the station's investment and then some, but the local media coverage for the event was a boon to business.

It was a good deal for all, and Van Mele wanted to make the trip special. The day of the show, he and his wife, Debbie, and Mark Murray took Limbaugh to visit the Notre Dame campus. Founded in 1842, the university was known for its traditions, including excellence on the gridiron. Not only that, but it was Ronald Reagan, then a twenty-nine-year-old actor, who had helped immortalize the school's famous coach in the 1940 film *Knute Rockne—All-American*. The movie had made the saying "Win one for the Gipper" a popular inspiration on game days across America.

The current "Fighting Irish" football coach, Lou Holtz, whose office was known to tune in to the show, was away, but Limbaugh met his son, Skip Holtz, and sat in the head coach's chair. "Rush was pleased with that," recalls Murray. "He's a real football fan." Van Mele also arranged lunch with some of the assistant coaches, who diagramed plays with Limbaugh during the meal. After lunch, Limbaugh toured an area of Rockne Stadium usually closed to the public. His guides took him to the locker room, where he saw pictures of the Notre Dame Heisman Trophy winners, and to the place where the team's battle-scarred game helmets receive a fresh coat of gold paint each week. "When we walked out of the stadium onto the field, he

was in awe," says Van Mele. "There's an awful lot of tra-
dition, spirit, an aura." And that's something, as listeners
well know, Limbaugh reveres.

That night, a sellout crowd of about sixteen hundred
showed up at South Bend's Morris Civic Auditorium.
Among the local heavyweights on hand were John Gour-
ley, the City Attorney, who would give Limbaugh a key
to the city of Mishawaka, and an assistant mayor from
South Bend who was to present him with a key to that
town. Prominent executives from Miles Lab, Coachman
Industries (makers of vans), Skyline (makers of RVs),
Notre Dame administrators, and local politicians—all
dressed to the nines—studded the audience. As the crowd
flowed in, Limbaugh paraphernalia was on sale, and
Murray gained an insight into Limbaugh's following
while watching the goods get swallowed up. "I was absolutely amazed that his stuff sold out as fast as it did,
T-shirts and coffee mugs and things like that. He was
not at all what he is today. He was not that big."

The organizers were supposed to hand out three-by-
five cards to the audience as they came in so that they
could submit questions for Limbaugh to key off during
the show. But, says Murray, "We kind of screwed up and
didn't hand out the cards. Rush was suffering almost an
anxiety attack because it was 10 minutes before showtime, and he didn't have any questions from the audience
yet. He was begging me or somebody in charge to go
get him some questions. And I kept saying, 'Hey we're
working on it, we're working on it.' We finally got him
some with just a few minutes to spare, and he calmed
down. As Murray helped Limbaugh fasten his tuxedo

bow tie, "He promised that tonight we're really going to push the envelope," says Murray.

It was Murray's job to warm up the crowd. "I did about eight minutes of light comedy," he recalls. "The mayor of South Bend, who was a Democrat, had left with a contingent of people to go to the new ex-Soviet Union. It was ridiculous—like we were going to have some kind of international trade deal between South Bend and the Soviet Union—and one of my jokes was: 'As soon as Mayor Joe Kernan learned that Rush was coming to town, he immediately took off to the Soviet Union.' " Murray poked fun at Limbaugh, too. "It was raining that day, and I was talking about how we had visited the campus," describes Murray. "It's a really old, corny joke, but I said, 'There was a reunion of the Notre Dame class of 1920 today. We were standing outside the Morris Inn— Rush had his yellow raincoat on—and two of the members of the class of '20 tried to jump inside him because they thought he was a taxi cab.' " Murray is embarrassed by his joke now, but it brought laughs and Limbaugh didn't seem to mind.

"When I introduced him—this is what amazed me— I'm the only one on stage, and we played his theme music. The crowd is going crazy because he's been introduced, and Rush just stands there in the wings. He doesn't come out. He doesn't do anything, and I'm looking around thinking, 'What is this guy doing?' He was playing the crowd. The guy's a genius. So as soon as he does step out, the crowd noise gets even louder, and they get even more excited. It was unbelievable. That's when I thought, 'This guy really knows what he's doing.' He's a tremendous entertainer. One of the first things he said was, 'Thank you, thank you, thank you, but enough fat jokes,' " says Murray.

Then Limbaugh went to work. With Bill Clinton not yet in the spotlight, he used Ted Kennedy as the butt of many jokes and in a particularly inspired moment, as Norm Burggraf, Jr., recalls, he did push the limits—of decorum, at least—when he parodied National Endowment for the Arts grant candidates. As an imaginary artist in search of public funds, Rush pretended to take into the NEA offices a plate of human excrement with a candle stuck in the middle. The mock explanation he offered the NEA board was that the "work of art" represented the state of the homeless in New York City. The candle, he explained, represented the Empire State Building.

"When he analogized that to a lot of the so-called art that gets government funding, it was hilarious," proclaims Burggraf. "It was right on the money as far as I am concerned."

Some 250 guests were invited to the Marriott after the show for hors d'oeuvres and drinks. Over five hundred showed up. "It was jam-packed," Murray recalls. "Walking over, people were coming up to me begging, 'I'm not on the list. Can I come in, Mark, please?' Just to stand close to him or take his picture. It was like the president of the United States was visiting South Bend. I knew they liked what he said, but it was a real obsession for some people. It amazed me because he hadn't been on the air that long," explains the incredulous Murray. "The fact that he had already developed such a following absolutely blew me away."

When it came time to sneak out for dinner, it was after eleven o'clock, and all the restaurants in this hard-working Midwestern town were closed. But Van Mele knew just the thing.

"I was really into Rush," says Norm Burggraf, Jr., now an attorney but at the time a Notre Dame undergrad working his way through school bartending and helping manage the River Bank. "My wife, Jeanne, and I had front row seats at the show, and they introduced us as being instrumental in bringing Rush here. When the owner of the radio station asked me, 'Do you mind if we go over to your restaurant?' I said, 'No, that'd be great.' So I called up my dad and said, 'Why don't you give last call? I'm going to bring Rush Limbaugh over.' " The elder Norm and his wife, Dorothy, the River Bank's master chef, were thrilled to host the man who had become something akin to the establishment's patron saint.

Escorted by an off-duty state patrolman, Norm Jr., Limbaugh, and company drove to the Mishawaka restaurant. "We pulled in, and Rush saw the big sign on the wall—we give away free peanuts during the Cubs games," remembers Norm Jr. "He got out of the van and said, 'Oh, boy, I know what I want already. I want some of those peanuts.' He came in and sat down. I was really just as nervous as hell—this guy was my hero, you know. He pointed at the Crown Royal bottle on the bar and said, 'I see exactly what I want.' And I said, 'How do you like that?' He said, 'On the rocks.'

"I wanted to impress him. I came around the bar, and I grabbed a big tumbler. I filled that baby full of Crown Royal, and I walked over and said, 'Here you go, Rush,

EIB, Excellence in Bartending,' and dropped it right in his lap. I was just mortified." But Limbaugh responded with a graciousness unusual for a big shot. "He moves good for a big guy," pronounces Norm Jr. "I had a bar rag, and I'm wiping it up, just apologizing all over myself. He said, 'That's fine, just get me another one.' He wasn't put out at all."

"A lot of people have the impression that a celebrity would look down his nose at common people," says Doug Burggraf, Norm's youngest son. "When we were getting ready for Rush, I kept thinking, 'Gosh, I wonder what he is going to think of this place, or us.' It's just a little family-run restaurant, nothing fancy. I mean, Rush goes to places in New York with fancy chandeliers and this and that." But Doug, who also worked the bar that night, needn't have worried. "Rush was very complimentary," he says. "He did not have this attitude of 'I'm better than everybody.' He felt at home. He talked to everybody." He even befriended Toma, the Burggrafs' blind German shepherd, whom he fed peanuts.

"He posed for pictures, posed with Toma. He hugged the dog," says Murray. "It was like having an old friend over who happened to have several million listeners. He's an incredibly nice, down-to-earth guy. He seemed totally unaffected by it all."

"We had CNN on, and he couldn't keep his eyes off that," adds Norm Jr. "He's a real news nut. He's like the guy next door. You wouldn't have known he was a celebrity at all. He treated my mom real nice." And well he should have. Mom, Dorothy Burggraf, has a reputation for great cooking. For Limbaugh, she served up an extra-hefty version of Saturday night's house specialty—prime rib, baked potato, salad, and bread. "It was a big piece of prime rib, and he ate it all," Dorothy recalls, laughing appreciatively. "He really enjoyed it."

"We found out he was about as common as an old shoe, just a really nice guy," says Van Mele. Of course, the talk eventually turned to politics. Rush extolled the Reagan and Bush era, and—years before Bill Clinton would make it one of the linchpins of his presidency and Limbaugh would lambast him for it—they talked about health care. "Otis Bowen proposed and got passed a long-term care bill," explains Van Mele, whose former boss, Governor Bowen, became Secretary of Health, Education, and Welfare under Ronald Reagan. "But the bill was later repealed by Congress." Always on the ball, Limbaugh commented knowledgeably on Bowen's ideas and told Van Mele how much he respected the former secretary.

"He's so easy to talk to. He's a person who listens to your point of view," observes Van Mele. "It would be, 'I understand what you're saying. I see why you think that way.' It was that kind of approach. There was a lot of give-and-take. He wasn't trying to command the situation at all. He wasn't condescending. Rush talked about back home. He said this was the atmosphere he really enjoyed, and you could tell, the way he consumed that prime rib. He was having a good time." So good, that dinner rolled into after-dinner drinks. The party finally broke up around three A.M. In the van on the way back to his hotel, Limbaugh told Murray that so many people took him to the expensive places in limousines but that he really enjoyed a place like the River Bank, which was relaxed. He liked spending time with real people.

Later that morning, the Van Meles whisked Limbaugh to the airport. But the feeling of camaraderie generated by that spirited weekend would last. On the air, Rush praised the Burggrafs and Toma, the blind dog, and recalled his inspiring walk around the Notre Dame campus. He called his brief visit to the South Bend area one of the best trips he had ever taken. For the people of Michiana, Rush Limbaugh was a role model who did not disappoint in real life.

The River Bank, for one, would never be the same. "Dick made a commercial for the restaurant out of Rush's comments about the weekend," says Murray. "And that's when it really took off for the restaurant—when that commercial hit the air with Rush talking about how it served great food but had just the nicest people you're ever gonna meet."

Among the legions who found the River Bank were Notre Dame football players and law-school students and at least one professor. "At a Rush Room, you get to know people who believe mainly the same things that you do," remarks Dan Foley, a third-year Notre Dame law student originally from Des Moines, Iowa. "Some people won't even bother to listen and critically evaluate what he says, but he makes a lot of sense. And the way he makes fun of the left using their own tactics and twisting them around to show how ridiculous they are really adds a lot of humor. His points are perfectly articulated, and he researches them well."

Pausing to carefully word his analysis, Charlie Rice,

a law professor who in his classroom proudly displays a diploma from the Rush Limbaugh Institute of Advanced Conservative Studies, asserts, "The Rush phenomenon is a result of the colossal failure of the ordinary media to provide people with information."

"The people who come here have a wide variety of experience and backgrounds—everything from lawyers to educators to law-enforcement officers," notes John Penn, a commercial artist and former River Bank bartender. "Some of them are just good ol' factory workers. They think Rush is right and that there is nothing wrong with pushing for excellence in life. The liberal premise of trying to make things better by handing out freebies just doesn't get you anywhere," says Penn, doling out the wisdom of one who has served both the democratic forces in Nicaragua and tequila sunrises in Mishawaka. "In my personal experience, I've never met anybody who had something handed to them who truly appreciated the worth of it.

"One fellow, Chuck Norton, came down as a Rush fan," Penn continues. "He had just gotten out of the Navy, a weapons expert, and he was looking for something to do. He tended bar for a while, and now he has his own talk radio show. Listening to Rush, I think, pushed him into a higher sense of political awareness. And he went out and did something about it."

"Rush opened my eyes to how to spot hypocrisy," asserts Norton, a libertarian with a fast tongue, whose afternoon talk hour on South Bend's WIWO has risen from forty-seventh to eleventh among listeners. "I tell the truth, and I am an equal-opportunity destroyer. I don't care if they're Republican or Democrat. If they try to BS people, if they talk one way and vote another, or if they vote one way on the big votes but on procedural votes exactly the opposite—just like our congressman, Tim Roemer, does—then I go after them. That's just the way it is."

While still a bartender at the River Bank and delivering pizzas part-time, Norton decided to test a Limbaugh assertion that liberals don't tip as well as conservatives. To do this, he poled six hundred pizza customers. On the Thursday prior to the Bush-Clinton vote, he called the Limbaugh show and reported that seventy-six percent of those who said they were going to vote for Bush tipped compared to seven percent of those who said they were going to vote for Clinton. A South Bend television station heard the phone call and decided to follow Norton on his route the next day. Norton's astounding statistics bore up.

According to Penn, it is Limbaugh's upbeat, get-active message—the same one that inspired Norton to take his case to the airwaves—that attracts people to him. "You may have no control over what comes to you in life, but the one thing you can control is how you react to it," he maintains. "If there's one piece of advice I hear reinforced in Rush's philosophy, that's it. He is constantly an upbeat individual. He refuses to let the American Dream die."

For many, the success and high spirits of the River Bank are a good example of that dream. "The conversations go on, but one ear is always on the radio, and every so often you hear a burst of laughter," says Mike Bernache, a small-business owner and one of Limbaugh's first advertisers in South Bend. About Burggraf's success, Bernache, who lunches at the River Bank when his busy schedule allows, adds, "I think it is a tribute to creative thinking. When he started the Rush Room, most people couldn't have cared less about Rush Limbaugh. But now look at all the great publicity it's generated—legally! You can get on the front page of newspapers illegally, but to do it legally and intelligently, like he has, is pretty unbelievable."

Although Van Mele agreed to sell WAMJ in November 1992—about fifteen months after WSBT, one of the area's larger stations, wrested *The Rush Limbaugh Show* from him—his alliance with the River Bank had already served the restaurant well. The next step in the rise of the River Bank was already underway. It involved not the tantalizing talk of radio, but the magic of TV. In the fall of 1992, when *Rush Limbaugh: The Television Show* began broadcasting, the River Bank was well equipped to take advantage. The Burggrafs already used a satellite dish to pick up sports events—mainly Cubs games blacked out in the area—so they were able to trump South Bend's tape-delayed eleven P.M. broadcast by tuning in to the one from New York at eight P.M.—while working people were still awake. At 7:30 P.M., they warmed up the crowd with a tape of the previous night's show, and then it was Limbaugh live and almost life-size on their eight-foot screen.

John Penn, bartending at the time, saw evening attendance increase dramatically. "Business went up, and it gave us a community-family feeling in those hours. People came in for dinner and a drink while Rush was on. We'd fill up about three quarters of the room. Sometimes we'd be full, and they'd be standing in the doorway. During commercial breaks, the conversations would pick up. As soon as Rush came back on, the voices died out again, and everybody's eyes would be back on the screen. In fact, I was forbidden to make blended drinks while he was on. And nobody had a problem with that. They wanted to hear Rush, not the blender."

"Now sports have taken a backseat, and Rush has moved up front," says Curtis Aschenbrenner, a printing company production worker who lives about a mile from the River Bank and who met the woman who would become his wife there. "It's your normal neighborhood bar where everyone used to go to watch the White Sox and Notre Dame football, and now it's where everyone goes to see Rush." But the River Bank's reputation traveled well beyond the neighborhood, too.

On August 16, 1993, *U.S. News & World Report* ran a story about Rush Rooms, and more specifically about the one at the River Bank. The magazine reported that according to EIB Chief of Staff, Kit Carson, there were now some three hundred Rush Rooms in operation around the country—from Orlando to Anchorage. When reporter Amy Bernstein showed up at the River Bank, Harold and Brenda Aldrich happened to be there celebrating their twenty-second wedding anniversary. Why? Quite simply, Harold told the reporter, "I can't think of a better place to spend it."

And then in a paragraph describing the River Bank group watching the Limbaugh show, Bernstein deftly showed the rest of the world why the Aldriches might feel that way: "The conversation quiets as the 40 people in the room focus on the show's first feed," she wrote. "They howl over a clip of Bill Clinton saying, 'Insanity is doing the same thing over and over again and expecting a different result.' They put down their burgers and beers as Limbaugh speaks of the brutal murder of an eight-year-old boy at the hands of neighborhood teenagers. Two or three women become visibly emotional. The segment closes with an argument for teaching religion in schools. 'Respect for the essence of humanity and life—when you can't teach that,' the host says solemnly, 'what we have in our society is no wonder.' The room explodes with applause."

Bernstein's description showed that through Limbaugh, the group coalesced almost like a family, responding to the humor, sorrow, and hope of the world—as expressed by Limbaugh—in unison, openly, honestly. For the Aldriches, it was like spending their anniversary among relatives.

"The Rush Room regulars," says Chuck Norton, "are first-class people, who care a lot, who will do you a favor. Many of them I've seen at gun shows or city council meetings. The school board goes to lunch there. It's a place where you get to know people."

According to Jeanne Burggraf, Norm Jr.'s wife, who cooks and waits tables at the River Bank and is a dedicated Limbaugh fan herself, the group is more fun to serve, too. "I find Rush fans are considerate and easygoing. On the whole, they tip better and their attitude is better. They're not looking for something for nothing." She also agrees with Limbaugh on his views about women. "I believe that women, if they are qualified, should be given an equal chance for a job at the same pay. But they have pushed a little bit too far, to where men are afraid to treat women as ladies. They're afraid to open doors. Men are basically afraid of women now for obvious reasons, like sexual harassment."

Soon after the *U.S. News & World Report* story ran, Rush fans started arriving from around the world. "I've had guests from as far as Madrid and from every state in the Union," boasts Norm Sr., who estimates that crowds are up about thirty percent from pre-Limbaugh days. They bring cameras and take family portraits in front of the River Bank's neon sign that proudly proclaims, "We were the first Rush Room." They have bought hundreds of prime rib dinners and over six hundred Rush Room T-shirts.

Although the Burggrafs turned a former biker bar— the kind you wouldn't want in your neighborhood—into a successful family restaurant, Norm Sr., who spends twelve hours a day, six days a week, at this town's gathering spot and social hub, doesn't profess to have any secrets. "People ask me all the time how to start a Rush Room," he says. "I tell them to buy a radio and then turn it on. That's about all there is to it." Apparently, America has gotten the message.

Charter Limbaugh Show Advertisers

The first Rush Limbaugh Show *advertisers in South Bend tended to be small-business entrepreneurs with views right in line with Limbaugh's:*

"I wake up to Rush Limbaugh. We have a TV with a sleep mode on it, and I have it set for 5:30 A.M. on Channel 28. My wife's hooked on it too. I get such a kick out of the way he can present things 180 degrees from how you think sometimes. I think his criticism of the bashing of Reagan and Bush, especially Reagan, is the part I agree with him the most on. Through those years we experienced a lot of prosperity. We got our dignity back in the world, and I agree with how Rush presents that.

"The show carries more weight than I think even he realizes. I had a stockbroker in yesterday. He made a comment, and I knew he had just listened to Rush. He is giving me a pitch on some stock to buy, and I said, 'Well, didn't Rush just say that this morning? And he looked at me, and I said, 'Are you a Dittohead?' and he said, 'Well, we're supposed to feel out the client before we start talking about it.' He said, 'I just love him. I'm really hooked.' "

—Bud Zolman, Zolman Tire Inc.,
Mishawaka, Indiana

"I was interested in advertising because Rush talked about a lot of things I believe in. He has a great sense of humor. I like his aggressive, entrepreneurial attitude, and I kind of like how vain he is. I am that kind of person but not as boisterous and sharp-tongued. His attitude says, 'Sure, I've got something, but I earned it, and I work hard. I expect to do a little better than people who don't.' I am impressed with his strong belief that in America you can do anything or be anybody you want to be as long as you put your mind to it. I am also for less government in business. That, he continually reiterates: 'Keep the government out of private business.' The liberals say, 'Give me, give me, give me,' and they spend it, spend it, spend it. I have a very small, growing company, and it's something we really have to be aware of. The less government involved in my business, the better. Every single day he says something that catches me by surprise and makes me say, 'Wow, this guy is so well read and prepared.' He amazes me."

—Michael Bernache, Michelangelo's Floral and Events Co., Mishawaka

"I like his conservative approach. I am very much in agreement, and I think he's entertaining. I'd urge clients, who were personal friends as well, to listen, not so much to our commercials as to the program because of its enlightenment, and often they did and commented favorably. A few friends, more liberal-minded, said, 'You listen to that garbage?' And I said, 'You're damn right I do, and I believe that garbage.' "

—Bill Bridge, retired owner, Bridge, Holland Insurance Agency, South Bend

"There are not many middle-of-the-road people. They either like him a lot or they hate him. Yet they continue to listen. I advertise because he has a large listening audience. People who don't agree with him still tune in. Maybe that's how they get rid of their frustrations. I like the way he comes across. I feel like he's telling us things the press isn't. I listen to him every day."

—Ron Martin, Martin Tire Co., Niles, Michigan

"It was a good format, even if it was controversial. Even if a customer didn't like him, they were obviously listening to him to not like him. So we felt it was a good decision. I think most of the country has probably experienced him in the same way. The more they have listened to him and become accustomed to him, at least they have realized that he is consistent in his opinions."

—Mark Koebbe, General Manager,
Gates Toyota, South Bend

The First Time I Heard Rush . . .

"The first time I heard Rush, I was varnishing my sailboat. It was a beautiful day, and I was wearing a Walkman radio. I was tuning around, and I heard this guy doing a commentary. The first word that I heard was 'Femi-Nazi.' I couldn't believe it. It was a word that just went right to the inner lobe of my brain. I thought, here's a word that grabs your attention right away, so I listened, and part of what he said sounded to me, in the context of the left-wing talk radio in the Bay Area at the time, very refreshing. The agenda being set by these people who he termed Femi-Nazis he contended did not represent the great majority of American women. They had their own agenda. They all showed up at the same protests, the animal-rights people, these feminist groups, the gay-liberation people all supported one another because they've all got their own agenda, but by achieving critical mass at these demonstrations, it helps them achieve their political objective.

"That made a great deal of sense to me. I was absolutely floored that some radio station in the Bay Area would give the guy time to say it. I started to tune in, and I'll tell you, the guy is a breath of very fresh air. He is a forum for reasoned discourse. I have found him to be very courteous to people who call in, certainly much more courteous than Larry King. With King, if you don't meet his agenda, you get hammered. You get clicked off. Limbaugh takes the time to talk to people, and I respect that."

> —Phil Gioia, investment banker,
> San Francisco, California

"Since the early 70s when I was a salesman driving around in a car all day long I have listened to talk radio. One day I was sitting in a Coney Island parking lot and the radio was tuned to WABC, and on came Rush. And I'm saying to myself, 'Hmm, this guy is crazy. Where'd they find him?' I was put off. Here's a guy who came out of the blue and started challenging the accepted notions. I was definitely not in his camp, but I kept listening. And after awhile, I realized he was saying things I believed in, even though it was in a way I probably wouldn't have. His way caused one to whip one's head around and say, 'Whoa! What'd he mean by that?' I started to realize that, hey, this guy is on to something. He's got a different way of looking at the usual bologna handed out by the press and by the people who are supposedly running our country. He made me realize there is more to life than just doing your job.

"I agreed with him on a lot of the things, but he pointed out reasons I had never considered before. For instance, I disagreed with the environmental groups because they interfered with the way I used my property, but Rush pointed out that they had not only that on their agenda but an ulterior motive: the whole thrust of their organizations is to raise funds. One night I was having dinner with my son's friends. One of them said a friend was working for Greenpeace as a fund-raiser. I asked, 'What does that mean?' He said, 'He goes from door to door collecting money.' I said, 'Wow, what a crummy job.' He said, 'No, it's a good job. He makes a lot of money. He works on commission.' When you donate to Greenpeace, he gets a cut, and the more he can get you to donate the more he makes.

"As time went on, I became aware that Rush was right on. I strongly agree with his belief in the American way of life. And that means you have to do it yourself or get people to act in concert with you to help you do it yourself. The government is never going to do it for you. We need somebody out there shouting that from the rooftops, blaring it on the television and over the radio, having it appear in the newspapers because unless that message is really reinforced and the tide is turned, we're going to go down the tubes. I don't think this country was created for that."

—Stu Buchalter, small-business owner,
Poughkeepsie, New York

"I had made a sewing room and I brought my radio back there. One day, I ate my lunch, sewed and listened to Rush. He struck me as someone who was sharp. He had facts. I not only thought he was funny, I found him stimulating. I wanted to learn more. I felt like prior to that I had just been listening to what my husband or someone else said. Finally, I felt I was getting it first hand. I was getting three hours of education on what was actually happening day to day. I don't watch Dan Rather any more. Tom Brokaw? I wouldn't give you 10 cents for any of them. I don't trust them. They give you one-sided news."

—Barbara Glover, nurse,
Monroe, Louisiana

"I have been a Dittohead since a few years ago when I was driving from Texas to Nebraska, where I lived at the time. I was listening to him talk about teenage sex, and it was odd to hear somebody who agreed with me on that. I listened every chance I got, subscribed to the newsletter and read both books. I really became informed and it exploded my interests in so many directions. Rush is an inspiration in everything that I do in the sense that he informs and invigorates me."

—Chris Kyle, high-school student,
Tigard, Oregon

"I was driving from Texas to Ohio. I had never heard of Rush Limbaugh until that day on a stretch of Interstate 55—Rush would love this—in Arkansas. It didn't take long for me to realize this guy was talking conservative ideas, which was very unusual on the radio at that time. He had a compelling voice and quite clearly was having a great time with his callers. What struck me initially was the combination of politics and humor. He was a little more outrageous then in the stories he told, so it really was unusual. I enjoyed it.

"A lot of my colleagues, of course, think that he over-simplifies, that he's guilty of distortions of logic. But I think you are hearing from them a reaction to the opinions he espouses. I think he does a good job presenting his case and understands his audience, which is a key rhetorical issue. He knows what his audience can take in in a certain time, and yet he elevates his audience, too. Quite often, he presents complicated economic issues with remarkable clarity, in ways that most people could not possibly learn from the TV news. Rush goes into detail, explains clearly, lucidly. He educates people about ideas the mainstream media sometimes think they're not smart enough to understand. He of course is a master of language. He knows how to take complex ideas and express them clearly.

"What amuses me, however, is that a lot of my liberal colleagues also apparently listen to Rush. At one faculty meeting, a very liberal professor mentioned something Rush had said on the radio. He went through all the elaborate business of, 'Well, I occasionally listen to him, but I don't really agree with anything he says.' But quite clearly the guy listens to Rush, and I find that happens all the time. Rush is very much a presence here at the University of Texas."

—John Ruszkiewicz, college professor,
Austin, Texas

Two

Rush Rooms Mushroom

This is probably the only bagel bakery Rush Room in the whole country. Not only the first one in a bagel bakery but the first one in a bagel bakery that makes the best bagels in the world. Excellence in Broadcasting and Excellence in Bagels.
—Stu Buchalter, owner, Mr. Bagel, Poughkeepsie, New York

What followed the birth of the Rush Room in Mishawaka can best be described as a Rush Room boom. Wherever people could gather to listen or watch Limbaugh, they did. Rush Rooms popped up in diners, steak houses, restaurant chains, car washes, country clubs, locker rooms, and student lounges. In San Antonio, a permanently parked, air-conditioned bus became the Rush Room at a burger joint called Rooty's. In Jacksonville, customers took a few extra minutes unloading their dirty laundry at the Diamond Dry Cleaner to catch a snatch of Limbaugh. The Clinton Barber Shop in Clinton,

Maryland, played Limbaugh and advertised, "Haircuts don't cost $200 here."

Among the national restaurant chains with Rush Rooms were Hooters, Little Caesar's Pizza, Mr. Gatti's Pizza, Popeye's, Steak & Ale, Western Sizzlin and Arby's, to name a few. Some Rush Rooms were commercial ventures, and others were just places where groups of like-minded people could gather. Virtually any place with a radio or television would do.

The Green Bay Packers started a locker-room Rush Room. And the Phoenix Suns claimed to be the Official team of EIB, a virtual globe-trotting Rush Room, which Limbaugh attended on occasion. The student lounges at Oklahoma University, Ohio State University, the University of Southern California, and the University of Detroit had Rush Rooms, and so did the law school at Notre Dame. For Dave Morken and Dan Foley, starting a lunch-hour Rush Room at Notre Dame's law school was a way to socialize and to see the previous evening's show, missed because of long hours at the legal library.

By far, the majority of Rush Rooms were started at restaurants where conservative owners knew they could attract more customers of the same mind during lunch. Capitalistic scheming? You bet. And they were proud of it. Limbaugh and profits went together like food and drink, and to restaurant owners, all four were even better. Broadcasting Limbaugh was like having a congenial bar customer to break the ice between strangers.

For restaurant owners, having a Rush Room was a matter of pride and patriotism, but it also had to serve the business's bottom line. Radio ads with the local EIB affiliate and banners outside the restaurant attracted hordes of hungry and good-tipping customers. And, of course, Limbaugh fanned the flames of the Rush Room mushroom on his time as well. He loved to boast about the new spot on the block, and when he did, visitors would show up from around the nation. If Limbaugh happened to visit your Rush Room, well, that put you in another league altogether.

Without a doubt, some Rush Rooms burned like hot stars with a brilliant but brief flash. But others, particularly those owned by committed conservatives, have maintained a steady clientele. In Houston, Texas, what would become one of the biggest and most celebrated Rush Rooms was taking off in May 1992. "I happen to be a Rush fan, and my customers are very conservative, strong folks. Rush is very popular," says Edd Hendee, owner of Taste of Texas, a steak house that is one of the busiest restaurants in Houston and has hosted the commentator twice.

"Rush understands the plight of the small businessman and the fact that the government can—without even knowing what they're doing—absolutely put you out of business through their tax bills and red tape," says the outspoken restaurant owner. "I liken being in business at this time—with the government having as large a part in it as they do—to sleeping with an elephant. In the middle of the night, the thing could roll over and kill you and never know it. I think they're clueless as to the damage their health bill will do.

"Rush speaks for me personally on the character issue and political involvement," adds Hendee. "America needs to consider character in all of its politicians, not just Mr. Clinton. There've been Republican presidents who didn't have as much character as they should have, so I won't get partisan. But we need to demand character and honesty from all politicians."

Hendee feels it's his duty as an American to make dining at Taste of Texas more than just a culinary experience. In the Rush Room, a garden room with large windows looking out onto a patio, separate speakers on the tables pipe in Limbaugh's show. The decor matches the entertainment. "I've got artifacts and displays around the restaurant that make a political statement because I think it's up to us who have an opinion to express it, to heighten the political awareness of our country," he explains.

Hendee, who includes Limbaugh updates in the restaurant's newsletter sent to twenty-five thousand customers, relies on his patrons to help decorate. "When they had that bake sale in Colorado, one of my customers said, 'Listen, I need to go to Dan's Bake Sale. Why don't I be your man out there?'" recalls Hendee. The restaurant owner laid out $200 for travel expenses and collected a bounty of bumper stickers, handouts and other paraphernalia in return.

Another customer, Trace Guthrie, gave Hendee a clay Clinton bust, which is prominently displayed in the middle of the restaurant. "Coming out of the back of Bill's head are two levers, like a bulldozer's, and Hillary's just driving this guy," Hendee describes. "A thousand people walk by on a Saturday night, and they laugh and take pictures. About one out of every thousand people will stop and say something like, 'Well, I don't think that should be in here.' "

Hendee accepts that ratio with glee. "A great number of people have thanked us for having a Rush Room. I can point to a substantial rise in the public awareness of our restaurant based on our association with Rush Limbaugh. There's no question it has increased our business. People make a statement by choosing to come here. Visitors come to town, and their Houston friend will say, 'We'll go over to Taste of Texas. They've got a Rush Room.' It fills up based on what the esteemed President of the United States is up to that day." Unless, of course, the Republican National Convention happens to be in town, as it was in August 1992.

"Rush was broadcasting from Houston, and, of course, the convention was pretty hot news, so we had a lot of people every day," explains Hendee. "There was a waiting list to get in the room, and two women walked in with two young children and sat down in the room. I walked up thinking they didn't know they were in the Rush Room, and I said, 'Well, ma'am, we're glad to have you. I just want to make sure you know you're in the Rush Room.' And she said, 'Of course we do.' I said, 'Excuse me for bothering you. It's just that sometimes people walk in here and don't know.' She looked at her two kids and said, 'These are Dittokids.' "

The fact that Limbaugh has visited Taste of Texas on several occasions adds to the restaurant's cachet. "The first time was during the convention," relates Hendee. "We did it during off-hours. Rush told his host, Dan Patrick, our affiliate president, that he couldn't figure out whether he wanted to have steak or barbecue. I already had the steak covered. The night before, I cooked barbecue for him at my house."

Limbaugh's second visit was with his bride-to-be, Marta, Kansas City Royals future hall-of-famer George Brett, and some other friends before the 1994 Oilers-Kansas City Chiefs NFL playoff game. Hendee snuck Limbaugh in through the kitchen. "When the customers found out that Rush was there, I probably could have gotten the Beatles out easier," says the restaurant owner. "It was amazing. They were absolutely pressed up against the doors trying to look at the guy, just to say hello. I had an employee stand there with a notepad, and the folks wrote him notes. People paid Brett almost no attention. I mean, that's like Sandy Koufax or Babe Ruth sitting in there, and Rush Limbaugh so overshadowed his presence. It was remarkable."

That night Limbaugh had a sixteen-ounce New York Strip and a cigar. "He's the only guy I'd let smoke a cigar in the restaurant," admits Hendee, who presented Limbaugh with a Guthrie clay statue. This one was inspired by Rush's ongoing joke that he battles liberals with half his brain tied behind his back. "It was a figure of Rush sitting at his desk with his microphone and his headphones on, and there was a hinge on the back of his head," describes Hendee. "It was open just a little bit, and you could see that half his brain was missing. When you spun it around, you could see his brain was tied up with a rope behind his back." The name of the statue? *Just to Make It Fair.*

Limbaugh is clearly a lover of red meat, and steak

houses are natural gathering places for Limbaugh fans. In Washington, D.C., Blackie's House of Beef, a labyrinthine institution of high ceilings, dark wood, and brick walls covered with political memorabilia, was the next jewel in the commentator's crown.

"We noticed other restaurants around the country opening up Rush Rooms, and we figured the nation's capital had to have one," says owner Gregory Auger. "So after Bill Clinton was elected in 1992, we decided to become the loyal opposition. Now it seems that anywhere I go in the country, everybody comes up to me and says, 'Hey, Blackie's, you're the one with the Rush Room.'"

Just off Washington's main business district, Blackie's was truly a feather in Limbaugh's cap because the restaurant had always refrained from partisanship. Photos of senators, congressmen, and other Washington dignitaries reveal much about both the restaurant and the city over the past fifty years. "My parents started this steak house in 1947," says Auger. "We've always gotten our business from both sides of the aisle and therefore never wished to take sides. We never favored one party over the other. We always wanted to be fair and equitable." Now several pictures of Limbaugh decorate the walls, as well. Hanging prominently in front of the bigger of the restaurant's two Rush Rooms, which together seat about one hundred people, is a poster of *The American Spectator* cover featuring the commentator.

Inside, the food is American, including such specialties as the Rush Platter, the EIB Burger, and the Live from New York Rush Strip Steak. The diners are mostly professionals, dressed in suits and talking business when not listening to Limbaugh. But even so, the staff at Blackie's makes sure things don't get too serious.

"I love Rush. He is great entertainment. He's a lot of fun," says Calvin Rolark, II, the scion of a prominent Democratic family in Washington and the manager of the Blackie's Rush Room. "He attracts a great crowd if you can judge by the people who come to hear the show at Blackie's," adds Rolark, who hands out what he calls "cheap and cheesy" gifts during commercials.

"Who is the only Quaker president of the United States?" he asks the lunchtime crowd. And then he hints, "He's tricky." A businessman from North Dakota answers, "Richard Nixon," and claims his prize, a plastic peach-shaped mug with a peach liqueur logo.

"For what U.S. Senator does Limbaugh play the song 'Movin' On Up'?" asks Rolark next. A consultant correctly answers, "Carol Moseley Braun," and also receives a plastic peach mug. While good times are had by all, Blackie's still gets its fair share of serious Washington brass. "Bill Bennett comes in fairly regularly," notes Auger. "Senator Kay Bailey Hutchison came in one day," he continues, referring to the Texas Republican who won a special race to fill the senate seat of Lloyd Bentsen and for a while symbolized victory over President Clinton. "She walked in one day not so long after coming to Washington and received a rousing standing ovation. Not even Bennett gets that kind of response. She said, 'Rush, that cheering is for you.' "

Over in Kentucky, red meat and Limbaugh have proven to be a winning combination, too. For Ron Vandament, owner of The Barbecue Shack in the town of Florence, about eight miles south of Cincinnati, starting a Rush Room was part of a natural evolution. "My employee listened to Rush on our radio in the kitchen. It fit my politics," declares Vandament, a retired insurance executive. "I'm a Dixiecrat. A Dixiecrat is a registered Democrat who votes Republican and drinks whiskey instead of wine spritzers. This way, I can vote against Senator Wendell Ford twice— once in the primary and once in the general election.

"Customers started asking us to turn it up, so they could hear it out front. One kept telling me I should turn The Barbecue Shack into a Rush Room. I didn't even know what a Rush Room was. When decided to become a Rush Room, I advertised on Rush," relates Vandament. "We put some speakers out, and I brought in a stereo system. WCKY 1530 in Cincinnati—now WCKY 550—gave me a great big photograph of Rush and a vinyl sign that says, 'Rush Room.' We put that in the window and let her rip."

Vandament first advertised on a Monday and saw no movement that day or the next. "There was a little stirring on Wednesday," reports the restaurant owner. "On Thursday it just went crazy. One of my customers had to bus tables. Luckily, he was the one who had asked me to start the Rush Room. The next day I hired somebody."

Then Limbaugh heard about The Shack's Rush Room and its politically incorrect menu and told the rest of the world. "Barbecued Clinton was a covered dish special, covered to keep it out of the draft," recounts Vandament. "Ted Kennedy was a smoking sausage. Perot was a surprise lunch—you didn't know what you were getting, and when you got it, you couldn't give it back. We didn't get too many orders for that." But Limbaugh fans came from

St. Louis, Philadelphia, Boston, New York, San Francisco, and even Canada to try The Shack's secret spicy sauce.

The Barbecue Shack was apparently a good place to find a spouse, too. "We had three ladies sitting on one side of the room who came in for the barbecue and three men sitting on the other side of the room," recalls Vandament, who has been married for twenty-eight years and is the father of two. "The ladies didn't know who Rush Limbaugh was. They were all about the same age, very attractive, and the guys were attractive, too. One of the girls started hollering, 'Who is that idiot?' And one of the guys hollered back, 'He's a genius, that's who!' And so they started bantering back and forth. Eventually they ended up talking to each other and handing out their cards and introducing themselves. This year, one of the couples was married, and another couple was in their wedding."

But not everyone fell in love to the tune of Limbaugh. Vandament lost one regular customer who was a Perot supporter, and another bowed out because he doesn't like Limbaugh. "You have to understand that Frank Sinatra is an entertainer, and he uses music as his medium," Vandament reasons. "Bob Hope is an entertainer, and he uses comedy as his medium. Rush is first and foremost an entertainer, and he uses politics as a medium. He'll tell you himself, 'Don't get that serious about Rush Limbaugh.' " But if somebody really objects, Vandament turns off the radio. That happened one day, recalls the owner: "A customer came in and asked me why I didn't have Rush on, and I told him we weren't going to have it today. That made him so mad, he slammed my front door. It cost me $70 to get a new door closer. But that's okay. He slammed the door on his pickup so hard he knocked the glass out of his rearview mirror."

On November 12, 1993, another Kentucky Rush Room opened its doors and invited a very special guest. Mr. Lee's Steak & Seafood in Madisonville, Kentucky, about ninety miles northwest of Nashville, Tennessee, draws its crowd from southern Illinois, western Kentucky and southern Indiana. "I agree with 99 percent of the things Rush says," declares owner Dan Griffin, whose parents opened Mr. Lee's twenty years ago. "He's the voice of America. This is a large restaurant, and we had a room that could be used for the Rush Room—and I thought, 'Why not?'

"A friend gave me Millie Limbaugh's phone number, and I called her up just as a friend, a fan. I didn't mention the Rush Room to her the first time we talked. The next time, I said, 'Millie, you know, Cape Girardeau is only about two and a half hours from here. Why don't you come over for the grand opening?' I felt honored that she accepted my invitation. You take someone like Michael Jordan, and his mother probably doesn't have the popularity that Rush's mother has. Rush is more in real life, and people can relate to that. The radio station WTTO came over for about four hours that day. And Rush said live on the radio, 'My mother and some friends of hers are on their way to Madisonville, Kentucky. The Blue-Haired Bloody Mary Gang is on its way to Madisonville for the grand opening of the Rush Room at Mr. Lee's Steak & Seafood.' I was tickled to death. The following Monday, Paul Harvey mentioned Millie and her trip to Madisonville on his show.

"We served them Bloody Marys—not to Millie, she didn't drink anything—but to her friends," recalls Griffin. People lined up to have their pictures taken with Millie and to have her sign copies of Limbaugh's books. "It was crazy," says Marie Vanhoose, a retired Mr. Lee's waitress, who eats lunch in the Rush Room with her husband, Bud, almost every day. "From the second we opened, it was nonstop. Speeches, book signings, giveaways. It was great. I miss that sometimes. Then again, it's harder to listen to Rush when you're working," observes Vanhoose. "Right on, Rush. I just love him. It's so much fun to come here and listen to him over lunch and chat with Bud."

At the grand opening, Griffin held raffles. Winners received Limbaugh books, T-shirts, and bumper stickers. "During the four hours, I'd say a thousand people came in," he notes. "We've got the largest buffet in the Tri-state—roast beef, prime rib, meat loaf, catfish fiddlers, barbecued chicken, fried chicken and hot wings—and we were offering a Rush special, which is all you can eat for $3.99. We're known for our desserts, too—apple and cherry cobblers, strawberry shortcake, pecan pies and all that."

When Millie returned home, she sent Griffin a letter of thanks for "the good ole Southern hospitality." She wrote, "I told Rush that I was queen for the day." Millie Limbaugh and Griffin still talk on the phone from time to time. She told one Mr. Lee's patron: "I'm so proud of my son. The only problem with his success is that I don't get to see him that much. I saw him over Easter, but that's not enough. He was in and out, just like when he was a boy. My other son, David, Rush's lawyer, also goes off to New York all the time. They are great boys. They really make me proud. I try to listen to young Rush as often as I can. If I'm not here, I tape the show and listen to it later that evening. Quite often I have to do that because my bridge game gets in the way."

A print of the Leroy Neiman painting of Limbaugh, *Fifth Anniversary Edition,* hangs in Mr. Lee's Rush Room. The tables are decorated with American flags and vases of roses. Sometimes Griffin puts out bowls of popcorn to support Limbaugh's defense of the snack against scientists who have called it a health risk. Police officers, detectives, and retirees often pack the room. Mayor Phil Terry and other local politicians stop in regularly for the buffet.

Among the faithful visitors is Kentucky State Policeman Jerry Amos. "Rush expresses opinions most people agree with," says Amos. "Things are getting bad in this country, and people have thought so for years. The liberals who run this country are getting out of control. I'm not in favor of heavy drinking and smoking, but now they say no booze, no cigarettes, no fat, as if people can't decide for themselves. Heck, the only fun thing left is Rush."

State Detective Lanny Allen declares, "I'm so sick of liberals running our courts and letting people out of jail. They are breaking down law and order. He is the only one out there who gets this message out. The TV doesn't do it. The newspapers don't do it."

Allison and Sam Kristin Goodman take their infant son, Daniel, to Mr. Lee's. Sam Kristin, an accountant, notes, "We tune in at work during lunch. It has started up a dialogue around the office. People are more informed and can talk more intelligently about political issues. Rush is so straightforward. He is so clear."

"We're drawing people from all over," asserts Griffin. "A couple from Washington State came in; they were visiting some friends in Central City, which is about 20 miles from here, and they wanted to eat here because of the Rush Room. We're a small town of about 20,000. It's really created a nice door for Madisonville. Thanks to Millie, Mr. Lee's is also an official Rush merchandise outlet. We sell T-shirts, lapel pins, wristwatches, bumper stickers, window stick-ups. Normally, when I order something, it's gone within a week."

While Kentucky Rush Rooms offered barbecue and a down-home buffet, Upstate New York added a different culinary treat to the Rush Room menu—bagels. Stu Buchalter owns what he bets is the only Rush Room bagel bakery—with a dining room that seats eighty. "Ever since we put in the Rush Room, business has been increasing and profits have been rolling in. It's been a good experience," says Buchalter.

"Rush Limbaugh and his people have absolutely nothing to do with the Rush Room that I run," asserts the proud entrepreneur, who owns two bagel bakeries. "This is something I have done purely on my own." His only complaint is that he can't have a Rush Room in his second store because the signals don't reach the town of Kingston.

To promote his business, Buchalter does his own radio commercials. "A number of years ago, I worked with a radio man who taught me how to read a commercial with energy," he says. "Now I sponsor a drive-time radio show every Tuesday morning. I'm on the air with the host, and we conduct a poll on a local issue, like whether to publicly fund a local sports stadium. Afterwards, we have a county legislator on the phone to discuss the issue, and we go back and forth on it." Listeners vote in a box at the bagel shop.

Buchalter advertised his Rush Room on the Limbaugh TV show. "I do a takeoff on Rush's gag where he inserts his picture in the corner of the screen and looks up at what's going on. Our billboard is on the screen, and it says, 'The first and only Rush Room in the Hudson Valley. Mr. Bagel, Route 9, Poughkeepsie, New York. Every day from noon to 3:00. Dittoheads, don't miss a word.' In the corner, I say, 'My name is Stu Buchalter, and I'm Mr. Bagel. I want you to come to our Rush Room, where you can get the best lunch in the valley, plus the Doctor of Democracy, Rush Limbaugh.'

"I became famous," boasts Buchalter. "I would drive over the bridge and pay my toll, and the toll taker would say, 'Hey, I saw you on the Rush show. Wow. Keep it up!' It was amazing, the outpouring of support. It was a total connection to our audience."

But there were some drawbacks at first. "I received a letter from a man who said Rush was a bigot and he, as a black American, would no longer patronize my business," Buchalter admits. "I had a woman who came in and said, 'How can you have Rush on? He is anti-woman.' I talked to her. She had never listened to the show. She had only heard what people said about him. Out of all the interactions we've had, maybe a dozen were very negative—people who said they would never do business with me again, it was the end of the world for me, I had gone over the edge.

"Other than that, it has been very positive," states Buchalter. "I can't say that everybody at lunch is here to listen to Rush, but most of them do. They come every day. They stay for an hour and a half. They listen and talk amongst themselves. There is a community. I have had people who have driven by and said, 'I saw your sign, and had to stop in for lunch.' When we were on television, I had people coming from 50 and 60 miles away to be part of the Rush Room.

"Then all of a sudden, the station, without any notice, took the show off the air. They never came out and said they did it because they were against the Rush Limbaugh show, but they did it very abruptly. It didn't make sense. There were always sponsors for it and a tremendous audience."

Because his shop was a locus for Rush fans, Buchalter started a petition campaign to restore Limbaugh's show to the airwaves. "We put up a sign that said, 'WTZA, we want Rush back. Sign up here,' " Buchalter relates. "Within nine weeks, we had a thousand signatures. Finally, we got a call from the TV station, and they said, 'Well, you guys won. So we put on the billboard outside our business, 'We won.' We were on the local news."

With the Rush Room's strong appeal to the politically active, it was only a matter of time before one found its way to the heart of a community's political arena. In Anniston, Alabama, Tom King co-owns and manages the Courthouse Cafe, a Rush Room.

"There's an alleyway between us and the courthouse," says King. "Whenever anybody goes to the courthouse, they usually come by. I get everyone from factory workers and shoppers to lawyers, politicians, judges and professionals. Everybody here is mostly conservative," he says with a laugh. "So Rush has a lot of fans. Now they can listen to him here."

King's restaurant serves up home-style cooking—chicken and dumplings, okra, corn bread, peach cobbler and the like. It also doles out individual servings of Limbaugh. "I hand out transistor radios because I don't have a real big place," explains King. "Some of them have earphones, but most of them, they just play at the table. I've even got one guy who sits up in front with his own radio. He comes in almost every day."

Business at the cafe is so good that King plans to expand soon. "There's a lot more I want to do with the Rush Room. I plan to open up a new room as soon as the landlord and I can come to an agreement on the rent," says King. "I'm going to decorate it with portraits of politicians and a big one of Rush by a local artist, and then I'll pipe in the show."

From courthouse squares to highway-strip malls, by 1993, Rush Rooms were creeping even farther into the mainstream, and on occasion they even appeared in the national restaurant chains. For a while, some Steak & Ale Restaurants, of the Dallas-based chain, offered a lunch haven for Rush fans, and Rush Rooms popped up in Virginia and Missouri Hooters Restaurants. In June, Rush Rooms opened at an Arby's in Louisiana and at a Ramada Inn in Maine.

Chris Popper, the general manager of Barnaby's in Bangor, Maine's Ramada Inn, was looking for a way to break out of the hotel mold. "I wanted to attract some attention," says Popper. "I'd heard about Rush Rooms in other places and thought we could start one that would be even better." Barnaby's signed an agreement with Limbaugh's syndicator so that they could rebroadcast the television show, which aired at midnight in Bangor. The restaurant plays the videotape from 11:30 A.M. to noon and the radio show after that.

But Popper didn't stop there. He ran with the theme. "We have red, white and blue balloons in the restaurant and a red, white and blue picket fence dividing it," he says. "We ask people if they want to sit on the right or on the left." People who can't make up their minds can eat their Free-Trade Burgers (U.S. ground beef, Canadian bacon, and Mexican jalapeño peppers) at tables along the fence.

Barnaby's also offers portable telephones for calls to Rush. "I got through on the first day," says Popper, "just to tell people that we were opening the first Rush Room in Maine. Rush wished us tremendous success." And that's what they've had, according to Popper. "Our covers have increased by at least 100 percent," he reports. "We've even had people in who are traveling the country, going to Rush Rooms."

A good distance south of Bangor, James Doyal decided to test the Rush Room ambiance in his Arby's. "I am what you'd call a fiscal conservative," says Doyal, at his Shreveport headquarters. "My offices are adjacent to my store, and every day I sit here during the lunch rush and watch the traffic flow. I work and listen to Rush at my desk, and it occurred to me that people in the drive-through and in the dining room didn't have the same opportunity. I knew that I enjoyed him. I knew that a lot of people I associate with enjoy him. And, of course, I heard Rush talking about this Rush Room and that Rush Room. It seemed like a logical decision to give it a try."

Doyal installed a receiver and tuner in his restaurant in June 1993 and quietly turned on the power. "We want to give customers what they want," Doyal explains. "We put Rush in the dining room to see what reaction we would get. This was an experiment. The reaction was very, very positive. We had people come up to the counter after lunch and thank us for putting him on. It was only after that that we began to trumpet that Arby's was the place to go to hear Rush and have lunch at the same time.

"Our dining-room business improved 20 to 25 percent, and we started to see new people with a different profile, more suits and ties than before," says Doyal. "Typically in the fast-food industry, you get a majority of your business at the drive-through. We saw the dining room, for the first time in this particular store, take first place, and our drive-through didn't seem to suffer. We just got new customers, and those customers were there because they wanted to sit in the dining room, eat lunch and listen to Rush.

"Several representatives from our headquarters have come through and seen what I am doing, and while Arby's Inc. has not expressed a position, they have not discouraged me from doing it. Their attitude is, if it's good for business, that's fine," assesses Doyal. "I am somewhat different from most restaurants that have a Rush Room. Most are individual restaurants, mom and pops, if you will. I don't know of many that are national franchises. I would imagine that most franchises wouldn't permit a Rush Room. It's not within the boundaries of their cookie-cutter operating procedures. Arby's has been very indulgent in that respect, and I appreciate it."

Doyal also has Arby's stores with Rush Rooms in Alexandria and Pineville, Louisiana. "I tried it in Lake Charles and didn't get the kind of feedback that warranted continuing it," he says. He is contemplating adding Rush Rooms to his Monroe and Ruston stores. "If people don't want it or are ambivalent, then I don't want to force it down their throats. I want them to enjoy themselves while they're in our restaurant and have a good meal."

Because Doyal plays Limbaugh in his Arby's dining rooms, some customers get the idea that he is in touch with the commentator. "They sometimes think I'm a pipeline through which they can get info to Mr. Limbaugh, particularly when it's a subject that they're opposed to and think that he would be opposed to also," remarks Doyal, laughing. "They'll call me and say, 'Did you hear about this? Can you make sure that Rush finds out about that?' Typically, I'll say, 'Knowing Mr. Limbaugh, he already knows it. He probably knew it before we did. Listen to his program. I'll bet you in the next day or so he'll say something about that.' And sure enough, he always does."

Live from America's Rush Rooms

"I think I have the first Rush Room. I started here in 1989. The girl from *U.S. News & World Report*, Amy Bernstein, spent two days here. She loved it, but she didn't write about us. And she said some place in Indiana was first. Since we don't serve alcohol, all types come to Bee-Bees—families, kids, Christians who don't drink, everyone. We serve 250 meals during Rush Hour, which is from 12 to 3:00. And since the entire restaurant is the Rush Room, people who don't want to listen can go to my drive-through window and listen to whatever they want in their cars."

> —William Melanis, owner, Bee-Bee's Restaurant, Greenville, South Carolina

"My patrons were the ones who encouraged me to do what I did. My Rush Room holds about 30 people and is set aside from the other rooms. It's quiet, and people can relax in there. There's a regular group that comes in to listen to him. Some people are very biased. They disagree with everything he says, but they still listen to him. I agree with almost everything he says. He is definitely entertaining."

> —Jack Tracy, owner, The Keg, Hartford, Connecticut

"Being a small-business owner I get discouraged with all the government taxes and regulations. Rush talks to that issue, and it's inspirational. The restaurant business is difficult, and I need all the support I can get. He motivates me. Rush is also a great topic of conversation.

This is a small town, and most of my customers are regulars. One day a guy told me I should listen to Rush, so I did. Then it became a way of starting conversations with him and other people, you know, 'Did you hear what Rush said the other day about? . . .' This is a fairly upscale restaurant in an upscale part of California. When I first decided to play Limbaugh, many customers came up to me and said, 'If you keep playing Limbaugh, I will never eat here again.' And they meant it. Many haven't come back. But so many more come because I play him."

—Michelle Schanel, owner, Schanel's Snooty Frog, Cameron Park, California

"The customer asked for it. They said, 'How come you don't put a Rush Room?' I said, 'A what?' And they said, 'A Rush Room.' They told me what channel, and I listen by myself. I like it, so I put on. I like it all. I get a lot of military people. They like Rush Room. We serve Chinese food, buffet-style, all you can eat. Maybe later on we put TV, too, but right now it's only radio."

—Chi Huynh, owner, House of Q, Lawton, Oklahoma

"Auburn University is a conservative campus. The first day we did it, we more than tripled our daily lunch business. It was about what a home football game would be, 150 to 200 customers between 11:00 and 1:00. Later we had problems with the radio reception. For some reason, this building doesn't pick up radio very well. The station sent DJs and everybody to look but couldn't figure out how to fix it, either. Outside you could listen to your car radio, and it'd come in crystal clear. But as soon as you walked in the building, the radio would mess up. So finally we just had to stop doing it."

—Brandon Potter, co-owner, Strutting Duck II,
Auburn, Alabama

"We've had the Rush Room since the first of January in an area set off to the side. There's been an increase in older customers and women. I think there's a great deal of women who really enjoy Rush Limbaugh. I recently had a table of four elderly ladies come in just to hear Rush, and they were excited about it. Rush's cousin, Andrew Limbaugh, who works for the Equity here in St. Louis, has come in several times. He was happy about it being here."

—Drew Christian, general manager,
Hooters, St. Louis, Missouri

"About once a week I meet some people to have a roundtable discussion about Rush's topics. The group's been as many as 10 and as few as two. At first, it was people from work. Then it expanded through word of mouth. Most of us are engineers. Some of the secretaries show up and various other people who work with us. I admire his respect for—I'm not going to use the term family values—I'm going to say individual values. I think those are paramount to a society, the recognition of individual rights. Sometimes we don't all agree on things, but we all like the pizza."

—Stephen Moss, customer, Terry's Pizza &
Lounge, Huntsville, Alabama

"I love Rush Limbaugh. The Rush people tend to be very vocal in what they believe, and they'll sit and talk to you about their viewpoints, whereas you're not going to go in my dining room and start talking politics with a family of four. You just have to deal with those people differently. They may have the same attitudes, but it's a different environment."

—Paula Pjeza, manager, Terry's Pizza & Lounge, Huntsville, Alabama

"One day a lady came into the restaurant and saw our sign advertising the Rush Room and turned around and walked out. She said, 'As long as you listen to Rush, I'm not eating here.' The customers looked at her like she was odd and kept eating. And I don't know why, but the next day the place was fuller than it has ever been."

—Dick Braegelmann, owner, Alvie's East Family Restaurant, St. Cloud, Minnesota

The 25 Most Popular Rush Rooms

Here are the standouts of the nation's Rush Room boom.

- Alvie's East Family Restaurant,
  St. Cloud, Minnesota
- Arby's Restaurant,
  Shreveport, Louisiana
- Aunt Teak's and Uncle Junk's,
  Strongsville, Ohio

- The Barbecue Shack,
  Florence, Kentucky
- Barnaby's,
  Bangor, Maine
- Bee-Bee's Restaurant,
  Greenville, South Carolina
- Blackie's House of Beef,
  Washington, D.C.
- Chit Chat Club,
  Bethlehem, Pennsylvania
- Courthouse Cafe,
  Anniston, Alabama
- Ditto's,
  Sacramento, California
- Flammini's,
  Dalton, Georgia
- Golden Bull Grande Cafe,
  Gaithersburg, Maryland
- Hanover Star Restaurant Company,
  Breeze, Illinois
- Hooters,
  St. Louis, Missouri
- Joe Morley's Smoked Beef Barbecue,
  Midvale, Utah
- The Keg Restaurant,
  Hartford, Connecticut
- La Piaza,
  Orlando, Florida
- Mr. Bagel's,
  Poughkeepsie, New York

- Mr. Lee's Steak & Seafood,
  Madisonville, Kentucky
- River Bank Restaurant & Lounge,
  Mishawaka, Indiana
- Rooty's Restaurant,
  San Antonio, Texas
- Schanel's Snooty Frog,
  Cameron Park, California
- Slick Willie's,
  West Memphis, Arkansas
- Smokey's Barbecue,
  Chattanooga, Tennessee
- Taste of Texas,
  Houston, Texas

Three

TV Dinners and the
Louisiana Supper Club

What Rush does validates and reinforces what America thinks. He's not saying anything that his fans don't already know and believe to be true. Family, faith, common sense and hard work—as corny as it may sound—that's what America is all about. Here's somebody on the national scene who has the politically incorrect ability to stand up and say, "This is what is right."

—Walter Abbott, Head Ditto, the Rush Limbaugh Supper Club

With more than five hundred radio stations and eighteen million listeners already in his fold, Limbaugh's prospects for kicking off a successful television career in the fall of 1992 were looking good. Still, there were skeptics. Would Limbaugh's humor translate from radio to television? Would a one-man, no-guest TV talk-show work? Could he generate the rave reviews—from the cranky, mostly liberal reviewers—needed to land an advertising base?

Forget whether it would be good—would the networks even air the show, and at a time when people would be awake to see it? After all, not everyone could be expected to set their TV timers for a 5:30 A.M. broadcast, the way a couple of Limbaugh devotees in Indiana do every morning.

Rush Limbaugh: The Television Show debuted nationally on September 14, but not in Monroe, Louisiana. And for Don Glover, a fifty-eight-year-old Church of Christ minister in the small northeast Louisiana town, that was a problem. "Rush is positive about religion," says Glover. "For a person in public life as he is, three hours a day on the radio and a half hour on television, to speak unashamedly about the place of religion in the development of our country is quite gratifying. Years ago it wouldn't have been a big thing at all, but now it's so rare." Glover and his wife, Barbara, wanted Limbaugh's TV show to be broadcast in Monroe, and they didn't plan to take no for an answer.

"We listen to Rush on the radio, and we enjoy him," says Barbara Glover, a nurse and mother of six. "He doesn't make up things. What I really appreciate about him is that he shows you what people say. He doesn't just say, 'Well, Bill Clinton said this.' It's a direct quote, and therefore it's true. We don't have the resources and the time to read as widely as Rush does. I learn a lot about what is going on from him," adds Mrs. Glover, who bought Limbaugh's books for her children and was given a subscription to his newsletter for Mother's Day. "It is something we can all talk about. The kids get together, have coffee and say, 'Hey, did you hear what Rush said?'

"When we heard he was coming to TV, we wanted to see the show, but nothing was said about it," Glover continues. So she called the three TV stations in town to see if one of them was planning to carry Limbaugh's show. "The ABC affiliate said, 'We're thinking about it,' " she reports. "NBC said, 'I doubt it.' "

On the other hand, when she asked Jack McCall, Program Director at KNOE, the CBS affiliate, whether he was considering airing *Rush Limbaugh: The Television Show,* he answered bluntly, "No, we are not."

"May I ask why?" she inquired.

"We do not want it," he replied.

"I said I was perplexed," she wrote in a letter to the editor of Monroe's newspaper, *The News Star.* "I pointed out that the program is received in Baton Rouge, Shreveport and Ruston, and that it would doubtless go over well here, especially since the radio program (broadcast daily over KMLB 1440-AM) is extremely popular. 'We are not interested,' McCall said.

" 'Sir,' I replied, 'you must not agree with his political views and wish to keep it out for that reason.' Silence. Click." Now the Glovers were mad and even more determined to bring Rush's program to Monroe.

"The director at the CBS affiliate basically said he thought Rush Limbaugh was a racist, and he didn't want the show," adds Don Glover, who wrote the letter but preferred to keep a low profile on the matter and asked his wife to sign it. The letter ran on September 20, concluding: "But what can you expect from those who believe that Phil Donahue and Dan Rather are the epitome of political balance, virtue and objectivity? Incidentally, anyone interested in joining the Northeast Louisiana chapter of the Rush Limbaugh Club, a primary goal of which is to see that Limbaugh's television program be carried in this area, should call me at . . ."

"That was just a statement thrown in as a little pressure tactic. We had no intention, frankly, of organizing it," says Glover, who had no way of knowing at the time that his tactical trick would turn into a statewide movement. "We got a tremendous response. In the space of about 48 hours, we had well over a hundred calls, one after another. We had to organize the club."

The letter united the area's Limbaugh fans. "It turned out that a lot of people around town had been calling the stations like I had," says Barbara Glover, triumphantly. "And when they found out that someone else had been calling, they said, 'Hey, we're going to get this done,' I never thought people would get up in arms."

Next, Barbara called Multimedia, the masterminds behind *Rush Limbaugh: The Television Show,* in Atlanta, Georgia. "Atlanta said put the pressure on," she relates. "The TV station said, 'Please, don't call. Mail letters.' " The Northeast Louisiana Chapter of the Rush Limbaugh Club—seventy members upset with their local television stations—convened at Catfish Cabin, a restaurant serving the local specialty deep-fried, and plotted its campaign. "I told all my group, 'Don't write letters. They can throw them in the waste can. Call!' "

And so they did. Inundated with telephone calls, KARD-TV, the local ABC affiliate, finally caved in and agreed to run the show. "When I found out from Atlanta that they were going to do it," says Barbara, "I went to ABC. I walked through the door, and the manager threw up his hands and said, 'We just signed.' "

Mission accomplished, a significant portion of the club—elated by their victory—wanted to continue discussing conservative ideas and to become a more active part of the nation's political process. With the eloquent and well-read Don Glover at the helm, about thirty-five people decided to continue to gather at monthly dinner meetings.

"We felt like we had accomplished a lot getting him on the air," says Barbara Glover. "We enjoyed discussing politics. We're conservatives, but we're not clones of Rush. I don't think he's any harder on liberals than they are on conservatives," she adds. "He's just got the guts to sock it back."

"Our group comes together, and we call it the Rush Limbaugh Club, but frankly we're not a fan club," says Don Glover, an evangelical minister and frequent guest columnist on politics in the Monroe newspaper. "At least that's what I emphasize. People say to me, 'You mean you agree with everything he says?' Well, of course not. I don't agree with everything anybody says. Anybody on the radio three hours a day is going to make some mistakes. They're going to pop off and say something that's not quite right. But I think on the whole he does an outstanding job. We are a conservative organization. We use Rush as a starting point. We have discussions. We share ideas. We have guest speakers. And we have fun."

Limbaugh's articulations made the minister's job easier. "His antiabortion argument is the best I've heard. At a time when people are emphasizing the sacredness of life on all fronts, particularly when it comes to animals, he simply takes the point of view that it is wrong to kill an unborn child. I think he believes people do have a right to choose, in one sense. He doesn't believe in a constitutional amendment to prevent it, but he does believe that nobody, or almost nobody, should have an abortion. He makes a religious argument, a philosophical argument. It isn't all that complex. It's just the way he puts it. He contends that the other people have the obligation to prove that life doesn't start at conception or thereabouts."

Glover continues, "The guy is engaging. He is very talented, and he makes ideas that are complex relatively simple. I do not think he is simplistic. There is a tremendous difference. But being able to make things intelligible is quite a gift."

Under the Glovers' leadership, the Rush Limbaugh Club continued to gather at Catfish Cabin for over a year. "One of the first questions we would ask anybody when they joined us was, 'How did you hear about Rush?' And they would tell us, 'I listened, and all of a sudden, boom, this guy was saying what I believed.'

"We weren't really trying to do anything big politically, like a Republican campaign or anything. We were just conservatives getting together," says Glover. "People of all ages—university students and teachers, small-business owners, laborers and others. These people were intelligent and gifted in expression. I found they read everything," says Glover, a *National Review* reader for twenty years who counts Edmund Burke and Adam Smith as two of his favorite authors. "We certainly didn't take Rush literally when he said, 'Don't read anything or watch anything because when you come back on Monday, I'll bring you up to date.' When we heard that, we read even more. We exchanged ideas generated by the news. Everybody got to speak. Rush was the motivating force. One thing I really like about Rush is the discussion he creates among average people."

The Rush Limbaugh Club also brought in outside speakers and showed films and videos. One night, it was a film of Thomas Sowell, the black conservative columnist. On other nights, Dr. Harry Hale, a sociology professor at Monroe's Northeast Louisiana University and a regular club attendee, delved into the moral and political issues concerning abortion and euthanasia. At the August 1993 meeting, Richard Hood, a pharmacy professor, and his wife, Rebecca, told the group about their trip to Dan's Bake Sale and showed their video of the occasion.

At the same time, Glover's voice in the community continued to grow. "I go to the university as a conservative, and they ask me questions about politics and the evangelicals. The liberals have never renounced their avid desire to have their way in politics, but they criticize the evangelicals for showing an interest. They used to criticize us for not being involved. You know, 'It's pie in the sky. It's a religion of heaven. It doesn't have anything to do with this earth.' Then when we got involved but came down on the other side of some issues, they decided it wasn't a good idea for us to be in politics."

Glover wrote a number of letters and columns defending Limbaugh in the newspaper. He also appeared on Monroe's Lanny James talk-radio show. Glover recalls,

"One of the callers, a lawyer, I think, said, 'I can't believe that a minister of the Gospel would be for Rush Limbaugh.' And I asked him, 'Why not?' He said, 'Well, Jesus helped the poor, and he was for the downtrodden.' And I asked him, 'Are you suggesting that Rush Limbaugh is not for the poor and the downtrodden?' He said, 'Why, yes.' He was very sarcastic. He said, 'The Democrats would be much better for a minister because they are doing something.'

"We don't think that socialism, which makes people dependent, is the way to do anything," says Glover. "And as far as Jesus is concerned, we have a lot of different interpretations of Jesus. But one thing for sure is that when he told people to help the poor, he didn't mean to send it to Rome and let Caesar do it for them."

Being so outspoken, Glover was also confronted by crackpots. One in particular was somewhat unnerving. "When I got out of class about eight o'clock, I came down here to the offices, and one of the deacons was on the phone with someone who was asking questions about Rush Limbaugh and me.

"It turns out this fellow was adamantly opposed to what we were doing. He threatened me. He called my house many times and left messages on the answering machine when we weren't there. He would say things like, 'You can run, but you can't hide.' Then he called my son, who is a local dentist—he and his wife are part of the club. He also called the restaurant where we meet and said he was going to come down there."

Glover, a former police chaplain, called the police. "He told me his name finally—he was a Perot supporter,

I think. He denied that he had ever called me, but I had him on tape. He took everything Rush said literally. He had no sense of humor whatsoever. He didn't understand parody or satire."

In the winter of 1993, Glover decided he needed to spend less time running the club so that he could concentrate his energy on his church work. Fortunately, an enthusiastic conservative named Walter Abbott, III, from the nearby town of Ruston was more than ready to take over. In fact, Abbott was already preparing to expand the club around the state.

"When my mother-in-law told me about it, she said, 'You need to go to one of those supper clubs since you're a big Rush fan,' " says Abbott, a forty-four-year-old project manager for WPS Industries, a construction/engineering firm in the wood-products industry. "I said, 'Well, I've heard about that. It's a Rush Room.' She said, 'No, no, no. This is something where they have monthly meetings at night.' So I hunted it down and went to it."

For Abbott, a self-described news junkie who listens to Limbaugh at the office and in his car, the commentator's appeal is simple: "What Rush does validates and reinforces what America thinks. He's not saying anything that his fans don't already know and believe to be true. Family, faith, common sense and hard work—as corny as it may sound—that's what America is all about. Here's somebody on the national scene who has the politically incorrect ability to stand up and say, 'This is what is right.' "

Abbott enjoyed the Monroe club's September 1993 meeting and returned for the next month. An organizer by nature, he decided to start another chapter of the supper club where he knew more people—in Shreveport, the area's largest city. "I wanted to spread the EIB virus," jokes Abbott.

To help him form the group, Abbott called his friend Jim Spradling, a Shreveport attorney whom he had met at a Buchanan for President get-together. The two had gotten to know each other better when both were delegates to the 1993 State Republican Convention. Abbott suggested setting up a Limbaugh club in Shreveport. "I said, 'Can you really do that?' " relates Spradling. "His response was, 'Well, why not?' I said, 'How do you do that?' He said, 'Who cares? Let's just do it.' And I said, 'Okay, let's do it.' "

To get things started, they decided to meet at Don's Seafood & Steak House, an advertiser on radio station KEEL 710-AM, the local Limbaugh show carrier. The day before the group's first meeting, Abbott called conservative KEEL talk-show host Dean Grau on the air and asked him to announce the meeting. He did. Three people who heard the announcement showed up, in addition to Spradling, his wife, Natalie, and Abbott. Matters of organization were addressed. Don's was established as the official meeting spot, and the first Thursday of each month was designated meeting night.

Abbott took on the title Head Ditto, and dues were set at nineteen cents a month to cover mailing costs. The one qualification for membership was also settled on: You must be a Dittohead, and if you have to ask what that means, you don't qualify.

Grau's show, then known as *Soap Box* and now called *Sound Off,* was a natural place to attract Limbaugh diehards. Started in February of 1993, *Soap Box* was a platform for the curmudgeonly copy-machine salesman, who had done his own quirky radio ads for seventeen years, to grouse about current affairs and issue paternal advice.

"You'd be surprised at how many people call me the poor man's Rush Limbaugh," says Grau, a soft-spoken senior citizen who lashes liberals with wry humor and who understandably relishes the comparison. "I don't have nearly the pizzazz he's got. But we've been successful at fighting some local tax increases. Without being vindictive, I hope, and without being personal, I enjoy picking on the bureaucracy. They're fair game."

"What really got the club going was when I went on with Dean Grau and pitched it," notes Spradling. "We did that over three months, and the membership just kept growing. After that, Dean had me on, and we discussed substantive areas. For several weeks, we harangued the mayor for shady deals she pulled on some construction projects, and pretty soon we had the mayor calling to talk to us."

With people phoning to vent their frustrations with the local government and Louisiana's notoriously convoluted politics, Grau's show, on the same station as Limbaugh's, became an everyday nexus for the growing Supper Club community. Thirty-eight Rush fans showed up at the November meeting. "We agreed that we'd never seen anything grassroots get going so fast," says Jay Murrell, a petroleum landman recruited by Spradling. "I am kind of an organization guy. I said, 'We need to have some kind of program.' But we didn't want to get too formal."

In December, Murrell, a journalism student in college,

began his own Limbaugh-inspired radio show, *The Grapevine,* on KEEL. "Rush forced me to use valid premises to derive a valid conclusion," he observes. Murrell wisely focused on state and local issues. "Why cover something at 10:00 A.M. that he's going to cover in more detail and with more art at 11:00 A.M.?" he points out. The fledgling host also promoted the Limbaugh Supper Club. It was a natural fit. "My show was a 30-minute compression of Rush's format, about half news and commentary and half calls," explains Murrell who admits, "I can be confrontational. I learned from Rush that you need to be of good cheer and that you turn people off if you're in their face all the time. He weaves irony and parody into his arguments. That influenced me."

Limbaugh was clearly motivating the city's conservative community to get active, and at the third meeting, attendance doubled to some eighty people. Among them was businessman Jim Doyle, who had opened Shreveport's first Rush Room at his Arby's restaurant. "I enjoy meeting people who have similar political and economic philosophies as myself," says Doyal. "I like the unstructured way the meetings are conducted. It allows for talking, enjoying good fellowship and having a good time."

Another of the group's core is retired U.S. Air Force Major Bob Worn, a man with Limbaugh's physical stature, a gregarious laugh, and a Shih Tzu who stands on its hind legs and salutes with its right paw when his master commands, "Attention!" A political gadfly, Worn often shows up at City Hall to levy handbills on passersby. Armed with a copy of the federal budget and various reports on Congress, he and his friend Dave Corley, the local chairman of United We Stand America, hounded their congressman, Republican Jim McCrery, when he strayed from the conservative path.

A die-hard Limbaugh fan, Worn keeps the broadcaster informed on Louisiana politics by sending a continuous stream of faxes, and he counts as one of his chief accomplishments the book he wrote, published, and sent to Limbaugh. It was entitled *All the Faults and Shortcomings of Rush Limbaugh,* and the pages inside were, of course, blank. Limbaugh displayed it on the show one night. Another copy of the tome was later auctioned off at a Supper Club meeting to help pay mailing expenses.

At that third meeting, Richard and Rebecca Hood showed their Dan's Bake Sale video and photographs. Local TV station KTBS sent a team over to shoot a spot for the ten o'clock news. Of his Dan's Bake Sale experience, Hood told the club, "It was an exciting once-in-a-lifetime adventure." For the Supper Club members, the Hoods' account and video was an express trip to a fine spring gathering for an inspirational cause.

"We try to get speakers who are lively, thought-provoking and catalytic in getting people to use their God-given brains to see what's happening to them," declares Worn, who, between speakers, fills in with a stream of stories about combat missions and other tales, like the time he tried to tattoo *Air Force One:* "I had a challenge from several friends to put a 'Rush for President in '96' sticker on *Air Force One* when it was here. I thought maybe one of the guys off the flight line would escort me out there on the pretense that I wanted to see the airplane. You know, 'just to see it up close, see how clean it is.' I was going to put that bumper sticker on one of the gear doors. That would have been a coup. Then I found out my cousin's son was assigned to *Air Force One,* and that would have caused him some consternation if not trouble. So I backed off that challenge."

Attendance at Shreveport's Limbaugh Supper Club had to level off sometime. Just how many Limbaugh fans could there be in a medium-sized Louisiana city who were willing to head out on a work night to discuss conservative politics? But January was a good month for Limbaugh, whose show for the week ending January 23, 1994, scored a 4.2 national household rating (meaning 4.2 million viewers)—a record high for the show. The supper club turnout once again more than doubled at that month's meeting, with new members driving from as far away as East Texas and South Arkansas, reflecting both Limbaugh's strong appeal and KEEL's powerful 50,000-watt signal. Abbott counted 175 people that evening.

Congressman McCrery was scheduled to speak but had to cancel because his wife had a baby that day. Instead, Shreveport resident Charlie Putnam, a retired bookseller with a very distinctive voice, talked about his twenty minutes on the phone with Limbaugh. "I am the most famous person in the Shreveport area," says Putnam, laughing. "Apparently Rush has used my call many times.

"I was speaking with Rush after Bernard Shaw interviewed Henry Kissinger concerning the Gulf War," explains the retired sixty-five-year-old. "Shaw asked Kissinger if he thought the Gulf War came about as a boost to George Bush's campaign. I thought that was very unflattering to the Presidency, and I asked Rush if he thought that was good journalism. Rush said, 'Well, it was a vacuous question,' and he joked that all the journalists were trying as best they could to instill some sign of life in Henry Kissinger." It was just another normal call until Limbaugh received a sign from his staff.

"Rush said, 'Could you hold on? The people in the booth are saying you sound just like Lloyd Bentsen.' So he came back and asked me a few questions, and I answered them in the Lloyd Bentsen vernacular," recalls Putnam, who, like Bentsen, speaks with a croaky but melodious Southern drawl.

Putnam played a tape of the conversation for the supper club. "I had to force myself to listen to it several times before I could halfway enjoy it, because I thought I sounded so stupid," admits Putnam. "I waited an hour to speak to him, and had I talked to him in the first 15 minutes, I would have sounded more like Mickey Mouse. I was hyperventilating. Here I am talking to millions of people, and was fumbling around trying to write down simple questions. But, looking back, Rush made it very comfortable. He was very patient."

Like many others, Putnam enjoyed his evening with the club so much that he joined. "These are nice people, and it's fun to talk to them. Everybody has a common interest and a belief that Rush is doing good and stirring the conscience of the United States," he says. "We feel we need to support Rush because, indeed, he is the voice of change."

"We've all become more outspoken on issues. We are not afraid to say, 'Now, wait a minute, this doesn't make sense here,' " says Abbott. The Supper Club's main contingent ranged in age from forty to sixty, with about an even male-to-female split, but as word spread, younger people were starting to drop in as well.

Meanwhile, Abbott also assumed the leadership of the Monroe Club, which now had some twenty members. He moved the meeting place to Mike's Catfish House, which had become Monroe's official Rush Room. With its big, open rooms, Mike's clapboard building and back porch overlooking a bayou was the perfect setting for Southern-style conversation and dining on fried catfish, okra, greens, iced tea, and peach cobbler with soft vanilla ice cream on top. In the format that had proved so successful in Shreveport, Abbott invited guests. Jay Murrell spoke to two dozen members in January, and Roy Brun, a conservative state representative from Shreveport and a member of the Republican National Committee, spoke in February.

February also saw the first meeting of a chapter in Baton Rouge. A handful of people joined organizers Sam and Jena Varnado and Chris Furlow to watch a taped version of the C-SPAN broadcast of Limbaugh's February 18 radio show. With Limbaugh surrounded by his Mac Powerbook 128, another computer terminal, a microphone suspended from a mechanical arm, and jugs of Florida orange juice, it was something like looking behind the curtain at Oz. But Limbaugh came off better than Oz's wizard. A woman who called to chastise him fretted about getting cut off when the show ended. "What happens at 3:00?" she asked. Limbaugh teased, "Are you asking me if I want to have coffee?" She suggested wine.

In Shreveport, February's meeting drew record attendance—some 250 people—if not the featured guest.

Southern Methodist University journalism professor Philip Seib, who had written a book called *Rush Hour: Talk Radio, Politics, and the Rise of Rush Limbaugh*, had to reschedule his talk for spring. But Henry Burns, the former finance director for the city of Shreveport, showed up and aired his grievances with the city's mayor, grievances that had led to his dismissal and a public outcry from local conservatives.

The friendly gathering was clearly growing into something more akin to a movement, a sounding board for local politicians as well as Limbaugh's national issues. The forum was starting to attract the state's top politicians, professors and others in the public eye, and soon the meetings would require serious logistical planning.

The March meeting drew a crowd of close to two hundred to hear *Sports Afield* writer Grits Gresham, a vocal defender of Second Amendment rights, talk about gun control and environmental issues. At the April meeting, Jeffrey Sadow, an outspoken conservative political science professor at Louisiana State University-Shreveport, lectured on liberalism in academia. "A lot of the people coming to power now at universities were dodging the draft through staying in academia. Find out where they are spending their money," he urged, in suggesting these liberals were giving short shrift to traditional Western Civilization academic subjects. Local School Board President Judy Boykin also talked about her ordeal in trying to exercise control over the Caddo Parish junior-high-school and high-school sex-education curriculum. The dispute that developed had ended up in court and had been a subject of a *60 Minutes* segment.

"We attempt, when there is some deserving soul, to recognize acts of heroism and courage in the face of the liberal onslaught," proclaims Jay Murrell. "Judy Boykin stood up for decency and family values and good bedrock conservative thought in the face of withering fire from American Way, Planned Parenthood, ACT-UP and from the local media."

According to Sharon Bowman, a twenty-four-year-old elementary schoolteacher who attended that meeting, it is the breakdown of the family that has caused children to grow up too fast. "I feel that sex education is something that should be taught at home through the family, and there has been a breakdown of families in the country. I'm completely old-fashioned," she says. "The woman's lib movement has ruined everything for the women of the Nineties. I am a teacher. I like to stay home in the summer. I want to be a mother and a wife. I don't get into being head of the household. I know my place as a lady and my boyfriend's or husband's place as a gentleman.

"Kids don't have parents when they come home any more," complains Bowman. "There is no one there to take care of them, to cook dinner for them. There are no parents out there." About Limbaugh, she states, "His message is right on target. I wish he could step up and take charge and really be able to accomplish his goals. I like his enthusiasm, his sense of humor. A lot of people comment that he is kind of obnoxious, but I like that. He gets his message across in a different way. I think it's inviting. I would like to see more younger folks at these meetings."

Bowman's boyfriend, Christopher Morse, a commercial credit analyst for Premier Bank, says, "It's good speaking with older people who have the same ideology as I do. It's good to reinforce your beliefs with other people. Rush's analysis of the growth of the public sector—what that's done to the economy and the socio-economic ramifications—is in line with what I believe. The public sector has usurped the private sector in job creation and growth."

An affinity for Rush's message and for meeting people is what links supper club members. "I like the fact that the people who come have the same values as Rush Limbaugh," explains the sixty-seven-year-old Grau. "We don't always agree with him, but we do agree with the basic principles that he stands for, and we appreciate his courage in telling it like it is. The club has no dues, no projects. It's social. We've been catered to nicely by the restaurants because now we are looking at 200 people," says Grau. "In fact, we are turning people away. We're looking for bigger facilities."

"We're meeting at one of the largest restaurants in Shreveport," declares Abbott, who recently moved the shindigs from Don's Seafood to Ralph & Kacoo's, another Cajun seafood restaurant with a large private meeting room in back. But between September 1993 and February 1994, Limbaugh's television audience increased nationally by thirty percent, outpacing everybody from Leno, who gained fifteen percent, and Letterman, up twenty percent, to *Nightline,* which lost five percent. And enthusiasm for Limbaugh's show was still growing. For Abbott, that could mean even larger gatherings. "We've seriously considered trying to have something at the civic center," he says.

But that might just be the start of another phase for

the Rush Limbaugh Supper Club. "We have talked periodically about going nationwide," discloses cofounder Jim Spradling. "There is interest from groups in South Carolina and Texas. The problem with a national organization is that now you're talking about dues, newsletters and that sort of thing. It becomes, at that point, an impersonal organization. Down here, we pass the hat to pay for postage. Nobody makes any money on these deals. It really was designed as a vehicle for people to get together just to enjoy each others' company, and Rush Limbaugh was the centerpiece for putting that together."

"Welcome President Clinton—
and Your Husband Too."

A special systems officer for electronic countermeasures assigned to the First Flight Detachment of the Study and Observation Group (better known as SOG), Bob Worn was shot down twice in Vietnam while flying in UC- 123Ks. Here Worn spins a typically not-so-typical Rush Limbaugh Supper Club tale about his activities during President Clinton's visit to Shreveport to promote his health-care plan. Earlier, Worn had refused to budge in the face of police German shepherds on the outskirts of a local GM plant where Clinton spoke.

"I wanted to have my last say as far as telling the President what I thought of her and her husband. So I parked my motor home out on my property on North Gate Drive and put my banner out. A few of my friends stopped by for coffee, and eventually two Bossier City policemen came up and knocked on the door. The youngest one said, 'Sir, we've had a number of calls from Barksdale Air Force Base, and they are concerned about you.' I just grinned, and I said, 'Oh, tell them not to be concerned. We've got enough coffee. We've got doughnuts and Coke.'

"He said, 'Well, that's not it. They're concerned about the banner on the side of your motor home.' And I said, 'By golly, at least I got their attention. That makes me feel a little better about spending the money.' He said, 'Could you take it down?' I said, 'I could. But I am not going to. I want the President's husband to see it.'

"So he excused himself, stepped outside and called his supervisor. Unbeknownst to him, we had the scanner on, and we were listening to the police and secret service frequencies. He said, 'I made contact with the subject.' Everybody in the police department knows Bob Worn, but I was 'the subject' that day. He says, 'He doesn't want to take the banner off his motor home.' And the response from headquarters was, Well, tell him to clear out.'

"He comes back in and says, 'Sir, headquarters asked me to have you move your motor home off the lot.' And I said, 'I can't do that. The President hasn't been by yet.' He says, 'We have to clear this out for security for the President.' I am sitting there with two other commissioned officers in the United States Air Force, and I said, 'Three commissioned officers in the United States Air Force are a threat to the President?' And he said, 'Well, we've just got to clear it out.' I said, 'You're going to have to arrest me then because I am not moving.' That threw another metallic object into the gears of his slowly turning mind.

"He went outside again. Now his partner is sitting in

there with us—by this time he has a cup of coffee too—and he's listening to this young guy, who calls and says, 'I spoke to the subject about moving his motor home and he says he won't move it but that I could arrest him.' And they said, 'No, don't do that, don't do that. Tell him he's trespassing, and he has to move the motor home.' "

"By that time his partner, who is listening on the scanner with us, is absolutely cracking up. He knocks on the door and comes back in. He says 'Sir, you've got to move because you're trespassing.' And I said, 'Is there a basis in law for what you just told me?' And he said, 'Yes, if you don't have permission for being on somebody's property, you are trespassing.' I said, 'Oh, oh, operative word—permission.' "

"He says, 'Do you have permission to be here?' I said, 'Well, yes.' He said, 'Who did you get that permission from?' I said, 'When I woke up this morning, I rolled over and I kind of grabbed my wife's hand, and I said, "Honey, can I put our motor home on our property over on North Gate Drive today?" ' His face just fell."

Walter Abbott's Easy Five-Step Plan for Starting and Running Your Own Rush Limbaugh Supper Club

Walter Abbott has learned all the tricks of organizing a club. He hands out Rush Limbaugh Supper Club membership cards certifying that the cardholder has, in fact, "tested EIB-positive." His stationery is topped by a Supper Club bulletin board that gives the time and location of the next meeting. Abbott boils down the daunting tasks of starting and operating a club into five easy steps:

1. Contact two or three fellow Dittoheads, preferably some with P. T. Barnum qualities, to help out.

2. Fix a time and location for the meetings. Choose a restaurant—preferably a Rush Room or an advertiser on the local EIB affiliate radio station—that has a large meeting area, since growth will be exponential at first. Plan to meet at the same place and time, say, the last Tuesday or second Thursday, each month.

3. Call a radio talk-show host at your EIB affiliate and invite him or her to your meeting. Ask them to publicize the meeting a couple of days beforehand. Remember, you are operating on a slim budget, if any, so use your imagination to stir up interest. For example, you could encourage the local NOW chapter to picket your meetings. Be sure to call television stations and the newspaper to let them know it's happening.

4. Keep a list of names and addresses of all the participants and send reminder cards before each meeting. Encourage everyone to bring fellow Dittoheads to join the club.

5. As membership grows, organize a program that includes guest speakers, membership cards and awards, and special events.

Four

Colorado Dan's
Dazzling Day

*One fellow in a three-piece suit had a little stand
with a stack of resumes. He was holding a sign that
said, "Will Work for 40K." Another guy walked
around with a bucket and a sign on a stick that said,
"Have home, have job, want airplane." People threw
twenty-dollar bills into his bucket. He had a great
product. All he had to do was show up. He's a lot
smarter than I am.*

—Joey Gerdin, T-shirt vendor,
Minneapolis, Minnesota

It started out as just another phone call to Rush Limbaugh. Like most callers, Dan Kay, a twenty-three-year-
old Colorado flea-market worker, waited on the line for
more than half an hour. Then he told Limbaugh that he
was so broke his wife wouldn't let him spend $29.95 for
a subscription to *The Limbaugh Letter.* He confessed to

the commentator that he was forced to photocopy a friend's issue each month.

What did Kay expect the fruits of this phone call to be? A little sympathy? Would a wealthy listener call in and offer to pay his subscription tab? Would Limbaugh—in an act of great magnanimity—confer the letter free of charge upon his penniless fan?

No, of course not. Instead, the commentator blithely suggested that Kay hold a fund-raiser—a bake sale, to be exact. Several weeks later, on March 10, 1993, Kay called Limbaugh again, this time to report that the bake sale was on. Little did either know what a colossal event they had set in motion. Immediately fans began to call, fax, and e-mail. Among the first was Jack Jolley, vice president of Root Outdoor Advertising in Ohio. Jolley had something to pitch into the effort, and Limbaugh read his letter on the air: "What a great idea you had for Dan in Fort Collins, Colorado, to have a bake sale to raise the funds to purchase your newsletter. I would like to help Dan. Root Outdoor Advertising owns billboards in Fort Collins and would be willing to design, paint and display a billboard to advertise Dan's Bake Sale at no charge."

It was an offer made in earnest and too good to refuse. "I wanted to help in any way I could," explains Jolley. "I liked the idea that we could demonstrate to the public how business, not government and charity, is the answer to our problems. After Rush read my letter on the air, we got to work." Jolley, it turned out, could offer the project not just one but up to three thousand billboards nationwide. Suddenly, the event's potential proportions became all too apparent. "Limbaugh's people thought it might get out of control. We ended up displaying 14 billboards, just in northern Colorado," says Jolley.

"When we heard Jack Jolley talking about putting up billboards, we told Kit Carson we would bring the Bananas Foster," says Kathy Abernathy, the general manager of Brennan's Restaurant, a New Orleans institution and one of Limbaugh's favorite restaurants. "Rush called and said, 'Oh, you don't have to do that.' I said, 'Well, we're going to.' Rush is a great supporter of the restaurant. The number of people who come to Brennan's and mention him is just unbelievable. He's also a great friend," adds Abernathy, who met Limbaugh in 1989 after inviting him to dine at the restaurant. "I like him because he's informative. He doesn't talk over our heads," remarks Abernathy. "Lots of the staff listen to him, too."

Meanwhile, Kay's crash course in running a civic event had begun. He had planned to hold the festival on the modest grounds of the flea market where he worked, but when the hype escalated, it became clear that this would not do. Kay asked the city of Fort Collins for permission to use Old Town Square, a quaint refurbished area downtown. The city agreed, but it insisted on managing the logistics—for a price. Each vendor would have to ante up $100. Half would go directly to the city treasury, and half would pay for security, cleanup and a country-music band. Kay would control the activities, themes, and who got to sell what.

On the air, Limbaugh was obviously excited, and news of the bake sale spread with the sonic boom of his voice. Sellers, buyers, fun-seekers, and people with a cause—from Maine, Alaska, England, Guam—began to mobilize.

Jolley's billboards went up around Colorado. "They were nice—'Rush to Dan's Bake Sale, Old Town Square, Fort Collins, May 22,' " says the billboard exec, "with a really good picture of Rush."

The first to make plans were the vendors. Westerly Miller, a thirty-one-year-old artist from Malibu, California, heard Kay and Limbaugh on the radio and called Kay. "I got permission to design the official bake sale T-shirt," she says. "It was simple and subtle. On the left breast, printed, 'Dan's Bake Sale, Fort Collins, Colorado, May 22, 1993.' " Phone calls poured in from providers of almost every imaginable form of food and souvenir, and one by one, Kay signed them up.

Joey Gerdin, who owns a T-shirt business in Minneapolis, Minnesota, had been listening to Limbaugh daily since the Persian Gulf War. "After a few months of tuning in, I made my family listen so they could tell their friends what kind of junk is going on in the world," she says. "I had never gone to a political caucus before I listened to Rush. Then I heard Rush and Dan talking about the bake sale. I was going whether I could sell shirts or not.

"I always listened to Rush by myself while I worked," explains Gerdin. "I consumed every word he spoke, and I figured others did too. And I always wondered who else was listening." Gerdin overnighted a check for $100 to Fort Collins to secure a booth. "A week later, I called Dan to see if I could sell the official shirt. He had already promised that to someone else. So I asked if I could do the signature shirt. He didn't know what that was, but when he found out, he was excited at the thought of everyone wearing his signature on their shirts. So he faxed us his signature.

"I printed as many shirts as I could with the line of credit I had," declares Gerdin. "When I heard Rush say he was going, I suggested to my husband, Gary, that we tap into his retirement funds. He said, 'You're crazy.' I said, 'I'm not crazy.' He goes to sleep at 9:00 and doesn't watch Rush's show." Unfortunately for Gerdin, her husband won the argument.

Each day during the week before the event, hundreds and then thousands of people began the journey to Fort Collins, a town that was once a supply stop for California-bound gold rushers. "People waved to us all across the country," says Helen Coman, an Asheville, North Carolina, quilt-pin maker who recruited her niece Kerry Hunt, who had just graduated from North Carolina State University, for the trip. "The work I do is great for listening to talk radio," observes Coman. "I can work and laugh and not have to look at anything. The moment I heard Dan, I called to sign up. Rush probably thinks we're a bunch of liberals, but there is no more conservative a group than craftspeople—especially quilt-pin people, like me," Coman asserts. "We rented a Ryder and spent a week driving cross-country. We had signs that said we were going to Fort Collins. Everyone in the country seemed to know about it. At a diner in the Midwest, people ran out to the van just to say how jealous they were that we were going to Dan's and they couldn't go."

That Tuesday, Miller and her mother, Loni, packed Miller's pickup truck with camping gear and T-shirts and hit the highway. "For three days, they drove the fifteen hundred miles to Colorado. At the end of each day, they camped at a KOA campground, cooking over an open fire, and sleeping in a tent. "It's a long drive for two ladies, but it was tremendous," remarks Miller. "We drove most of the day and listened to and talked about Rush. I never would have thought of politics if it weren't for him. I joined the Malibu Women's Republican Club because of the excitement for politics that he gave me. I disagree with him on the environment, though. He says it doesn't matter. He should see how beautiful this country is. But the way he presents it is so funny. Besides, I mostly agree with him. The whole experience of driving and camping out was great. My mom loved it."

Gerdin had planned to drive out alone. Then her twenty-nine-year-old brother, Chip, who worked on the family's nearby dairy farm, insisted on going. "I'd been talking about Rush's show for so long that if I hadn't let him go, he never would have forgiven me. But I was happy to have the help," Gerdin concedes. At dawn, two days before the bake sale, Gerdin and her brother cruised past the farm's stone wall in her green Ford pickup packed with T-shirts and began their nine hundred mile journey. Gerdin's sister and husband, an engineer, would fly to Fort Collins later, and a cousin from Kansas City would drive out for their miniature family reunion at the bake sale.

Also among the hordes heading West was David Levesque, who listens to Limbaugh while working on cars in his Marion, Illinois, machine shop. "I'm relieved that finally someone expresses the things I've been saying for years. Only Rush does it a whole lot better," says

Levesque, who likes to drive his classic cars to places like Opryland and Daytona Beach. "When I heard Dan and Rush talking about having a bake sale, I had to go," he states. "I printed thousands of bumper stickers to sell to pay for the trip, but I really went just to have fun." With that in mind, he filled up the trunk of his bright red 1962 Studebaker Hawk with boxes of "Dan's Bake Sale: I Was There" bumper stickers, revved the engine, and headed West.

In Buckeye, Arizona, Paul Winn, a retired attorney for billionaire Howard Hughes, took similar measures. Winn had heard about Dan's on his Walkman while biking through cotton fields surrounding his vacation home. He called pal Steve Reta, a horse trainer, and talked him into a week-long tour of the Southwest—culminating not in an inspirational gaze on the Grand Canyon but in a rip-roaring, right-and-ready Fort Collins revival.

Winn and Reta drove east on Interstate 70 from Las Vegas. "We saw all sorts of cars, Broncos, vans and buses with signs and stickers that said, 'Dan's Bake Sale or Bust,'" reports Winn. "I had a simple little sticker on my Buick Park Avenue that said, 'Rush Is Right.' It was a Rush Limbaugh road trip. We'd pick up muffins and coffee and find a nice field, roll out a blanket and listen to Rush."

They came by air, too. That Friday, the McClures of Fort Worth, Texas, had been looking forward to a quiet weekend at home. Devoted Limbaugh listeners, Brian, a telephone service salesman, tunes in daily during lunch, while Nedra listens at home. "The answering machine picks up even though I'm there," she announces proudly.

"For about the last year, each week I've turned a new person into a Dittohead, and that's no exaggeration. I say, 'Just tune in for a week.' After that, they're hooked."

When the McClures heard that Aviation Solutions, a Dallas-based charter company, was filling a plane destined for Dan's the next day, they couldn't resist. They paid the $250 for round-trip tickets and scrambled to get a baby-sitter. They weren't the only ones. "Within five hours after WBAP announced our charter, we received 1,300 requests," says Dave Meyers, CEO of Aviation Solutions and a Limbaugh fan himself. "If we had had another day, we could have filled five or six planes."

"I tend to be very conservative in not doing things at the spur of the moment, taking time to make the right decision based on all the facts," says Richard Hood, a Monroe, Louisiana, college professor. "Well, this came up about noon on Friday before the bake sale on Saturday. Something sparked my wife and me to say, 'What the heck, let's do it. We'll always remember this.' My wife was tickled because it was totally unlike me.

"People flew into Dallas from all over the United States because they couldn't catch a plane from their home cities directly into Denver," notes Hood. "The airport was totally booked. It seemed as though at that last minute the only flight in there was through this charter out of Dallas."

By Friday, the bake sale was already consuming the town of Fort Collins. Signs of Rush Limbaugh were everywhere—hats, T-shirts, buttons, and books. A recording of Limbaugh boomed from somebody's portable cassette recorder. "I drove 24 hours straight, without stopping—

except for gas and food," recalls Levesque, who arrived that afternoon and immediately began peddling his bumper stickers.

June Peterson, from the Downtown Business Association, walked through Old Town Square that evening to check on developments. "We'd gotten a lot of phone calls and interest in booths, but I couldn't believe so many people were there so early," Peterson recalls. "What will it be like tomorrow?" she wondered.

Saturday, the official day of Dan's Bake Sale, arrived in Fort Collins with mild and clear weather and the generally ignored promise of noontime showers. "We brought a lot of stuff, and we set up at six o'clock that morning," Gerdin says. "I always like to get there well before the crowd. But even at 6:00, people were wandering around. I knew stuff would sell, but not so fast so early. I have never seen anything like it. We were overwhelmed." And the tide was just beginning to roll.

With every seat occupied, Aviation Solution's 727 took off at 6:00 A.M. Two hours later, the McClures, the Hoods, Meyers, and 175 others landed in Cheyenne, Wyoming, and hustled onto three buses. "We crossed some beautiful prairies with mountains in the background," recalls Hood. "There was a tremendous amount of traffic, large vans and vehicles of all kinds from many states with 'Dan's Bake Sale or Bust' and other travel messages on their windshields. That was the first real sign that we were there."

Because of the unprecedented traffic into town that day, some of the buses from the Denver airport would never make it to Dan's. But the Cheyenne buses narrowly beat the worst of the jams. "In fact," Nedra McClure reports, "the bus driver announced as we entered town that the police had closed off the roads behind us, and a round of applause erupted. I would have walked if the police stopped our bus. There was no way they were keeping me away."

By 9:30 A.M., just an hour and a half after opening shop, Westerly Miller had only a few dozen of her five hundred official Dan's Bake Sale T-shirts left, and she was out of change. With the crowd pressing in on the booth and hands reaching out with cash to buy one of the rapidly vanishing shirts, could Miller escape to get change? Running through the back of her mind, she remembered debating whether to borrow money to print more shirts. She could do nothing about that now, but with seven hours of bake sale still to go and very few shirts, she could make one bold move. Instead of trying to rustle up some small bills, she simply raised the price from $15 to an even $20. "Nobody complained—not even the people standing there when I did it," she laughs. "They were happy just to give me their twenties." Within half an hour, the last shirt was gone.

"It took me 18 hours to fly from Guam and less than two hours to sell all my cookies," reports Bob McLaughlin, owner of Eagle Enterprises, a cookie company. "It was a pain getting them here, but wish I'd brought an entire planeful." McLaughlin, who listens to Limbaugh on K57-AM in Guam, toted three hundred pounds of chocolate chip and macadamia nut cookies in his luggage.

By ten o'clock, the festival had kicked into full gear. The streets were swarming with costumed people wearing funny hats and signs. Others handed out fliers advertising everything from newsletters to burritos. One booth hawked "Impeach Hillary" shirts, another "Limbaugh for President" hats. Gourmet food, cookies, political pamphlets, computer software, paperweights, American flags, and even certificates verifying attendance flowed from other stands. The Colorado State Republicans, including Senator Bob Schaffer, who represents Fort Collins in the Colorado legislature, handed out literature and flogged their own goods—T-shirts, hats, buttons, and wooden cookies engraved with the words "Dan's Bake Sale."

A thriving black market sold everything from buttons and wursts to Snapple from backpacks and unauthorized booths. "One fellow in a three-piece suit had a little stand with a stack of resumes," relates Gerdin, who had already sold out of Dan's signature T-shirt and started to take orders. "He was holding a sign that said, 'Will Work for 40K.' Another guy walked around with a bucket and a sign on a stick that said, 'Have home, have job, want airplane.' People threw twenty-dollar bills into his bucket. He had a great product. All he had to do was show up. He's a lot smarter than I am."

"Some guy was wearing a barrel and a sign that said, 'Clinton took everything. This is all I have left,'" recounts Paul Winn. "Two other guys nearby had signs saying, 'Taxation without representation is tyranny,' and 'Taxation with representation ain't so hot either.' I talked to Dan's wife, Kelly. She's really nice," he concedes, ignoring the fact that she was vocal about not being a Limbaugh fan. "I bought 50 T-shirts for my nephews, nieces and grandchildren, and a wooden key chain with 'Dan's Bake Sale' painted on it."

"A young guy walked around with a tall sign that said, 'Haircuts $200.' He wormed his way through the crowd, and everybody fell out laughing when they saw that," says Hood. "The basic conversation we heard over and over was that we're not Rush worshipers in the sense that we think he never says anything we disagree with or never goes a little overboard, but for the very first time somebody—other than occasionally Paul Harvey, now that's a personal observation—is saying something that sounds like what we have thought all along.

"Somebody is saying something like what my daddy taught me, like what my values are. Rush is the only person I hear talk about the World War II generation of my parents, who I love so dearly, and the struggles they went through. That's one of the philosophical reasons we listen and why we went to the bake sale. For the very first time, somebody is saying what we have always thought. I definitely don't get that from Dan Rather or Peter Jennings or Tom Brokaw, or somebody like Larry King."

Almost without exception, people were well behaved. A group of teenage punk-rockers rambled through the packed town square. No trouble resulted. In fact, they conversed with the crowd, then rode away on skateboards. A small group of protesters carried banners saying, "Flush Rush, We Love Clinton." They were chided but mostly ignored. "The Rush fans were clean and decent people, just happy to be alive," says Gerdin. "At state fairs, people are really grumpy. At Dan's, people genuinely cared for each other."

Old Town Square was far more crowded than anyone had predicted it would be. Outside town, at Hughes Stadium, where the Colorado State University Rams play, all eight thousand parking spots were taken. Another thousand cars parked at the school's Moby Gym. "It attracted five times as many people as they expected and double what the national media reported," says Colorado's U.S. Senator Hank Brown, who was on hand to welcome Limbaugh.

While the hordes mixed it up, the crew from Brennan's sweated over gallons of ice cream. "I brought my executive chef, two day chefs, my purchaser, director of sales and my husband, Steve," reports Abernathy. But it was friend Missy Ochsner, an emergency-room physician, who proved to be invaluable. "We brought 80 cases of bananas, several hundred pounds of brown sugar," Abernathy relates. "We called restaurants and banquet halls to find a place with vats large enough to cook our sauce. Nothing. With Missy's help, we wound up using the kitchen in the Poudre Valley Hospital." The Brennans crew and a unit of volunteers worked all night Friday making the sauce and storing ice cream in thirty plastic coolers.

"We're used to the crowds because of Mardi Gras," Abernathy emphasizes. "There was no drinking at the bake sale, but it was as fun as Mardi Gras. People shoved books, T-shirts, arms and legs in front of us to sign, just because we knew Rush and were from Brennan's. It was a big, positive feeling." Abernathy and her crew dished up over eight thousand servings of Bananas Foster, while the Jaycees collected $3 a plate for charity.

Without a doubt, Dan and Kelly Kay's booth attracted

the most attention. "My wife, a friend from Oregon and I stayed up really late baking, so I was running on very little sleep," recalls Kay. "Most of the day is a blur of meeting people, shaking hands and signing autographs. As soon as we got there, crowds of people surrounded me. I had to lead the crowd away so they could set up our booth." The trio sold cakes and cookies—gone in an hour—spatulas, Hawaiian shirts, candies, certificates of attendance, and other goodies contributed by friends and Limbaugh fans. "Someone sent us a case of homemade jams and jellies, and a company out of Detroit sent us cases of spaghetti sauce, barbecue sauce and pasta sauce," says Kay. "Another person gave us sets of a game he designed called Lawn Dice, where you throw big dice into lawn circles. Many people sent things general delivery, and the post office would call us and say, 'We've got all these packages for you. Where do we deliver them?' " relates Kay. "From April through the day of the bake sale, if we didn't answer the phone for a day, there'd be 25 messages."

Fans circled the Kays' booth to have Michael Lynch, the official photographer, snap their pictures with Dan. "I heard the inspirational moment on Rush's show," says Lynch, who lives in Seattle. "Then sensed the snowball rolling. I was psyched. I had always been politically opinionated, and Rush validates what I think. I called Dan and said, 'You'll be a popular guy, and I'd like to be there to photograph it for you.' It was an unbelievably good time. I worked my ass off and didn't get any sleep, but I didn't care. It was a complete honor to go to Dan's Bake Sale."

Just before noon, Limbaugh circled overhead in a helicopter, surveying the scene, taking videos for his TV show. Limbaugh later reported what he saw from his helicopter as he came into town: "There were seven miles of buses lined up on the interstate." The police estimated that while there were sixty thousand people in Old Town Square, some thirty thousand more were still trying to get to Fort Collins.

Then came the rain. "I was in my booth watching the crowd and the clouds building overhead," says Helen Coman. "Then it just started pouring. During the morning we had been talking to the people from *The Limbaugh Letter* and the radio show, who were in the next booth. When the rain started, they came into my booth, which was covered. I asked them to sign my copy of *The Way Things Ought to Be,* but they wouldn't do it because it wasn't their book. It was neat meeting the people who work for Rush, anyway."

Meanwhile, a crowd had gathered around the stage in the center of Old Town Square, where a country-music band was playing. Finally, the mayor began the speech-making that would build up to the arrival of Limbaugh. Paul Winn was in the throngs around the stage, where he met an English woman named Tia. "She wore a formal beige dress, pearls and a ribbon in her hair. She looked as if she were going to a banquet," describes Winn. "Tia and her brother, who wore a dark suit, were dancing around, full of life. When the rain started, everyone was worried that their clothes would get ruined. Some guy in Dan's booth gave them garbage bags to wear. Tia was trying to get to the stage, but she couldn't get through the dense crowd," Winn recalls. "So my friend Steve—wearing a ten-gallon hat—ushered her up there, calling out, 'Make way for Tia! Make way for Tia!' Everyone laughed. The crowd teased us, but they let Tia up to the stage."

At last, Limbaugh's helicopter landed, and Fort Collins police escorted him and his entourage through back streets to Old Town Square. Security took to the roofs to search out would-be troublemakers. The rainstorm passed just before Limbaugh's arrival, and the cheers began: "Ditto, ditto, Rush, Rush, we love Rush!" Mounted police officers and private security cleared a path through the mob. It was time for the main event.

Ostensibly, Dan's Bake Sale had one goal—to raise enough money for Dan Kay to purchase a subscription to *The Limbaugh Letter.* It was time for Kay to present Limbaugh with a check for $29.95. Senator Brown waited by the microphone until the broadcaster was close enough to approach the stage. "This is a bigger party than a Broncos game," he shouted, amplifying the crowd's volume level.

Sales halted and all heads turned toward the stage as Limbaugh, wearing a blue suit and signature splashy tie, ascended the steps. "The excitement when Rush hit that stage right after that thunderstorm was just incredible," recalls photographer Michael Lynch. "I'll tell you, I've never seen anything like it."

After riding to Fort Collins from Denver with a group of fellow motorcycle enthusiasts, Ken Hamblin, the conservative broadcaster and columnist, was swept onto the stage. "He recognized me in my black leather jacket and chaps even though he had seen me only on CNBC in a fedora, white shirt and braces," notes Hamblin, incredulously. "He said, 'I'm pleased to be here in Fort Collins with brother Hamblin, who I watched on CNBC recently.' "

"I love you all from the bottom of my heart," Limbaugh yelled to the cheering crowd. Although the stage-mounted speakers reached only about a third of the crowd, those in the back listened to Randy Keim's live broadcast on KCOL, as Limbaugh described the beautiful sight the gathering created for him from his plane, *EIB One*. "I was going to be here earlier," he said, "but the barber was running late." He was referring, of course, to President Clinton's recent snafu at the Los Angeles airport where air traffic ground to a halt while the President, in his plane on the runway, received a $200 designer haircut. The crowd roared with laughter.

"Capitalism caused this to happen—the pursuit of a $29.95 newsletter," announced Limbaugh. He congratulated everyone who had traveled so far to exchange goods and services and Dan Kay for instigating it all.

"Where *is* Dan?" Limbaugh beseeched, looking around the crowd. Having been swamped by autograph-seekers, the man of the hour now slinked onto the stage. "Everywhere I looked there were faces," says Kay, who is somewhat shy and admits he was nervous. "I was amazed that all those people could fit into that small space, get along so well and have such a great time." His speech was brief and unpolished—but sincere. He presented the broadcaster with a giant fortune cookie made with the help of a friend who owns a Fort Collins Chinese restaurant. Inside the cookie was a rolled up check for $29.95. Limbaugh handed over a copy of the latest newsletter, bound in a photo album. The crowd cheered, cameras whizzed.

Afterwards, the band kicked off another round of tunes. Limbaugh dodged copies of *The Way Things Ought to Be*—thrust forth to be autographed—as he passed by. Excited and exhausted, Kay was greeted by well-wishers. Richard Hood snapped a photo just then. "It shows his tiredness but his smiling through that," observes Hood. "His eyes are saying, 'Gee, I've been up all night, and I want to be here, but I surely am ready for a nap.' " Drained from months of preparation and at least one sleepless night, Kay fainted beside the stage, but he revived and even returned to his booth for more photos.

Dan's Bake Sale ended in the late afternoon as planned. By all accounts, the event had gone off with a bang. CBS News reported: "The spectacle was enough to drive a stake through the heart of liberalism." The next morning, papers around the country called it, "Rush-stock," a "patriotic Woodstock," a "right-wing love-in."

"It was a genuine effort to celebrate patriotism," asserts State Senator Schaffer. "There's skepticism when politicians try to do stuff like this, because they have something to gain. Rush really brings out the best in people. It was a chance for many Americans to celebrate their patriotism—and, yes, their conservatism. They were united by common sense and simple decency."

At the day's end, Dan and Kelly Kay told *The Denver Post* they wanted to "sleep, count our money and count our blessings." Several good causes were able to count theirs, too, as more than $20,000 was donated in the names of Dan and Kelly Kay to the United Way, the Red Cross, and the American Cancer Society.

Fresno's Dittohead Barbecue

Inspired by Dan's Bake Sale, Fresno, California, radio station KMJ organized the March 1994 Dittohead Barbecue. With a national plug from Limbaugh and plenty of hometown hot air, KMJ attracted ten thousand strong to the Madera Campgrounds for contests, a cookout, live tunes, and the day's special event: the Miss Dittohead Swimsuit Competition.

"We wanted Rush to visit us again, like he did in 1989. But he doesn't travel as much anymore, so we had to have our Rush event without Rush," says KMJ promotion manager, John Broeske. "He's a fantastic personality, with a great message, so we knew we would get great people"—and some pretty good cooks. The Politically Incorrect Cooking Contest was one of the day's highlights. The k.d. lang division was for beef and pork dishes (lang's a vegetarian). For fowl, there was the Spotted Owl division.

Twenty Limbaugh impersonators entered the Talent on Loan from God Contest and were judged by the crowd's applause. The winner was flown to New York for a taping of Limbaugh's TV show. Meanwhile, Tree-Hugging Contest participants lined up to toss a heavy bundle of processed lumber, but the brawny boys took backseat. "The Miss Dittohead Contest was the most popular," declares Broeske. "Each girl wore a black Coor's Light one-piece bathing suit. They were all very beautiful." At the end, the contestants all turned to a video camera and yelled, seductively, "We love you, Rush."

"When Rush talked about the barbecue on his show,

he said, 'Make sure you send the winner of that contest to New York,' " says Broeske. Limbaugh showed a videotape of the event on his show in April.

Five

Talent on Loan
from Dittoheads

I took the nation by a landslide, and we were rolling
*   along,*
But now I'm flat on my backside, wonderin' where
*   I went wrong.*
Well, I get a funny feelin' every time I turn on the
*   news.*
Yeah, there's no doubt about it, I got the White-
*   water blues!*
I got them Whitewater blues, the press won't leave
*   me alone.*
I got them Whitewater blues, and I just wanna go
*   home.*

> —"Whitewater Blues," written by Greg
> Sublett; sung by Paul Shanklin

Dan's Bake Sale had proved that Limbaugh could in-
spire people around the globe to travel thousands of miles
to celebrate his conservative message. That message had

also created a deluge of correspondence at EIB head-quarters in New York. Not only did fans want to heap compliments upon the commentator, but they wanted to contribute their talents to the show. Where else, after all, could a would-be conservative comedian turn to show-case his act?

And Limbaugh was receptive. In fact, look-alikes and sound-alikes were a specialty. In February 1993 when Charlie Putnam, of Shreveport, Louisiana, called in, Lim-baugh even fed him lines live over the air and taped them for future gags. "Can I ask you a favor?" said Limbaugh, obviously gleeful at the mischief he was about to get into. "You sound just like Lloyd Bentsen. Would you let us . . . have you say some things that we would like to have the Secretary of the Treasury say in the coming weeks and months?" Limbaugh scripted some lines dur-ing a break.

While Putnam was a serendipitous find, others were pros. One of the earliest and most prolific behind-the-scenes contributors was Springfield, Missouri, DJ Rob Carson. "I was working with Rusty Humphreys, who was with the TM Comedy Network in Dallas, and heard Rusty had done the Mike Tyson imitation that bumpered Rush's breaks," says Carson. "I'd been writing comedy for radio for a while, and I thought this might be a great way to do some political satire and reach a larger audi-ence. I said, 'Man, how'd you get that on Rush?' " Hum-phries put him in touch with John Donovan, WABC's production director, who introduces Limbaugh in his classic radio-announcer baritone.

In 1990, Rob Carson wrote "I Use My Wealth," a send-up of Ted Kennedy set to a pop hit called "I Touch Myself" by The DiVynils. Carson's new lyrics were a hit: "I use my wealth, The Kennedy motto. Don't go home with Ted, Or drive in an auto." Next, Carson, now a morning-show host with Springfield's ROCK 99, KWTO-FM, turned Joe Cocker's "You Are So Beautiful" into "Ted Is So Pitiful." A friend, Norman Jolly, sang and played the piano and also collaborated with Carson on "Shalala," to the tune of Eric Clapton's "Lala," and "Rush Is the Right One, Baby," a spoof of the Ray Charles Pepsi commercial. The gag commercials and song parodies became a signature of the Limbaugh show.

"The classics," says Carson, "are 'The Capitol Hill Bank' and 'The Capitol Hill Post Office.' We did those in the summer of 1991 when the Capitol Hill Bank scam was in the news. That was just a whim. It came out of nowhere. I wrote it in about 20 minutes. A friend, Bruce Jones, did the senator's voice, and I did the young pup's voice, the bank teller, and I got John Donovan to do the announcer voice. John has the voice of God, that marvelous seasoned 50-year-old radio announcer voice, and he makes things sound so authoritative." Donovan delivers the tag line: "Capitol Hill Bank, member FLEECE, a special-privilege lender."

Limbaugh liked the commercial parodies so much he published both in *The Way Things Ought to Be* in a chapter about Congress. "I had an instinct about it," claims Carson. "I read a lot of news analysis in the papers. Rush still talks about how insightful it was two years ago to what is going on right now with Dan Rostenkowski. I don't know how it happened—I guess we got lucky."

Carson had developed a close relationship with Donovan. "Johnny is the guy I talk to about ideas," says the DJ. "I speak to him almost every day. He is genuinely enthusiastic about what he does there. He feeds me what he thinks Rush'd be interested in, and then I throw it down. Or I listen to Rush and say, 'Aha, he's talking about whatever.' Generally, if I send it, he'll play it."

Among the parodies that Carson worked on with Donovan was *Bram Stoker's Taxula,* with Carson playing Count Taxula. "That's where Algore came into being," says Carson. "Come on, Algore! Let's go to Congress. I'm hungry!" In another spoof, Carson parodied *Jurassic Park* with a gag movie trailer for *Geriatric Park,* featuring such frightening monsters as Barneyfrankus Liberalis and Arkansaurus Taxandspendus."

Carson's movie parodies and other gags spurred others to creativity. Jeff Hines, an Indianapolis recording-studio manager, had been a Limbaugh fan for several years before he contacted the show. "I moved to Missouri in 1991 to do production work for a radio network called Missouri Net, and I began listening to Rush there," explains Hines. "I don't agree with everything he says, but for the most part, I think he says what needs to be said by the regular media. You almost have to go to Christian radio to get some of that, and many people who listen to his show wouldn't listen to a Christian station.

"I worked two years at Missouri Net, and the reporters were all liberals—every one of them," asserts Hines. "There's no way they were objective. One thing I like about Rush is that, yeah, he's subjective—he sure is—but at least he admits it. And I don't care if he makes money," declares Hines. "We're all trying to make money. A lot of his critics point at that: 'He's in it for the money.' Well, so are you. If you work, you're in it for the money, unless you're a charitable organization or a church ministry. You have to make money, or you'll go out of business.

"Rush articulates what a lot of people want to say, and he does it in a way that's entertaining and humorous, not as a crybaby. Marlin Maddox has been doing what Rush does for 10 years, but he's not as entertaining," maintains Hines. "Rush is funny and fun to listen to. The more I listened, the more I thought of ideas to send in, but while was in Missouri, I never did.

"When I moved back to Indiana in 1993 to work for a radio station," Hines recalls, "I was in the car a lot, so I listened to the show just about every day. In September, I was walking around my apartment one night— my wife was at work—and I had this idea to write a parody of John Lennon's 'Imagine.' It just hit me, and I wrote it in about an hour. I wrote about half of it after I called my buddy David Patton in Jefferson, Missouri, and said, 'Hey, you've got to hear this.' " Patton, a high-school vice-principal, contributed a new line referring to a world without high schools handing out condoms. Then Hines saw Matt Roush, a jingles singer and one-man rock band, at a gas station and asked him if he wanted to record the song. Roush said yes, and they recorded it the following week.

"I knew somebody who had worked with Johnny Donovan, and they told me he was now the production guy. So I called Johnny and sang the song to him over the phone. He said, 'That's great,' and I said, 'Well, it's produced, and I'll send it to you.' They got it at 10 o'clock the next morning by Fed Ex and played it twice on the show that day. They played the heck out of it. A lot of people I know heard it. That was exciting. My wife got a charge out of it. This is a way for me to tell 20 million people what I think. Not too many people get to do that. Anyone can sit at a coffee shop or a bar and rant and rave, but how many of us get to tell 20 million people what we think?"

Of all the talent that Limbaugh attracted, Paul Shanklin, a thirty-one-year-old impersonator, is by far the most recognizable to listeners. To them, he is the raspy-voiced fork-tongued warbly-singing Bill Clinton. The Tennessean found his way to EIB in early 1993, but it wasn't easy.

Shanklin, who with his wife, Angie, owns a commercial carpet-cleaning business in Memphis, was an immediate Limbaugh convert. "When Limbaugh came out, it was great," he says. "Taking nothing away from Buckley—he would get up in front of his peers and say what they didn't want to hear—Rush was doing the same thing, but it wasn't just to polite society. He was doing it on the radio, and he was saying, 'You don't have to listen to me, but that's just the way it is.' I had apolitical friends who I could never interest in *National Review,* but they latched on to Rush Limbaugh."

The would-be comedian, who says his talents were passed down from his paternal uncles, was discovered at a fair in the fall of 1992: "They had a contest booth, 'Can You Moo?' " recalls Shanklin, a longtime conservative junkie. "I did Ross Perot: 'Well, I'm only gonna moo if the volunteers ask me to. It's just that simple. I just work for them.' " Shanklin didn't win the contest, but Oldies 98, the radio station cosponsoring the event, hired him to work on their morning show. A friend, Mike Ramirez, the Pulitzer Prize-winning editorial cartoonist who works for *The Memphis Commercial Appeal,* advised Shanklin to send a tape to Limbaugh.

"Here we had a very creative and very, very funny guy with a tremendous amount of talent, and he was just doing it for fun," says Ramirez. "From the moment I met him and discovered this ability, I encouraged him to do it for a living. I introduced him to radio personalities, and whenever I had an opportunity to include him in an interview, I did. He's kind of shy when it comes to a multitude of people," observes Ramirez, laughing. "When you're one-on-one with him, you can't get him to shut up."

When Limbaugh called Ramirez, whose cartoons also appear in *USA Today* and *The Wall Street Journal,* for permission to reprint one of his cartoons in *The Lim-*

baugh Letter, Ramirez wrote back, "Sure, you can use the cartoon for a certain donation to charity and if you listen to this guy's tape of impersonations."

"We sent in a demo tape—things I'd done at Oldies 98 during the campaign and through the winter—with Mike's cartoons," says Shanklin. "We sent this Fed Ex with a *Commercial Appeal* stamp on it, trying to get somebody to pay attention to it. But we never got any response." Even so, Shanklin didn't give up. "I called Johnny Donovan after sending a second tape," says the impersonator, "and he said, 'No, I didn't get it. Send me another one.' Real short, terse. I sent him another one and called back later. He said, 'Yeah, you really got it. It was good. We'll be talking to you.' "

"Paul called me one day," relates Ramirez, "and said, 'I guess they're just not interested. I don't do a good enough job at it.' And I said, 'That's ridiculous. What voice did you use when you talked to them?' He said, 'I used my own.' I said, 'You dummy. Call them up and pretend you're Bill Clinton and that you're a little hostile over the things they've been saying.' "

So Shanklin called Donovan again. This time, he summoned up his three-star hangover sub-Adam's apple Southern drawl—his hangdog Clinton impersonation: "I said, 'Ah ahhh, I'm sorry. This is Bill Clinton, and I'm sorry if I've offended Rush in any way. I didn't mean to. Maybe we just didn't get started off on the right foot.' " Donovan loved it. "He said, 'Send me a demo tape.' And I said, 'I've sent you three!' He said, 'Send me another one,' " remembers Shanklin, who did, and then he sent two original gags.

"The first was some jokes," says Shanklin. "It was right after Clinton had told the joke at the press roast, 'Did you like the way Rush took up for Janet Reno? He only did it because she was attacked by a black guy.' I had him saying, 'No, no I got another one.' And it was Clinton sitting down with his joke writers, and I can't remember what I said now, but Mike and I thought up some awful racially charged jokes. The second was meant to be Clinton trying to read a straight speech, but he couldn't make his way through it because it said things about honesty and truth, and he started laughing," says Shanklin. *The Rush Limbaugh Show* incorporated Shanklin's second gag into a piece about the President's $200 haircut aboard *Air Force One*. "I said, 'Ah ahhh let's see, where's that speech?' " croaks Shanklin in Clintonese. "Let's see, ah ahhh I'll just run through it a couple of times: 'My fellow Americans, I just want to tell you the truth and be honest . . .' and I start laughing. 'Man, I can't get this right. I can't stand this. You're gonna have to take this part out.' "

Limbaugh used both gags. For Shanklin, airtime on Limbaugh's national show was a dream come true. "I never really felt like I fit into any artistic community," he quips. "I have short hair, I'm married, and I was a conservative long before Limbaugh came along."

All Shanklin, a virtual human Tower of Babel with a run-on sense of humor, had needed was a tad of encouragement. He later told a *Commercial Appeal* reporter that his secret was figuring out who people sound like: "Al Gore is like an accountant telling a joke to small children. Ross Perot is the uncle who's got the answer to everybody's questions. He knows what to do with Cuba: nuke it and blacktop it." To Shanklin, George Bush is John Wayne on Halcion: "We're gonna go over the hill, there, get those Indians, gotta get those Indians." Shanklin could do them all. Between jobs and playing golf with Ramirez, he cranked out ideas on the dozens of yellow legal pads he kept for that purpose.

In July 1993, Shanklin scored a big hit with his first song parody when he tinkered with the lyrics to the Beatles song "Yesterday" and delivered them in a rendition of Clinton's battle-weary drone.

> Yesterday,
> All my troubles started with the gays.
> Oh, we believe in yesterdays.
> Suddenly, the media, ah heck, they're
>   all over me.
> Maybe it was just Hillary.
> Or it could have been that haircut.
> Oh, our polls fell so suddenly.

A month later, Shanklin followed up with "All Your Money," a parody of the Beatles tune "All My Loving" with the refrain:

> All your money, I will tax from you.
> All your money, I need revenue.

The song was an instant hit. " 'All Your Money' is the favorite of a lot of people," says Shanklin. "I Lied to You" followed and was based on his favorite Beatles tune, "Do You Want To Know A Secret." Both songs received frequent requests. "I thought that couldn't be right," states Shanklin. "People wouldn't call just to ask them to play a song, but, oh yes, they do."

According to Shanklin, "I Lied to You," was an easy parody to write. "I could keep the original premise for a long time," he explains. "Clinton thinks he's been able to fool everyone and then he decides to come clean as if they didn't already know."

"Basically when I have an idea, I do it, send it up and see what happens," explains Shanklin. "If I have an idea but don't know where to go with it, I might call Johnny, or usually Mike and other friends, and pick their brains. Everybody says, 'Do you get to talk to Rush?' 'Next time you talk to Rush . . .' No, I never talk to him. I get ideas from what he says, and use that as a guide, but they don't call me and say, 'Do something on so and so.'

Not everything I send in gets played," admits Shanklin. "They edit, change, delete. Two minutes is what we shoot for. Some songs have to lose verses. Rush listens to everything. He directs the show. Sometimes by the time you get it there, it's too late. It has to be fresh or evergreen, a song they can play over and over. In that case, it has to fit many situations."

Other gags happened on the spur of the moment, like the before and after additions to Shanklin's Ross Perot parody, "They're Coming to Take Me Away," which Lim-

baugh played in the fall of 1993, the day after the Al
Gore-Ross Perot NAFTA debate. "First Johnny called to
say, 'Hey, we're playing your song,' " recalls Shanklin.
"Then he said, 'I've got an idea for doing Al Gore re-
questing it.' He wanted Gore saying, 'Gee, would you
play that song again? I really liked it.' And I said, 'Wait,
I've got another idea. Let's have Ross Perot try to buy
it back from Limbaugh.' So we had Perot say, 'Well, okay
then, how much do you want for it? I'll pay. Just look,
I've been blackmailed before.' " Live, Limbaugh took
them as phone calls, Gore before the song and Perot right
after.

Shanklin recorded another instant winner on April 1,
1994. "April Fools' snuck up on me," he says. "I called
Johnny and said, 'Hey, you want to do something for
April Fools'?' I had worked with somebody that morning
on a live radio show, and they had written something
similar . . . ahem, I didn't steal their idea exactly, but in
radio, theft is a bit of a compliment. Basically, it spring-
boarded me into something a little more revealing. I told
him how it would go, and then he turned on the tape,"
says Shanklin, metamorphosing into Clinton: 'I just want
the American people to know that I'm gonna come clean
and that ah ahhh I'm gonna disclose everything and admit it all . . . April Fools'!' It was one take and thank
you very much. We did it over the phone, but most things
aren't like that."

One of the show's biggest hits was a parody of "A
Whole New World" from the Walt Disney movie *Aladdin*.
Jeff Hines wrote the lyrics and sent them down to Paul

Shanklin. "When anybody has an idea that needs Clinton's voice, Johnny says, 'You need to talk to Paul,' " says Shanklin. "Jeff had a good idea, and he had some good lines in it. But it was in third person, and since I was doing it in first, it needed to be changed. It was a good idea, but I hated the song by the time I finished with it because I worked on it forever.

"It's like anything you do, you write something and you don't like it, and the more you work with it, the less you like it. You just don't want to think about it anymore. It had gotten to that point. And one morning, I was thinking, 'be like Russia,' and I thought 'Boris and Natasha,' from *Bullwinkle*. Hillary's thinking of Mother Russia as a good socialist would, and Bill's thinking more like, 'Yeah, we can be like Boris and Natasha!' I love that. Our parody is a parody of a parody.

"Really, Clinton isn't usually that silly until he starts talking on autopilot," admits Shanklin, who says he couldn't capture the President's voice until he realized that Clinton sounded like someone with a bad hangover. "Like, 'Well, I mean, I had a pickup once. Ah ahhh it was a El Camino. It had Astroturf in the back.' That's when he starts ah ahhh, sounding like a real—probably it's his real persona. 'Ah ahhh'—do you hear that when he talks? Basically, when he gets nervous or mad, whew. But he's smooth. Boy, he's so smooth."

" 'A Whole New World' took about two months to get on the air," says Hines. "Rush made a huge deal out of it because of the Grammys. The next day, they said,

'Number one song of the year, and we have it right here.' That was a huge hit."

Donovan has also teamed up Carson with Shanklin, who has now performed some forty pieces for the show. "Our latest one is 'The Clintstones,'" says Carson. "I wrote the movie-ad parody, which is 'The Clintstones, from the town of Little Rock. They've torn a page right out of history and run it through the shredder.' Paul, obviously, did Clinton's voice, and his sister did Hillary's voice, and I did the Razorbackasaurus. John had the jingle done by somebody else, and he put it all together in New York."

Although Shanklin does his work in Memphis, he has made the trip to New York to visit EIB headquarters. "I wanted to see the TV show, meet Johnny Donovan, and, of course, Rush," says Shanklin. "I wanted to see them in action. Sometimes, I send things up pretty rough," admits Shanklin, "and Johnny figures out where to cut them, and he comes up with the beginning. The other day, I sent in a segment with Bill talking to his lawyer, Bob Bennett, who is pulling his leg about technology that takes fingerprints off skin, and Bill starts getting worried and halting in his speech: 'Well, ah ahhh I ah ahhh I didn't know that they could . . . quit kiddin' me!' Johnny gave me the idea for that. He'll make it a 'Behind the Scenes at the Clinton White House,' no doubt."

Donovan took Shanklin and his wife, Angie, to the studio to see the radio show live. "I was just as nervous as a cat because I felt out of place," recalls Shanklin. "But they all told me their favorite stuff I'd done and put me at ease. I loosened up. Limbaugh and I talked during the breaks."

That night, the Shanklins were in the TV show audience. "They have a warm-up where James Golden, aka Bo Snerdley, talks and gets everybody feeling good about the show and not nervous," says Shanklin. "Well, before he came out, they were playing my songs. I couldn't believe all these people laughing and carrying on and holding their stomachs. Even I don't laugh at it like that. After his routine, Golden says, 'Does anybody have any questions?' Somebody asks, 'Yeah, who does those songs?' Golden smiles, and he goes, 'That's not any big deal. Anybody could do that.' He comes over to me and says, 'Like you, sir.' And I go, 'Ah ahhh I'm sorry. I wasn't listenin'. Could you repeat the question?' And they all go berserk."

During the show, Limbaugh introduced Shanklin. "I stood up and thought, 'Oh yeah, remember to smile.' And I turned pink, purple and sat down, totally embarrassed," recalls the Tennessean. After the show, Shanklin and his wife headed down front where Limbaugh was signing books. "These ladies come up to me and say, 'Will you sign our books?' And I thought, 'Oh my God, I can't do this.' I said, 'That's Rush Limbaugh's book. This is Rush Limbaugh's TV show. That is Rush Limbaugh,' and I pointed to him. I didn't want to steal anybody's thunder, but Angie said, 'Come on, Paul, it doesn't matter.' So I signed their books, and the first thing my wife does is say, 'Hey, Kit, look. Paul's signing books. Paul's signing books.' And I'm really embarrassed. A couple more people come along, and I sign their books. I don't know what to sign. I just put 'Paul Shanklin' or 'Paul Shanklin, aka, Bill Clinton.' Nobody'd ever asked for my autograph before.

"Here's the funny part," chuckles Shanklin. "When Rush was leaving, I had my back turned. I think I was signing another book, and he goes, 'Hey, Paul, don't get the big head.'

"So I'm avoiding getting the big head. It's been a lot of fun, and it'd be nice if it turns out to be bigger things. . . . It's a world of fun."

Six

On-Line: Where Dittos Do Battle

In the late Eighties, when I first began doing on-line meetings, people would ask me on the computer if I was Rush Limbaugh. I was talking about news items, opinions, commentary. People knew me only by my user name, 'moneysmith,' and I guess some of what I said sounded like Limbaugh. The point is that while there wasn't much public discussion about him, he was very much a known entity among on-line people. When KFYI in Phoenix picked up his show, there was an instant audience waiting.

— Tom Smith, Mesa, Arizona

One morning shortly after he started a Rush Room at the University of Notre Dame Law School, David Morken sent Limbaugh an e-mail message to tell him about the new conservative haven on campus. Morken, a second-year law student, had first heard the commentator a few years earlier while driving home from a shooting range at Camp Lejeune, North Carolina, where he had been qualifying to operate an M16. "I was amazed," says the former Marine about that first time he tuned in. "He was expressing a point of view about a multiplicity of topics that I agreed with. It was so different from the dominant media culture. I was shocked that it was on the air.

"After class I got into a car with a friend," recalls Morken. "I asked him, 'Have you ever listened to Rush Limbaugh?' " He hadn't, so they tuned in.

"I turned on the radio, and not 15 seconds go by before Rush says, 'Okay, I've been on CompuServe,' and he reads my letter," says Morken. "My friend almost dropped dead. Here I was in his car, and Rush Limbaugh is reading my message on the air. I got calls that night from relatives, friends and even old high-school teachers."

In many ways, Limbaugh's ongoing excursion into the "arena of ideas," as he liked to call it, and on-line communication were made for each other. On-line services linked millions of people in the most effective way for Limbaugh's listeners—and Limbaugh himself—to continue issue discussions during and after the show. They also provided a channel for conservative activists to rally concerned and like-minded citizens for political causes.

"Our system operator, Georgia Griffith, noticed among the political debates taking place within CompuServe a great deal of talk about Limbaugh," says a spokesman for CompuServe, an on-line service with some two million subscribers, which has access to Internet, a web of networks, connecting twenty million worldwide.

In October 1991 CompuServe set up a forum where fans could gather to contact Limbaugh, to trade information, to argue, to meet new friends, and to mobilize for political action. The Rush H. Limbaugh forum on CompuServe, which the broadcaster has been advertising since 1992 on his radio show, and similar forums on other electronic networks became in a sense electronic Rush Rooms. "What goes on?" CompuServe's Griffith asked rhetorically in an e-mail message. "Bedlam, grin. The users sometimes discuss what Rush discussed the day before, whatever is hot in the news, but it is always what concerns them at the moment."

In May 1993, it was Dan's Bake Sale. "You should have been there," cheered Michael Fussell of Little Rock, Arkansas. "Cars were backed up on the interstate for over seven miles. The day was certainly memorable. It was great to see so many young children, with a mother *and* a father. Some of you who made that trip, or anyone out there reading this message, should come see Arkansas. Just because Clinton is screwed up, doesn't mean the beauty and friendliness of the state he's from are too."

Bill Frazier, who missed Dan's event in Colorado, had a special request related to the bake sale. "To Bill Frazier," responded Timothy David. "I noticed that you were interested in getting a T-shirt from Dan's Bake Sale. I happen to have an extra. The front features the words 'Dan's Bake Sale' over a small map of the U.S. with a Colorado state flag in it. Under the U.S. map is the quote, 'More Fun than a Human Being Should Be Allowed to Have.' The back features a large chocolate chip cookie, with a bite out of it. Above the cookie are the words, 'What a Rush.' In the bite area of the cookie it says, 'Bake Sale Dittos.' I paid $20 for it. It is a large. If you are interested leave me a message." The sale went through.

CompuServe quickly became the easiest and most effective method for contacting Limbaugh, who often spent his limited free time grazing on on-line fodder. "Finally found an issue of *U.S. News* yesterday—the last issue at the particular store," wrote Thomas Auth of Greenville, South Carolina, to Limbaugh on August 10, 1993, referring to *U.S. News & World Report*'s cover story on the commentator. "Only disappointment was that Amy Bernstein left Bee-Bee's Restaurant (Greenville, S.C.) out of the Rush Room feature.

"I was also surprised to see your name on the cover of this month's *Penthouse*," Auth continued in his e-mail to Limbaugh. "Though I won't make a habit of buying *Penthouse*, I had to get the article. Haven't read it yet, but looks to be a very good one. Was a little surprised that you haven't mentioned this feature."

Limbaugh wrote back to Auth, saying that he had been quoted using profanity in the *Penthouse* story, when he said he had not, which is why he wouldn't discuss it.

Granting interviews to adult magazines was a sensitive subject for Limbaugh. When *Playboy* published one in December 1993, fans flooded on-line bulletin boards. Jason Ulmer from Springfield, Massachusetts, asked the commentator, "How could you lend yourself to *Playboy?* Sure you said you were teaching them values, but your being in there only sells more magazines."

"I personally think magazines like *Penthouse* and *Playboy* are very bad things," posted another fan. "In a way, they're worse than the overtly filthy magazines, precisely because many people tend to view them as being in the social mainstream. Of course, having interviews with reputable folks like Rush only serves to reinforce this." The banter went back and forth with others supporting Limbaugh in his effort to take the message directly to the center.

While debates like this crackled on almost every topic, fans e-mailed the commentator to report, make suggestions, or challenge him. Others, including a Tennessee franchise of the Hooters of America restaurant chain were looking to catch his attention, too. "The advertising agency of the franchise had an idea for getting Rush to do a local radio spot for them," recalls Mike McNeil, vice president for marketing of the Atlanta-based chain. "So they wrote a very funny script for Rush advertising Hooters. It started out: 'Attention, Environmental Wackos and Femi-Nazis: You may be missing a unique opportunity to protest the shameless exploitation of women and animals at the same time. That's right, two politically correct protests for the price of one. How? Go to Hooters. Yes, Hooters. Think about it. Where do you think chicken wings come from? Chickens, that's where. Cute little chickens. And who do you think serves those chicken wings? Women. Attractive women.' "

"Some people at Hooters had tried to reach Limbaugh by traditional means but were unsuccessful, probably because this was a local ad," says Geoffrey Proud of Jester/Proud Writer-Producers, creators of this spot. "We knew that he had a CompuServe mailbox, so we wrote the commercial and a note and e-mailed it."

"Evidently, Rush couldn't sleep one night and went on-line and was reading some material and came across that script," relates McNeil. "He loved it. He told Kit

Carson, his chief of staff, 'I love this spot. It's the best radio spot I've ever read. I want to do it. Find these Hooters people.'

"Rush cut the commercial," adds McNeil. "It aired in nine or ten markets nationally over a six-month period. It was very effective, and it garnered a great deal of publicity. *Forbes* wrote about it, and several local newspapers picked up on it as well."

Hooters wasn't the only one to find the commentator's on-line home useful to its business. Other organizations looking to identify conservatives began to log onto Limbaugh forums. Among them was the American Land Rights Association, a grassroots interest group to protect the rights of private landowners from federal regulators.

"I have been on CompuServe for about nine years," reports Charles Cushman, executive director of the association, based in Battle Ground, Washington. "I had mainly used it in the past for buying computer equipment and retrieving press clips. Then in December 1993, we were planning a White House phone-in and I had the idea to go into the Limbaugh forum. I experimented with going through and finding people with similar philosophical interests. If they are on the right side of an environmental debate, for instance, they're likely to be interested in what we're doing. We collected their CompuServe numbers and sent them a message with the internal White House numbers and a brief explanation of our position against White House policy. It was tremendously successful. I know we got through to the White House.

"People tend to look at faxes as a nuisance," reasons

Cushman. "On CompuServe, not only do people want messages, but it's easy to respond to them. You just hit a key and write a short note—either, 'Get me off your damn list,' or 'I'll call the White House every hour.' The key to a response is that we get people's names who are interested. We can then send another message offering a free poster so that they will send us their address for our mailing list." In just a few months, Cushman gathered about five thousand new names on-line. "The key was that we knew people in the Limbaugh section would be conservative, mostly well-educated and active. That's what we need."

The primary function of the forum is to provide a meeting place for discussion. Going on-line is like entering a town meeting. It enables people whose jobs and daily duties prohibit them from keeping a close eye on the wide-scale events of the political world to keep in touch from their living rooms any time of day or night.

"I need help locating two items," said Jim Weitz in a message to anyone who might care to help him out. "The first is Bill Bennett's *Index of Cultural Indicators*. Does anyone know where on-line I can find it? Also I was hoping to find the text of the speech in which Clinton called Rush a racist." Within two hours, both of his questions were answered.

"I've spoken to Rush's guy Kit Carson a couple of times about putting a Rush Room list together," says Auth, who keeps track of the nation's Rush Rooms on a spread sheet for anyone on-line who might be interested. "Limbaugh's people can't do it themselves because it changes so much. It is up to us to do it," Auth concludes.

Such easy access to well-informed minds proves useful to Limbaugh fans having trouble knocking down arguments or countering false claims. Rather than wading through back issues of conservative journals or researching at the library, one can simply send a question into the forum. "The day Clinton began saying he'd never promised tax cuts to the middle class back in 1993," Tom Smith explains, "the full texts of his old speeches were available from Internet nodes worldwide. In a stroke, Clinton's credibility suffered crashing rejection."

"For the most part, people on-line like to go into the Limbaugh section to debate issues that Limbaugh has addressed on his shows or on-line," says Chris Pressley, who monitors the Heritage Foundation's Town Hall, a branch of CompuServe that also allows access to the Limbaugh forum. "The Limbaugh section is as much a conservative debating society as it is for fans to hook up with each other. Rush is the entree. There are debates about Ollie North's senate race or the latest legislation in the House. Abortion, health care, guns and taxes are probably the most popular topics to debate."

Few assaults, no matter how minor, go unanswered in the Limbaugh forum. "I appreciate the fact that Mr. Limbaugh speaks out on infringements on personal liberty," wrote Travis Wheatley. "However, I am concerned that during the time that the crime bill was being debated in the House, Rush was ranting about popcorn rather than informing his audience that the Second Amendment was in danger of being abolished under the guise of crime prevention."

"He may have spent time talking about popcorn, but

that is part of his shtik. That's part of the fun," responded Jeremy Hill. "Besides he must have spent at least three days talking about how horrible the crime bill was. He may not have talked specifically about the guns, but he can't talk about everything."

When the topic is gun control, Thomas McAleer, who works in management at Pizza Hut in Milford, Connecticut, joins in the debate. "I typically log on and scan the message board," he explains. "It annoys me that the same people who want to give condoms to teenagers don't want adults to have guns. Limbaugh is a defender of liberties. He talks about it occasionally so a lot of people on the computer have a fair amount to say, and some tend to use his arguments."

For McAleer, some of the best on-line discussions took place in the summer of 1993, when Clinton's budget was making its way through Congress. "When Rush was comparing Clinton's 1993 budget to Bush's 1990 budget, I ran up my CompuServe bill," McAleer remembers. "Rush showed these guys—Panetta, Sasser, all of them—saying the same things as they were saying in 1990: 'This is the best piece of deficit-reduction legislation we have ever had.' Both of course were equally bad. Rush compared quotes, charts, numbers, everything. It was great. Everyone on-line was joining in and offering their own quotes and numbers they had found in the papers or that they had remembered from three years before."

From time to time, the impact of these debates extends further than the confines of the computer network. In February 1994, Democratic Congressman George Miller from California proposed an amendment to an education bill that would have required adults teaching students—including private-school teachers and parents who instruct their kids at home—to be certified by the government. Limbaugh took up the cause on radio and helped lead a call-in campaign that eventually killed it.

"I remember seeing messages on CompuServe days before Rush brought it up or anyone in Congress seemed to take notice," says Sally Pearson from Dallas, Texas. "I thought it an obscure issue. Next thing I know it's a big debate in Congress, and it seems to have started on the computer."

"Now we can exercise influence and give advice to the power brokers who have the good sense to listen to the people," declares Christopher Blaney, a college student from Long Valley, New Jersey, who spends many evenings on-line. Of all the powerful to tune in, Limbaugh, for now, is king of the hill. Computer communication has enabled the commentator to converse with many more people than he ever could have by phone, mail, or fax. "He is a major part of the revolution making our media interactive rather than passive.

"Not many TV hosts invite people to e-mail them," elaborates Blaney. "I have become a good deal more involved in political discussions on-line after I found out that Rush is on CompuServe. And I have made friends that I otherwise would not have. For me, being shy and taciturn around strangers, the friendships and camaraderie here are just great. I love this place!

"Rush has among the best news-clipping services available. Readers constantly fax and e-mail him news stories from out-of-the-way places and backcountry weeklies. This enables him to have that Paul Harvey-like global local flavor," observes Blaney. "Rush is on the vanguard of the interactive revolution."

By mid-1994, Limbaugh was receiving more e-mail than he and his staff could handle, many packed with just the sort of interesting news Blaney refers to. Of course the vast majority of e-mail goes unanswered, but Limbaugh tackles questions and sends comments whenever he can. Kurt from Clovis, New Mexico, called the radio show and asked Limbaugh: "Why don't you answer my letters on CompuServe?" The broadcaster said he was sorry, but he receives some six hundred messages a day on CompuServe alone. The average user, however, can browse through dozens of conversations and jump into one of his choice or continue an ongoing discussion, perhaps begun the night before.

For Jim Witten, an insurance executive in Utah, going on-line is instant access to interesting company. "I'm starved for political dialogue. I tune in regularly to Rush's radio show, but I can't talk back to the radio. I can't ask Rush or one of his callers a question. But on the computer I can send a message, 'Can anyone tell me more about the value-added tax Rush talked about yesterday? I would like to chat with someone about it.' Sure enough, messages come in and sooner or later I'm in a discussion with someone about VAT."

For others, it's a fun and productive way to fill downtime rather than talking on the telephone or turning on the TV. "I do some proofreading at night and find myself enduring long waits for material," says Julie Crane in Manhattan. "I just enjoy watching debates while I wait. Rush's marriage to Marta, who he met on-line, produced a spate of comments and speculation—many from women who felt they might have missed their chance to snare conservatism's more eligible bachelor," notes Crane. Indeed, Marta Fitzgerald sent Limbaugh messages after he had responded positively to female fan mail.

Limbaugh's eventual marriage to Fitzgerald provided hours of endless discussion. Many women pondered what type of dress she wore, what their first face-to-face meeting must have been like, where they went on their honeymoon, but there was also a long list of messages about whether or not it was hypocritical of Limbaugh to speak against premarital sex while living with his fiancée. "Rush and his defenders need to realize that when someone makes a living and a reputation criticizing others for what he perceives to be their moral transgressions, those standards will be applied to his life as well," insisted Hazel Staloff a few weeks after the Memorial Day weekend wedding.

"Rush didn't use the police to pick up women, nor did he give his sexual partner a government job," responded Walter Wilson, referring to allegations against President Clinton.

"I couldn't care less about his and Marta's personal life," said the dismissive Brenda Jinkins. "To me, his premarital behavior is hypocritical but not immoral."

"I recall Rush discussing celibacy and saying it was right for him at the time," pitched in Madeleine Kopp. "I don't think he took priestly vows. I don't recall him saying he would never have sex with a fiancée before marriage."

When Harvey Caras learned that Marta Fitzgerald's message to Limbaugh that led to their eventual marriage may have come via Internet from a network other than Compuserve, he said: "If it wasn't Compuserve, I'm outa here!"

Pretty soon the discussion progressed from the wedding and the nature of illegitimacy to family values. "It's getting late, and I am running up my bill," said Cathy Hoffman finally. "Besides, it's nearly nine o'clock, time for the TV show to come on."

Part Two

In Your Face Nationwide

Seven

Students to Rush:
Right On!

They made up a lot of silly rules for us that no other clubs had to follow, like saying we had to encompass all points of view. Yet no other club had to encompass all points of view. The disco club didn't have to teach the square dance for 30 minutes at every meeting.

— Kurt Busboom, Acalanes High School, Lafayette, California

It was the beginning of the 1993 school year, and Kurt Busboom and his friends thought they had a pretty good idea. The senior and his pals planned to start a club at their high school in Lafayette, California, to discuss politics from a conservative point of view. But they wanted to name the club something a little less stiff than "High-School Conservatives," something fresh and relevant, a name that even the rest of the "grunge" generation could relate to.

They decided to call it the Rush Limbaugh Club. And why not? In addition to having a recognizable voice—the only one fighting the battle loudly and clearly for conservatives—here was a personality that led hard-driving, focused discussions and challenged listeners to think with their own minds. With his credo "Words mean things," Limbaugh, as much as any schoolteacher, urged listeners to test ideas, to seek the truth through analysis, never to accept others' opinions without comprehending and consciously agreeing with them. This was very much in the spirit of American education.

Perhaps most importantly for the students, the socially astute former DJ and Kansas City Royals front-office man, was hip enough to relate to their generation. And Busboom, for one, was convinced Limbaugh's message mattered, "The time I was really attracted to Rush Limbaugh was a time of my life when I was really down and out." Busboom later told a columnist at the Bay Area *Contra Costa Times.* "I was really questioning some of the values in my life because other people were questioning them. I didn't have a whole lot of faith in myself because it seems that in America today, everybody is pro-drugs, pro-alcohol and pro-sex. And the message that I got was that everything I believed in was wrong.

"Just to have someone out there saying, 'Hey, you're okay, and there are people out there thinking the way you do, and what you're thinking is right,' really attracted me to him," says the eighteen-year-old Busboom, a senior at the 1,100-student Acalanes High School. "We called it the Rush Limbaugh Club because we were going to use Limbaugh's discussions as a start for our conversations and debates. But the club wasn't just for Ditto-heads. It was for anyone who wanted to discuss politics. We welcomed everyone." In fact, they figured, being associated with the media phenom would help attract more members to the club and thus more diversity.

"Initially I didn't want to join, but I was encouraged by my friends, Benjy and Kurt," recalls Fred Solomon, a self-described liberal. "They said it wasn't a strictly conservative club. It was open to anyone. So I signed up. I'm not a big Limbaugh fan, but I'm listening with an open mind. There are times when he'll say something and people will applaud, but I'll defend the other side. For example, when Rush was talking about how Vince Foster's suicide was mysterious and all that, I didn't agree with that. In my heart, I'm still a liberal even though I've become more conservative about some things, such as cultural and social programs and welfare. Rush has had a pretty profound effect on me. I'm beginning to take some of the conservative views—but not all."

The impulse to start a Rush Limbaugh Club turned out to be a good one. "Seventy people signed up at club day, and about 30 were showing up on a weekly basis," relates Busboom, who became club president.

"My youth pastor told me to listen to Rush Limbaugh," says Kathryn Dunn, who became the club secretary. "All during the summer, I watched his show, and at school, when Kurt started the Rush Limbaugh Club, I said 'Oh yeah, that's for me, that's for me.

"I met new people," says Dunn. "They believe what I do. It's not like you tell them you're a Republican or a conservative, and they go 'Ooooh.' Or that you like

Rush Limbaugh, and they totally freak out. I met this guy at a church activity the other day. He asked me, 'Do you know Kathryn Dunn?' I said, 'I am Kathryn Dunn,' and he said, 'You're the secretary of the Rush Limbaugh Club, oh my gosh.' And he picked me up and swung me around."

"Sometimes I'd pass out articles from *The American Spectator, National Review* or *Conservative Chronicles,* and we'd open the floor for debates," says Busboom. "Another thing I'd do was edit the best of Rush on TV that week and show the tape. People could come in at lunch, sit back, enjoy their lunches and the best of Rush Limbaugh. It was a good time.

"I don't agree with everything Limbaugh says, but I think he's right most of the time," adds Busboom. "He makes conservatives feel good about themselves. That's why people are so attracted to him. No one else is voicing these opinions on the radio every day and saying so many things that people agree with. It's good for America—whether you're liberal or conservative—because he opens up discussion and debate."

But the fun lasted for only about a month. "In late September I was told by the student activities director that we could no longer have our club because it didn't fit into the school curriculum," says Busboom. "Acalanes is what they called a closed-forum campus, meaning that all clubs must be curriculum-related. They said we weren't, and then they made up a lot of silly rules for us that no other clubs had to follow, like saying we had to encompass all points of view. Yet no other club on campus had to encompass all points of view. The disco club didn't have to teach the square dance for 30 minutes at every meeting. But our club had to have the liberal point of view. They told us we couldn't have our club. Yet they had never looked at our club charter. They never came to any meetings. They knew nothing about us except for our name."

With the possibility looming for shutting down the club, tensions were high between students and administrators. "At first I didn't know what to do," admits Busboom. "I was gathering my case when an article came out in the school newspaper. Some concerned citizens gave it to the *Contra Costa Times,* and from there the news stations got ahold of it. And once they got ahold of it, everybody got it."

By the time the *Contra Costa Times* ran a front-page story on November 9, 1993, Principal Leo Petty was scrutinizing many of the school's clubs, including Amnesty International, the Disco Club, and Friday Night Live, a group that offered entertainment and antidrug education. "The Rush Limbaugh Club was the lightning rod that set this off," explains Busboom. "They basically said, 'You can't have your club. Every other club is going to be here except the Rush Limbaugh Club.' And then I started saying, 'Wait, how does this tie into the curriculum, and how does this tie in?' So more clubs came under this umbrella of clubs to be disbanded."

Still Busboom claimed that his club was being singled out. "Mr. Petty says the Disco Club ties into the [physical education] curriculum," Busboom told the *Contra Costa Times.* "I think that is a broad interpretation. My club ties into government and economics."

"There's a double standard here. The administration said the club didn't fit into the curriculum, but you could clearly see that it tied into current events or government classes," agrees Fred Solomon, who after the publicity and an appearance on CNN, was dubbed the Most Famous Anti-Rush Fan by his pals.

"I know they were trying to do what was best for us, but they were treating us like kids," says Solomon. "We're 18 years old. I think they have a pretty deep resentment against Limbaugh himself. That's what it is. Other clubs didn't tie into the curriculum, but they weren't under fire—only ours. It's really strange because the administration would say one thing, and then do another. And they didn't tell the students; they didn't even tell the faculty."

The club's position was supported by at least one faculty member. "The social studies curriculum requires the study of individual political behavior," Acalanes Social Studies Department Chairman Larry Freeman told the *Times*. "And Limbaugh is definitely an example of individual political behavior. The question is: who gets to decide if a club relates to the curriculum? I think there's a due process question here."

The controversy began to spread beyond the Bay Area. *"The Frank and Mike Show,* which airs mornings on the EIB affiliate here, faxed the story to Limbaugh," relates Busboom. "It's just something they had fun with on their show, and they thought Rush would have a good time with it, too."

And they were right.

Limbaugh immediately ran with the story. He read

portions of the newspaper report to his listeners and championed the group of young conservatives fighting the liberal California education establishment in his name. He wanted Busboom live on the air and so did others in the media. Three Bay Area TV crews as well as CNN interviewed the high-school senior and his club officers within a day. Two days later, Kit Carson, Limbaugh's chief of staff, tracked down Busboom in Seattle, where he was visiting the University of Washington as a prospective student.

"I was staying in my sister's sorority, and he called me there and said, 'We want you on in about five minutes.' It was pretty funny," says the high-school senior, who was understandably nervous. "I was going to be talking to millions of people, and I was crammed into this little phone booth in a sorority house. Maybe I can put it in perspective this way: I had wanted to ask Rush a question all summer, and I had called so many times. Getting through was just impossible. Now, they were calling me. They wanted *me* to be on. I remember getting off the phone, and it didn't seem real. 'Oh yeah, I just got off the phone talking to Rush Limbaugh on *The Rush Limbaugh Show.*' It was the most unreal experience I'd ever had."

That day, Limbaugh used the Busboom ordeal to focus a discussion of discrimination against political conservatives in America. On several other occasions, he would reexamine the Rush Limbaugh Club's battle with Acalanes High School's administration on television.

Busboom, who would eventually meet the commentator in person in Los Angeles, received hundreds of telephone calls and letters, including a call from Guam and a letter from New Zealand. He also received Limbaugh T-shirts, financial donations, books, periodical subscriptions, and an invitation for the club to dine at a San Francisco Italian restaurant.

"I think my feeling at the time was one of pride and one of humbleness," reflects Busboom. "I was proud because we as kids—the officers of the club—were able to stand up for what we believed in, equal treatment for everyone. I was also humbled by all the support. Our phone lines were inundated, and everybody asked, 'What can I do to help you out?' I didn't know those people were out there. I'd always felt alone as a conservative."

Acalanes High also felt the impact of Limbaugh's attention. "The Rush Limbaugh connection sparked national interest and the wildfire took off," reported the *Contra Costa Times*. "The campus swarmed with television reporters competing for footage. Office phones rang off the hook, as raving Rush Limbaugh supporters called to express outrage." One angry parent told the newspaper, "Part of the learning process is to explore, learn and evaluate. Whether it's conservative, the Rush Limbaugh Club, or liberal, call it The Hillary Clinton Club, that's not the issue. It's thought police and McCarthyism in reverse."

During Busboom's second appearance on the Limbaugh radio show, the commentator called him "the new poster boy of free speech." All this might have gone to another high-school student's head, but Busboom, who during summers built homes for the poor in Mexico, New Mexico, and Seattle, with his church group, remained levelheaded. "It's a little overwhelming," he told the *Contra Costa Times*. "I don't care about the publicity. I just want my club."

And he did get that. "You could see when the media came that the administration didn't know what they were talking about," assesses Busboom. "The Pacific Legal Foundation, a Sacramento nonprofit, drew up a 16-page legal brief documenting the fact that we were discriminated against because of our conservative views, and there was a school board meeting at which about 20 students and community members spoke. The administration decided to let the club remain for the rest of the year."

At the very least, the controversy provided the club with a windfall of provisions. Every Wednesday, Busboom brings in the periodicals and books that comprise the Limbaugh Club Library for Advanced Conservative Studies. But beyond that, the club has decided to keep a low profile. "We were going to have guest speakers, but we thought we had had enough controversy for one year," says Busboom. "We have a pretty good foundation for a great club, and maybe the people who are involved in it next year can do more."

Although Busboom is still not satisfied with the treatment he and the Rush Limbaugh Club received, he wants to put the controversy behind him. "It scared me because here you have this school administrator, the principal, entrusted by the community to oversee students, who then thinks he's empowered to strip me and the other club members of our freedom of speech. We were treated with total disrespect. I've never gotten an apology. The principal and the administration never admitted they did anything wrong." In fact, states Busboom, "There's still a lot of hostility in the administration towards me."

But Busboom's battle may have a positive effect on other groups around the state, or so hopes Jesse Binnall, who formed the Rush Limbaugh Teenage Republicans in Rancho Cucamonga, east of Los Angeles, because he didn't agree with some of the things he saw happening at school.

"Political correctness and multiculturalism are two things we try to focus on," points out Binnall. "At my school, I can't call someone black who is black. I have to call him African-American. I have to keep up with the latest politically correct names, whether it's Chicano or Latino or whatever. Instead, everybody should be American. They have gone against one of America's founding principles, being united as one. We need to remember our motto, 'e pluribus unum'—'from the many, one.'

"Another effect of political correctness is that it has made it so I have to say that Thomas Jefferson and George Washington were evil because they may have done some things that were bad," notes Binnall. "However, the good things definitely outweigh them. It is now politically correct to say the people at the Alamo were not heroes, that they killed innocent people. This is slowly tearing down our American heritage and splitting us up.

"We try to promote conservative principles, and Rush Limbaugh is the main person doing that right now," emphasizes Binnall. "That's why we named our club after him. We meet to discuss issues and to help register voters or work on campaigns. Our members come from schools all across San Bernardino County, but no schools right now are letting us open clubs. Many are in violation of the law by refusing us.

"I go to a private school," the fifteen-year-old club chairman says. "Their excuse was that they'd lose their tax-free status, but that's not exactly true. The state cannot take away their tax-free status under the Equal Access Act of 1984. The West Virginia College Republicans put out a packet for Teenage Republicans that explains the act, and that's what we're going on right now. Next year there should be clubs in our area. We owe a lot of it to Rush Limbaugh. He helped Kurt Busboom, who has set a precedence that may help us."

Meanwhile, Rush Limbaugh was also sweeping college campuses around America. So many requests from students poured in for tickets to the filming of Limbaugh's television show that the producers decided to hold a college week. On one show, it was primarily students from the Northeast. The University of Delaware, Villanova (Pennsylvania), Norwich University (Vermont), Fairfield University (Connecticut), and Holy Cross College (Massachusetts) all sent representatives, wearing their college colors instead of coats and ties, and issuing hearty standing cheers when Limbaugh introduced their schools.

In the fall of 1993, members of the West Virginia College Republicans at the thirteen-thousand-student Marshall University in Huntington, West Virginia, were planning their own journey to see the show. But it wasn't college week, and they had to scramble to get tickets. "We called, and the assistant said we could get only three," remembers Clinton Gillespie, president of the club. "But then we were talking, and we found out her boyfriend goes to WVU. And that did it. We got our 30 tickets. It was a long wait. We had to call in June to get October tickets.

"We told everyone throughout West Virginia, 'The College Republicans are going to see the Rush Limbaugh show live,' " declared the sophomore International Affairs major from Charleston. In addition to Marshall students, West Virginia College Republicans from West Virginia University, West Virginia State, West Virginia Tech, the University of Charleston, and Wheeling Jesuit signed up for the ten-hour road trip.

The group rented a van and drove up on a Friday night to spend the weekend and go to the Monday show. "When you fall asleep with four other guys right beside you, it's pretty uncomfortable," Gillespie relates. "You have to make sure your head doesn't fall down on someone's shoulder or anything. Everyone was grouchy after being so close together, crammed in the van, and everyone wanted to stop here, stop there. It was probably the most miserable trip ever, but we wanted to see Rush Limbaugh."

"We all had to wear dresses, and the guys had to wear jackets and ties to the show, and it just gave it such a nice feeling," says Christina Dexter, a Marshall University junior who made the trip. "Kaye Copley is dying to meet him. She just thinks he's the most handsome man. He's such a charmer on the radio with women. He would open doors and pay for dinner—that's the kind of guy he seems to be."

"I listen to him on the car radio when I'm running errands," says Copley, a senior majoring in social work. "I don't skip classes to listen, but if I do have an extra minute or so, I put him on. I will not go to bed until I watch him on TV, so I go to sleep about one o'clock. I'd be too embarrassed ever to call in though. My mind would go blank. I'd probably stutter and be a moron if I tried to talk to him."

"Rush came out before the show and said, 'Where are you guys from?' " recalls Gillespie. "He was very nice. He talked to all of us. We presented him with a plaque, and the WVU chapter presented him with a Mountaineer carved out of coal with a brass plate that said, 'To Rush Limbaugh from WVU College Republicans.' He had it on his table by the window for about a week and a half, and he used it in a publicity spot, saying, 'Does this look like something that would offend you? Watch my show tonight, and see why they're getting rid of the mascots.'

"Once the show started, he said, 'The West Virginia College Republicans are here.' We all stood up, and the cameras panned us," recalls Gillespie.

"We all went 'Whoo whoo whoo whoo,' " says Dexter. "It was so fun. I had a ball. He was better in person than he is on TV or on the radio. There's a stereotype that conservatives are so boring, and they don't have any personality. He proves that wrong."

"The show that night was about smoking and how the smokers of America are going to pay for Clinton's health-care plan," says Kaye Copley, whose sister, Christie, is also a College Republican. "He was just making fun of it. He was applauding the smokers of America, because, you know, they're going to be paying for our health care. His sarcasm is so unique."

"He had a dinner afterwards, so he couldn't sign

books, but everyone got a thrill to actually be on the show," says Gillespie, who adds that news of the club's trip to see the Rush Limbaugh show has increased membership. "Before the Rush show, we had about 150 members," notes Gillespie. "We were in the paper so much for going up there. They did a special about it and everything. At Marshall University, we now have 300 members. Bill Clinton is our honorary membership director. He's helping us out a lot. In April 1993, we had about two College Republican chapters in West Virginia; a year later, we have 23."

The Marshall club meets weekly and sponsors a Rush Room in the campus cafeteria. "When Hillary Clinton came here to indoctrinate us about her health-care plan, we dressed in doctors' uniforms and held signs that said, 'The health-care plan has the compassion of the IRS and the efficiency of the post office,' " says Gillespie. "A lot of people showed up for that. Hillary noticed us. She said, 'And for you Young Republicans in the crowd, Richard Nixon supported a national health-care plan.' Of course, one of our pet peeves is when people call us Young Republicans because there's a big difference here in West Virginia between Young Republicans and College Republicans. College Republicans tend to be more conservative. I don't know what it's like around the nation, but we don't like to be called Young Republicans.

"For big events like that, a lot of people show up. For our weekly meetings, we see anywhere from 15 to 60 people," says Gillespie. "We try to keep the meetings informal. We talk and plan strategies, and everyone's always like, 'Oh, did you guys hear what Rush Limbaugh

Dan Quayle is one of the few guests ever to appear
on *The Rush Limbaugh Show.*

Too young to sit in the TV audience, Brian Downs
got to chat with Rush and the crew backstage
before the show.

Founded in 1947, Blackie's House of Beef in
Washington, D.C., which attracts Capitol Hill
heavyweights, joined the Rush Room mushroom
after Bill Clinton was elected.
(Photo credit: Geoffrey Morris)

Sergeant at Arms Bob Worn and Head Ditto Walter Abbott auction off a copy of *All the Faults and Shortcomings of Rush Limbaugh* to raise money for The Rush Limbaugh Supper Club in Shreveport, Louisiana. Published by Worn, the book is, of course, blank inside. *(Photo credit: D. Howard King)*

Two-hundred strong, the members of The Rush
Limbaugh Supper Club fill the back room at
Ralph & Kacoo's in Shreveport.
(*Photo credit: D. Howard King*)

Dan and Kelly Kay take a moment away from their
busy booth at Dan's Bake Sale in Fort Collins,
Colorado, on May 22, 1993, and pose for the
cheering crowd. *(Photo credit: Michael Lynch)*

Some people didn't attend Dan's Bake Sale just to
buy brownies. They came to make a statement.
(Photo credit: Richard Hood)

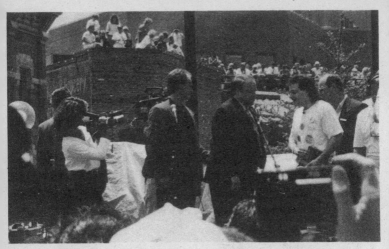

"Capitalism caused this to happen—the pursuit of a $29.95 newsletter," proclaimed Limbaugh as he presented Dan with a bound copy of *The Limbaugh Letter*. (Note: Limbaugh's future wife, Marta Fitzgerald videotapes the event.)   *(Photo credit: Brian McClure)*

In Fort Collins, James Golden, fondly known on the air as the contrarian Bo Snerdly, as always, charms the crowd.   *(Photo credit: Richard Hood)*

Some Limbaugh lovers flew to Dan's Bake Sale, some drove, some even came on all fours. (*Photo credit: Richard Hood*)

Clinton impersonator Paul Shanklin and his wife, Angie, visit the studio. "Angie and I got our picture made with Rush. . . . Okay, I wanted my picture taken with a famous person," says Paul.

Before the 1993 White House Correspondents'
Dinner, Limbaugh chats with fellow conservatives,
including (left to right) former Secretary of Education
William Bennett, his wife Elayne, *National Review*
Publisher Ed Capano, and Clarence Page, *Chicago
Tribune* columnist. (*Photo credit: Fred Hirsch*)

Two of Limbaugh's biggest supporters—Alyse O'Neill (left) and Millie Limbaugh—get together in Florida to raise funds and rally conservatives for Phyllis Schlafly's pro-family values Eagle Forum.

Kurt Busboom helps Rush celebrate at a book party in Los Angeles in December, 1993.

Limbaugh shows his appreciation for Alyse and Paul O'Neill's support.

Four Florida citrus growers—Carolyn and Jim Hull (front) and Ed and Joanne Sullivan—clink their glasses of orange juice in a toast to Rush Limbaugh at New York's Waldorf-Astoria before attending a broadcast of *Rush Limbaugh: The Television Show.*

Florida orange-juice activists Carolyn Hull (left) and Ron Calfee (rear left) gather with their cohorts at Hull Groves in Plantation City, Florida, before waging one of their many battles to support Limbaugh's promotion of citrus products.

The kings of spoken and written conservatism, Rush
Limbaugh and William F. Buckley, have a meeting of
the minds at the University Club in New York City.

Rush Limbaugh knows the way things ought to be.
After the broadcast of the TV show, he signs his
books for audience members, who have traveled to
New York City from around the nation and beyond.
(*Photo credit: Geoffrey Morris*)

On a sunny Florida day in March 1994, feisty Limbaugh supporters wave placards outside the Orange Blossom Indian River Citrus Market in South Orlando, before storming the market to buy up all the OJ.

They walked, they ran, they lumbered to the
Dittohead Barbecue—an afternoon of feasting and
frolicking—in Fresno, California.

At the Dittohead Barbecue, no dolphin is safe near
the booth ("made from old-growth redwood")
sponsored by Bron Concrete ("We pave paradise
and put up a parking lot").

Ever since Michelle Schanel started a Rush Room at her restaurant *The Snooty Frog* in Cameron Park, California, her competitors have been green with envy. (*Photo credit: Michelle Schanel*)

Business is booming ever since Stu Buchalter started a Rush Room in his Mr. Bagel shop in Poughkeepsie, New York. *(Photo credit: Stu Buchalter)*

said?' and 'Did you hear about Joycelyn Elders? She said this.' And you ask, 'Where did you hear that?' and they say, 'On the Rush Limbaugh show.'

"We also have a Rush Room in our cafeteria," reports Gillespie. "It's just a little corner. During lunch, one of the College Republicans always brings out a tape of Limbaugh that he's recorded. When he first did it, we said no one would come by, but we've had people that we've never seen before just come over with their friends and sit in the corner where they could hear it.

"Most College Republicans get their information from Limbaugh," claims Gillespie. "Where else are you going to hear that type of information? You're not going to hear it on CNN. You're only going to hear it from him. He is exposing the truth, the tactics of the liberals.

"The young people of America have a renewed interest in politics, the conservative message and truth," Gillespie continues. "There has never been a conservative as strong as Rush Limbaugh who reaches such a diverse audience. William Buckley, with *National Review*, reached only a limited audience. Not many college students read it, until now. They subscribe to it because of Limbaugh."

But the Marshall University College Republicans have taken their search for the truth one step further. In January 1994, they started their own newspaper, *The Statesman*. "We wanted another voice on campus to allow students who do not agree with certain things to voice their opinions," declares Dexter, a journalism major. "Nobody else had an inkling about journalism, so I took it on myself to be the editor. We have an open editorial policy, but it's primarily conservative. Our news pages are non-biased."

"Our paper is funded completely through advertisements and private donations," notes Gillespie, *The Statesman*'s founder and chairman. "We're capitalists, and we don't believe in getting funding through the government. Our official school paper, *The Parthenon,* is funded through students and through taxpayers' money since this is a public school."

The staff of *The Statesman,* which publishes five thousand copies every other week, produces the twelve-page paper using a computer desktop publishing program. In it is reporting and commentary by staff volunteers, with syndicated material from columnist Pat Buchanan, cartoonist Chuck Asay, and others. *The Statesman* regularly covers issues ranging from state politics and abortion to TV reviews and manners. One of its weekly Top Ten Lists, *à la* David Letterman, was " 'Top Ten Things Overheard at a Socialist Conference'. . . . 6. Ouch, Senator Kennedy, I said grab a handful of *chips.* . . . 2. President Gilley, I'm so glad you made it. 1. Of course, the Clintons are late again."

"It's been a tremendous amount of work, a course in sleep deprivation," says Dexter. "It seems that every time a paper comes out, we have to start working on a new one. There are now about 11 of us who are fully dedicated to producing the paper and around 20 in all."

"We've found that when we are writing it and laying it out, there is a touch of Rush Limbaugh's style there," Gillespie says. "It has a combination of humor and more serious commentary, like Limbaugh."

The Statesman staff has quickly learned the hard realities of the publishing business. "Sometimes we have a problem with our advertisers not paying us in a timely way, but we've worked that out with the printers," reports Gillespie. "They're very understanding. Basically advertising is coming in, and we're able to pay for everything.

"We have found out that some people, possibly members of the school paper, have been calling and harassing our advertisers, saying that if they continued to advertise, they were going to boycott," Gillespie adds. *"The Parthenon* thinks we are rivals, but we believe that *The Parthenon* has a place on campus. But it's not for the students—it's for journalism majors. They don't like our conservative message at all, but I think they understand we're going to be here. *The Statesman* has become the most popular newspaper on campus. When we put it out, it's gone that night.

"There is a conservative movement. The pendulum is swinging towards the right," insists Gillespie. "M.A.P.S., which stands for Marshall Action for Peaceful Solutions, is the long-haired maggot-infested hippie group. It has been around for 10 years, and they are officially disbanding because no one's joining their group. *The Free Forum,* their alternative paper, is folding, too. I talked to the Non-Editor—that's what he's called—and he said, 'You guys have taken all our energy. No one wants to write for us.'

"We're here at the right time, at the right place, because it's here at the college that they're trying to get us, and it's here that we have realized that needs to stop," continues Gillespie. "We're hoping by 1995 to come out weekly with distribution through College Republican chapters around the state."

So, do the Kurt Cobains and Howard Sterns really control the hearts and minds of Generation X? Or is that just what you hear from the liberal media? Is Limbaugh only for old fuddy-duddies? "I think students are probably Rush Limbaugh's biggest followers," states Gillespie.

Students on Limbaugh

"Even though people lead a pretty busy life during law school, they find the time to watch Rush during our lunchtime Rush Room. As a third-year student, you can get pretty detached. This is a good way to meet first-year students. Normally everyone just eats and watches Rush."

—Dan Foley, Notre Dame Law School, South Bend, Indiana

"Many of the dorm lobbies are actually Rush Rooms. No one has ever called them that, but quite often there are 20 to 30 people watching his TV show when it is rebroadcast here during the day. I don't think Reagan, Bennett or Buchanan could draw the type of crowd that Rush draws. People certainly wouldn't sit around on a couch to see any of them speak. Somehow Rush manages to say serious things in the simplest way and really be entertaining. He puts Letterman-style humor into things. And all the time he lets the liberals dig the holes, and then he just buries them."

—David Bobb, Hillsdale College, Hillsdale, Michigan

"I watch his show almost every night with my parents and my sister. We pick it up out of Denver on a satellite dish. He's fun, he's entertaining. I like his political views and the way he expresses them. We talk about him over dinner. We can't get the radio [program] here. But I hear it when we go to Washington State on vacation. I read *The Way Things Ought to Be*. I really love it. I got the book from one of our employees, who likes Limbaugh. There is no way to get his books nearby, so I haven't gotten to read *See, I Told You So* yet. He has made me more active politically. But that's difficult. Palmer, the nearest town, is 80 miles away. The only thing around our lodge is wilderness and snowmobile tracks."

—Claudia Berkley, Glacier View High School, near Palmer, Alaska

"I started listening right before he got humongously popular. I was working on a cattle ranch with a friend. But he still really hits things on the nose. After reading *The Way Things Ought to Be,* I would get thoughts when I would be arguing a political point with someone. And then I realized that I got that argument from Rush. I'm the president of the senate at college. I think that listening to Rush helps me deal with a lot of the problems I have to face, and he helped me hold myself up in debates."

—Darrin Dykstra, University of South Dakota, Pierre, South Dakota

"When I'm on the tractor in the summer or on days off from school, I listen to Rush. He is the only person out there giving the conservative point of view and not apologizing for it. I had my grandma drive me 40 miles to Fargo to buy his first book. I just asked her, and she said yes. I have read both books, but I enjoy the radio show the most. You can get more involved. You can understand more where he is coming from. He has more time to explain things."

I'm going to North Dakota State University and am going to major in agricultural economics. I'll join College Republicans and would love to get into politics after college, but I think I'll have to come back and take care of the farm."

—Randy Melvin, Maple Valley High School,
Buffalo, North Dakota

"A friend of my dad got me tickets to Rush's TV show. In order to be on the show you have to be 18 or older, so I had to stay in the back. After being backstage a few minutes, Rush came out. I said, 'Hi, Rush I think you're doing a great job.' And I told him how much all the Teenage Republicans loved him. He said, 'Oh, it's nice to meet you, Brian. I'll see if I can mention you guys on the show.' A few months later, he did mention us. During the show, I got to watch Bo take calls from people who were going to be on the show. I had expected Bo to be shot off in a limo to get away from a crowd, but he was just like an average guy. We even walked down the street together and no one said a thing."

—Brian Downs, Catholic Central,
Northville, Michigan

Eight

From Wall Street to Boise: Businessmen Tune In

I heard him take apart Ross Perot's book chapter by chapter. It was the most devastating thing I've ever heard. It was simply the best defense of NAFTA. Rush combines a fantastic radio personality with terrific insight.

—P. J. O'Rourke, conservative humorist

"One of Rush's best moments came in the summer of 1993, when he was helping lead the charge against the Clinton budget," explains Larry Kudlow, former chief economist at Bear Stearns, a top Wall Street investment firm. "He would call me to discuss the budget, and I would give him numbers and graphs and pertinent op-ed pieces to help clarify his arguments. Obviously what he did on the air went over well. Whenever he mentioned that he'd talked to me, I got hundreds of phone calls. He once read on the air an op-ed I wrote in *The Wall Street Journal*. After the show, the phones at Bear Stearns lit up. We must have gotten 200 calls. The receptionist called and said, 'Mr. Kudlow, it's happening again.'

"He just loved when he heard me saying on *Wall Street Week* that Clinton should follow the lead of John Kennedy, who as President had cautioned against higher taxes," Kudlow continues. "I read this long quote by Kennedy saying that we need to lower taxes in order to have the economy grow. Rush ran with that. I heard he used it on his show for days. When people across the country talked about the Clinton budget, they were using Rush's arguments," remembers Kudlow, now economics editor at *National Review*. "He was quite effective in stopping the stimulus package from going through and for making the vote on the final budget so close. He excelled at crystalizing the message, explaining to his listeners how higher taxes affect them, how the Clinton budget was bad for their pocketbooks."

Jim Clark, like many businessmen who work for smaller-sized firms, concurs. "I loved the way Rush dissected the Clinton budget," observes Clark, marketing director for Premium Coffee, in Lakewood, New Jersey. "He did it better than anyone else out there. That budget is anti-business. That budget threatens to put people like me out of business, and he helped rally opposition to it. Rush is a champion of business."

"Wall Streeters generally like the line Rush takes on economic issues, but they don't need his advice because they deal with the issues in a more complex way than he possibly can on the radio," Kudlow asserts. "But they use Limbaugh as a way to talk about his ideas on other topics. In that sense, Rush is like a pulling guard. He plows through and opens up a big hole. Once the hole has been opened with a conversation about Rush on interest rates, guys who normally don't talk about social issues may get into social issues, too."

From Wall Street to Maple Street, businesspeople use Limbaugh's antitax, free-market, pro-growth exhortations as an entree into conservative conversation. A discussion that is kicked off with "Did you hear what Rush said about the bond market?" often leads to Limbaugh on family, health care, or feminism. "I have been surprised to see these Ivy League moderates, who claim not to like Rush, recounting his skits. And that's good, because once you've got them talking about Rush," Kudlow states, "then you can use his argument to tear the guy open. Deep down he really believes those things, but he's just been taken in with conventional thinking."

On the twelfth floor of a Manhattan skyscraper, Bill, an institutional salesman on a sometimes rambunctious floor of two hundred investment bankers, sits concentrating at his desk. The bank is European-owned, but Bill is an American. To his friends and colleagues selling domestic and foreign equities, he is an outspoken Limbaugh proponent, but his business is customer-sensitive, and he deals in large dollar numbers, so the loss of one customer could be very expensive. He does not want his last name or the bank's name to go on record. Bill takes a deep breath and considers his words.

"Rush is a phenomenon in that he is a source of truth you don't find anywhere else," he says. "The news reported by the three major networks and the written press reports, with the possible exception of *Investor's Business*

Daily and *The Wall Street Journal,* has a liberal bias, not perhaps as draconian as Rush portrays it, but there is definitely a liberal slant. Rush gives you the other side of the story, the things the others have chosen not to report for lack of time or space or because of their political orientation. So you get a lot of information from him that you wouldn't find anywhere else.

"The Republican Party does not have a strong leader right now," Bill continues. "People don't look to Bob Dole as the party leader. You don't have a Dan Quayle or a Jack Kemp in command at this point. Bill Bennett is something of a leader, but you don't have anybody who is *the* voice of the Republican Party. People are groping for that, and right now Limbaugh is providing that voice.

"At the same time, he's an excellent entertainer. That's unusual. People who are conservatives aren't funny!" says Bill, laughing. "People enjoy listening to him. He gives us a conservative take on the news; he's the de facto head of the Republican Party; and he's amusing. Those three things have drawn me to him."

As far as analyzing Wall Street and placing it in the political arena, Bill gives Limbaugh an above-average score. "As an economist, he's okay," Bill allows. "Sometimes he makes statements that are true in an economic textbook but aren't in the reality of Wall Street. I give him credit because when he does get something wrong, he admits it at the front of the next show.

"To me, his hottest issue is the Clintons—whether it be Whitewater, health care, NAFTA, their character, their policies, whatever," says the salesman. "His forte is focusing on how he disagrees with them in politics. Rush doesn't dislike Bill Clinton as a person. That got blurred in the beginning. He would really go after Clinton, and he didn't make the distinction that, 'Hey, I don't dislike the guy; I disagree with his views.' But I think he's cleared that up. He's taking the high road, and that's good."

That doesn't mean that Bill wants Limbaugh not to be tough on the Clintons. "I'll tell you what my take on the cattle-futures affair is," Bill says. "An attorney representing Tyson Foods placed orders for Hillary Clinton. She made $100,000 during the very short period of time he placed orders for her. At the same time, he lost a lot of money. I've heard figures from $800,000 to $2.5 million. The point is, he lost money during the time he netted her $99,000 and change.

"Rush had a good take on it. But I actually go a step further," Bill continues. "Look at what Tyson Foods has done in Arkansas. They have been given tremendous leeway regarding the environment. The river by the Tyson plant is evidently one of the nation's most polluted. When it comes to wetlands, streams, rivers, sites, variances for construction, those are all state and local issues. This leniency came at a cost. Was it a political cost where they contributed to the campaign? Was it a personal cost?

"Think about how you'd get money to the Clintons," suggests Bill. "I don't think it was this blatant, but here's the example: you go long on gold, you go short on gold. If the price of gold goes up, you take the loss on the short, and you give the gain on the long position to the Clintons. You've just basically taken money and laundered it through a broker and given it to the Clintons.

It's now clean. It's not a campaign contribution; it's nothing. I think when they dig into this, they may find that Hillary's profit, if the attorney took that big a loss on the commodities market, might be the tip of the iceberg. Other people may be involved. Maybe some profits went to legislators, some to EPA regulators.

"The papers seemed to downplay the whole thing as just another Hillary-bashing or Hillary-pillorying, as they say, and Rush definitely pursued it. This is what he does. They seem to just feed him. The Administration seems to give him ammunition daily. He just loads up the gun and fires away."

Although he is careful about discussing his political opinions with clients, the conservative corner around Bill's desk on the bank's open floor does sometimes voice its opinions. "There are about four of us," says Bill. "The guy who sits next to me is a huge Republican, and he and I discuss Rush. He is a recent convert. On vacation, his parents had radios in the kitchen, at the pool and in the living room, all tuned to Limbaugh. He couldn't get away from him. So he sat out by the pool and listened three hours a day every day. He says, 'It was great. I loved it. That was vacation to me.'

"If I had three hours to kill beside the pool with a piña colada, I'd listen to three hours of Rush, too," says Bill. "Unfortunately, I don't. Yesterday, I was on the road traveling home from Philadelphia, and I had half an hour to listen. He has five-minute segments that are excellent, concise, well thought-out. They get his political point across. They present his news message for the day. That's great. But for me, because my free time is so limited, the entertainment value of his books is best."

Bill does have at least one client he discusses Limbaugh with—the conservative who introduced him to the show in the first place. "I was working at home about two years ago, and this client called me and said, 'You've got to tune in to this,' " Bill recounts. "I said, 'Tune in to what?' He goes, 'You've heard me mention this guy before. Turn on 77, WABC, that's the station he's on in New York.' And I said 'OK, I'll turn it on.' And he had a really funny parody going. I listened, and thought 'I've got to listen to this guy again.' " Bill was hooked.

"Bill is a broker who works with me and executes orders," says Dennis Gibb, a Seattle investment manager. "We became friends over time, and one day we were talking about Clarence Thomas. At that moment, I was listening to Limbaugh, and there was something going on, and I said, 'You've got to listen to Limbaugh.' He turned on a radio, and he got a kick out of it. Most of us work, and we can't necessarily listen live, but we tape him."

An Army helicopter pilot and field artillery officer in Vietnam, Gibb also first heard of Limbaugh through a friend. "Phil Gioia, an investment banker in San Francisco, was always talking about Rush Limbaugh. Phil is one of the genuine heroes of the Vietnam War, and he's nobody's fool as far as intellectuals go. This was a very powerful mind—a VMI and Georgetown graduate with a Stanford MBA—that listened to Limbaugh and loved him, so I took notice. But this was back in 1989, and in Seattle, no station carried Limbaugh yet," Gibb recalls.

"So all I heard about him was through other people's comments."

"I called Dennis one day and said, 'You've got to hear this guy. This guy's so straight he sleeps in a quiver at night,' " says Gioia, who founded the Bay Street Group, a merchant and investment banking firm, after completing his second tour of duty in Vietnam and receiving an MBA from Stanford. "If scapegoating and blame-shifting and divisiveness and victimization, empowerment, entitlement, and subsidy is your game, then you're going to hate this guy. But if personal responsibility, integrity and hard work are what you really believe in, you should listen to him. It's as simple as that.

"All I wanted to do since I was a little kid was be an infantry officer because my father was an officer in World War II, and thought he was the greatest guy I'd ever met," Gioia continues. "I wanted to be like my dad. Rush teaches that you should respect your parents. I was raised to tell the truth and to take responsibility for my actions, and that's what Limbaugh teaches. My father died when I was a cadet, and my mother carried the ball. Neither one of them made a lot of money, but they put us through school. They raised my brother and me with a terrific set of values. That's the greatest legacy you can have. That correlates directly to Limbaugh's message. I hear him refer to his father all the time. He learned a lot from his father. As counterpoint to the collection of journalistic harpies, like Molly Ivins, Nina Totenberg, Ellen Goodman and all these left-side sob sisters, Limbaugh is a great guy to listen to. I catch him three or four times a week in the morning when I'm going someplace. Rush is probably 90 percent good old-fashioned common sense and maybe 10 percent showmanship, pitch and bombast. But I think you need that in there. I think that leavens the show."

In Seattle, Gibb started listening to Limbaugh when a local station finally picked up his show. "I gave him the six weeks he requests to figure out what the show's about, but it took me far less than that," he recalls.

Gibb, however, is careful with whom he directly discusses Limbaugh. "Most of my clientele don't listen to him. Actually, I'm sure they do, but they don't talk about it. You have to be reasonably careful about talking about Rush because people who consider themselves to be intellectuals, particularly if they have a liberal bent, will sneer at you if they think you're listening to him. They consider Limbaugh to be anti-intellectual."

Gibb, who holds sociology, psychology and history degrees from the University of Iowa and a graduate business degree from the University of Chicago, disagrees. "There has always been a strong anti-intellectual bent in America. You can go back and read *Power Elite* and other books of the Fifties and Sixties that put down people who appear to be smart. George Wallace's famous comment about pointy-headed intellectuals is another example. But I don't think Limbaugh is anti-intellectual. He does speak in terms a mass audience understands. Buckley will never have the mass appeal Limbaugh has because he's so intellectual that he can't bring himself down to the guy who isn't educated that way. George Will also talks over the heads of people who should be listening to him. Rush Limbaugh is just doing what's necessary to sell a product.

"I try not to paraphrase or to telegraph my thoughts to people with Rush Limbaugh's name," asserts Gibb. "I try to use my own thoughts, which may be similar to his. That's Limbaugh's real strength. He doesn't say anything all that original. What he is saying is what everybody has thought for a long time. He voices the frustrations of a lot of people who are out there trying to do the right thing.

"What Limbaugh does for me is put the news and issues in a different perspective," says Gibb, who after Vietnam worked for Ross Perot at DuPont-Walston brokerage firm, Morgan Stanley, and Bear Stearns before founding Sweetwater Investments in 1989. "He comes up with things the news media don't cover, and that's valuable. He provides input, which I then analyze in terms of my beliefs and my principles.

"I also find Rush Limbaugh hilariously funny," adds Gibb. "What he's making us do is laugh at how stupid we are. Will Rogers did the same thing. He made us laugh at our own foibles and our own stupidity. The fastest way to deflate pompousness is with humor."

Gibb believes the most important issue facing America is the preservation of individual liberties, which he thinks are under attack by the Clinton Administration. "The book next to my bed is called *Road to Serfdom* by F.A. Hayek," he says. "I'm a great believer that individuals without the benefit of government regulation actually will perform better than with government regulation. Every time we let the government regulate more—whether it's health care or whatever—we lose a piece of our personal intellectual freedom. Limbaugh is on the same track. His position on health care, for example, is that it's wrong in principle, and that's my argument, too. I'm concerned about the willingness of people to give up individual freedom to the government."

Like Gioia, Gibb has spread the Limbaugh bug to his business associates. "I turned Duncan Naylor onto Limbaugh," says Gibb, proudly. "He and another fellow in his office, John Harris, have become politically active as a result of listening to Rush. Limbaugh has made people who used to sit around and take this crap take action. They're now writing letters, calling their congressmen; they're now raising hell. I can't tell you how many meetings I've been to with local congressmen where someone has stood up and said, 'How do we think we're going to get to prosperity by taxing ourselves to death?' You know, just straight out of Rush Limbaugh's mouth.

"Duncan is in the unfortunate situation of being represented by both Barbara Boxer and Dianne Feinstein. He watches their voting records in the Senate to see what bills they're for or against, to see what they're sponsoring," explains Gibb. "And he calls them all the time. He's a thorn in their sides."

"Dennis Gibb called me and mentioned Rush Limbaugh more than once," says Naylor from his Los Altos, California, office of a major Wall Street brokerage. "He was so up-to-date on what was happening in the government. It took me a while to get it. He said, 'You've got to listen to this guy.' And I said, 'Dennis, I can't: 9:00

to 12:00 on the West Coast—which is when he's on—is crunch time, and I'm a broker. I can't listen to him.' He says, 'You've got to tape it or do something.'

"So finally, I taped it at work, and I enjoyed it. And then I became fixated on it," Naylor recalls. "He has an unbelievable way of making a visible picture of the way government runs. Indirectly, he has shown us that we have a responsibility to give feedback to our government. The picture that he paints on a daily basis with facts and figures is convincing. He does an extremely good job of dissecting issues and comparing ideas and showing a lot of times where there is a double standard—where a certain type argument has been accepted from the Democrats but not from the Republicans."

Naylor listens to the tapes on the way home from work and at home. "He's on for three hours, and if you fast-forward the ads, you get about two hours of tape," says the broker. "I listen almost religiously every night. When I saw his show on C-SPAN, I was fascinated. I watched the whole damn thing. Rush is terribly brilliant. I don't agree with him on everything—I'm not for smoking—but I love his general conservative philosophy. Finally somebody voices my views, adheres to my values."

Despite his enthusiasm, Naylor is subtle about working Limbaugh's ideas into business conversation. "I don't bring up his name, but I do bring up the issues," relates the broker. "There's absolutely no doubt in my mind that I'm better versed on them and can better discuss my conservative philosophy after listening to Rush. I have conservative clients who are absolutely for Rush, and it unites us. We'll discuss our normal business, and we might get off into politics, like when Bentsen told the Japanese to lower their taxes. Forget Japan. Forget Mexico. Forget England. Lower *our* taxes. Don't worry about them. We can't even manage our own economy. These are the things I'm more aware of now.

"I'm more aware and more active now," insists Naylor. "I'm more concerned about the responsibilities that we, as citizens of a democracy, have. We can't sit back and expect things to be done for us. Everybody's got to do it, and I mean above and beyond voting. I've written a lot of letters to Feinstein and Boxer. I have a complete list of all the congressmen. I've either sent letters or called everybody from Alan Greenspan to the White House. Greenspan does a good job, and I called to congratulate him, to tell him to keep it up, not to kowtow to the White House. I would say that even if a Republican was in. It's important that the Federal Reserve remain independent."

Naylor is impressed by the passion and sincerity of Limbaugh's callers, too. One in particular hit home. "A guy called and said, 'My body is starting to give out slowly. I'm hanging in there, but you've really made a difference in my life. I really live just to listen to you.' Rush was totally taken aback. He didn't know what to say. Rush has made a change in many people's lives."

For Naylor, Limbaugh has made an impact closer to home as well. "My wife and I went to a family reunion down in Santa Barbara, and when I talked to my wife's aunt, Jean Smith, we were like two peas in a pod," he says. "Jean lives in Idaho, and runs a cattle ranch, but we have a lot in common." Part of her day also revolves around listening to Rush. "She'll need something welded and go into some shop in Boise, and some guy'll have Rush on in his back room. Rush works for everybody from a welder, to a rancher, to a stockbroker, to a friend of mine who is the president of the largest company in Oregon. It's amazing."

"Some friends of mine told me about him four years ago," recalls Jean Smith from her thirty-thousand-acre ranch near Boise, Idaho. "I have a cattle business, so I'm in my Blazer a lot, up and down the highway. My friend said, 'Jean, there's a great fellow on by the name of Rush Limbaugh who you ought to listen to, because I think you'll appreciate him and understand him.' They told me he was different, and I sort of like the ones that are different. So I turned Rush on in my Blazer, and I've been listening to him ever since."

Since the death of her husband in 1980, Smith has run a cow-calf outfit of fifteen hundred head, forty-five head of purebred Herefords and seventy-five bulls. "Rush is for free enterprise," reasons the rancher, "and since I'm an owner of a small business, my feelings are strong in that direction. Before, no one expressed how I felt about private enterprise. The fact that he likes meat, which helps me, too, attracted me. But I like his whole philosophy. After this man was elected, I just wondered what was going to happen to me and my business. And of course, it's been as bad as I thought. If I didn't have Rush to listen to, I'd think I was alone in this.

"Rush brings together people like me who do not go out and carry banners and do that type of thing. He gives all of us who are a little backward in expressing ourselves the courage to talk about how we feel. To me, it is necessary to get the word out. The older I get, the less I hesitate," she says. "I just think, 'This is the way it is, and I'd better say it.' Rush does that with humor, and that makes a difference. I love Rush's takeoffs and his music that entertains and makes a point. And of course, I'm used to his extravagant statements, so I don't pay any attention to those. I think they're fun. He *should* be egotistical. That's what drives the liberals crazy. And if we can laugh at those people, it's so much better than crying. When he fights the battle, I feel he's fighting it for me, too."

Businessmen on Limbaugh

"I'm out here trying to scratch a living with an oppressive government on my back. I just listened to Rush for the last two hours while driving home. People swallow this country club liberalism hook, line and sinker, and they've got to learn better. They need to understand where these people are coming from. Rush is about the only one out there right now with national recognition who speaks out against liberalism. He exposes the liberals, no question about it. He really makes people think."
—Mat Pope, president, The Pope Company,
Courtland, Virginia

"Rush Limbaugh has attained a status where people will act on his comments and decisions. That's a problem media stars always have. His famous bet with the Democratic National Committee for a million dollars that five years from now unemployment, taxes and the deficit will be higher than when Clinton took over is almost scary because it's starting to happen. His call on the effect of the taxes . . . if you notice, this market started down about 30 days before tax day. I have many clients who have paid more taxes than they thought they were going to pay. Sometimes Rush can be scary with the forecasts he makes. One of the problems he's got to be careful about is that if he makes a forecast that we're in a bear market or something like that, people are going to act on it."

—Dennis Gibb, Sweetwater Investments, Seattle, Washington

"At first I wasn't a fan. You see, I grew up in a family with a very different political viewpoint. But it has since changed. I like his business views. He likes to encourage small businessmen. He says just get out there and do it. His greatest contribution to this country is that he motivates people to do things: start a business, work hard, call a congressman, whatever. He is leading a great debate right now between the Clinton Administration and the working people of this country. Clinton thinks that we are just an endless source of money, to be taxed and taxed. But anyone who owns a business knows that quite the opposite is true. I really like Rush now. And I just want more people to hear and read about him."

—Devin Hollends, owner, Pacific Distribution Company, Penfield, New York

"I have listened to Rush ever since he came on the air in August of 1988. I was visiting a client in New York and flipping through the dial when I came across him. Rush epitomizes what an entrepreneur is. He was making $12,000, pulled himself up by his bootstraps, and succeeded. He champions the values and work ethic I was brought up with. Rush wants everyone to be able to keep the rewards of their labor, and he's against state control. Now, Rush is dissecting the health plan and pointing out what a disaster it will be for businesses and the American worker. He calls it like it is: socialism. He says. 'Name one thing that government has done well.' He's right. Welfare, Medicare, all of them are a mess. There is no accountability. He interprets the news in a very clear-cut common sense way, and he gets his point of view across with a sense of humor. His radio show is spontaneous, lively, and he cuts people to pieces. Each one of my 43 sales reps, to a person—secretaries, staffers, owners—listens to Limbaugh whenever they can.

—Jim Clark, marketing director, Premium Coffee, Lakewood, New Jersey

"I have been listening for about three years. I really love his audacity. Secondly I think he does an excellent job—particularly on the budget, business, and government intrusion—of talking matters through for the average listeners. I come from a business career. Limbaugh is merciless on Perot and that miffs me a little bit. I'm sure it really miffs Ross. Ross and I go way back. He's a terrific fellow, but Rush really goes into him. He is

really a great source of discussion. I like the radio show just slightly better than the books, but it's pretty close."
      —Orson Swindle, state director, Empower America, Honolulu, Hawaii

"I love the way he sticks it to the liberals. A lot of people in this town really don't like to hear this kind of stuff, you know, anti-government and all that. As long as they are getting what they want, they just want more of the same. It's a good thing he keeps these ideas alive."
      —John Greenlee, railway consultant, Capital Railway Consultants, Washington, D.C.

"Here in Florida, Rush enjoys good support. The man is out there trying to change things for the better. He speaks accurately. He is effective. I'm like a lot of the Dittoheads. We're frustrated with things, and we want to see something changed. I believe Rush Limbaugh is a phenomenon that will never be repeated. I don't know how long the wave he's riding is going to last, but right now it's a tsunami. He's speaking to the heartstrings of America."

                    —Al Clark, Southeastern Realty Group, Orlando, Florida

"I cannot see the American public electing that silly SOB again, and if they do, we're doomed. Even Rush Limbaugh cannot save us. He's a good entertainer who talks the truth. He talks to middle America. He brings out facts and lets you draw the conclusions. Everybody says they're for less government, but when it comes to cutting their foot off, they don't want to do it. I think Limbaugh is great. He's the conscience of this country right now. He's the only one we've got. Do I hear people talking about him? Goodness gracious, I have 15 or 20 friends who quote him daily."

—Thomas Redford, owner, Tram Construction, Richmond, Virginia

"I am amazed at the cross section of society that listens to Limbaugh. Their level of political knowledge is so high because of him. I have a friend who owns a lumber company, and although he doesn't quote Rush or even mention him, I sense that what he is talking about has come from Rush's show. He talks about taxes more than anything else, how ridiculous he thinks taxing the rich is when you want to promote growth. People take Rush's ideas as their own. They have thought these things for years, but he expresses them better. They borrow that."

—John Lewis, Gardner, Lewis Asset Management, Wilmington, Delaware

Nine

Routing the Liberal Media

That night after the show, I sent him flowers and a note that said, "Performing your duties 99 percent mistake free. Now I know what you had tied behind your back all this time."
—Markie Post, actress, *Hearts Afire,* on Limbaugh's guest appearance on the show

As Rush Limbaugh's show revolutionized talk radio, as his first book set best-seller records, and as he took his act to television, the press reluctantly paid closer attention. It had to. Limbaugh was becoming too powerful to ignore. Of course, that attention came mostly in the form of deliberate put-downs and open hostility.

But no matter how hard the media tried to push public opinion against Limbaugh, he bounced back. Limbaugh's very vocal fans were always there to back him up. Newspaper columnists soon learned that there was a price to pay for attacking the commentator without firsthand information. Negative columns boomeranged with twice the force. Limbaugh's detractors, not Limbaugh, were finding themselves hung out to dry—by angry readers.

The tables were turned in another way as well. Often, it was the letter writers who sounded reasoned and even-handed, and the professionals who sounded hot under the collar and bitter. Limbaugh's listeners had learned from his techniques. "Words mean things," the commentator is fond of saying. Limbaugh's fans were themselves becoming adept at calmly nailing the perpetrators of vapid diatribes with the weaknesses of their own arguments.

The press could no longer write with impunity. When *Arkansas Democrat-Gazette* editor Paul Greenberg wrote in a June 1992 syndicated column, "The Sister Souljahs and Rush Limbaughs grant us a kind of spurious moral permission to gibe at others," the response was immediate and emphatic. Among the letter writers was Ralph Vitale, Jr., of Arlington, Virginia, who retorted, "Mr. Greenberg does not offer a single quote from Mr. Limbaugh. Mr. Limbaugh never preaches hate, which is why Mr. Greenberg can't quote him on the subject. The trouble with Mr. Limbaugh is that he is all too articulate in both his defense of conservatism and his perception of the flaws of the liberal-left agenda."

In November 1992, *St. Petersburg Times* writer Margo Hammond blasted Limbaugh: "His callers are followers, who agree unconditionally to his ranting." One letter writer responded, "Pish posh. Hammond implies that Limbaugh fans are simply stupefied zombies . . . mumbling 'ditto' every time we are confronted with a substantive situation. His depth of philosophy and serious tackling of the issues are what keep listeners. Limbaugh remains because of his ability to engage in intellectually stimulating discussion of vital issues."

The pattern repeated itself in newspapers across the nation. Columnists attacked, and Limbaugh supporters parried. "At first the press thought Rush was a buffoon," says L. Brent Bozell, III, whose Alexandria, Virginia, Media Research Center monitors the coverage of events and personalities. "As his listenership began to flourish, the media's impression of him assumed the Andy Warhol model: his 15 minutes will soon be up and at that point, the world will come to its senses."

But Limbaugh and his growing number of fans wouldn't go away. Indeed, Limbaugh supporters showed just how persistent they could be in February 1993 when they sent the media world a resounding message. It was the month after President Clinton's inauguration, and the news event of the day was Clinton's first major initiative—to allow gays to serve openly in the military.

Although a committed liberal, *Washington Post* columnist William Raspberry opposed lifting the ban on allowing gays in the military. Raspberry knew the column would be controversial, but he was prepared to brave the criticism of his fellow liberal columnists on this issue. He could defend himself against the best.

What Raspberry didn't foresee was the possibility of something even worse, to him, than the scorn of his colleagues. He didn't know that Rush Limbaugh, of all people, would publicly agree with him. His stance on gays in the military no longer mattered. In the long run, that would not affect his career, but finding himself in the same camp as Limbaugh was more than he could bear.

Being a skillful professional writer, Raspberry knew he could rely on one thing. He could write himself back into the good graces of his readers and more importantly his fellow liberal columnists. How? By denouncing Limbaugh.

"There are approximately 243 million Americans whose praise I'd prefer to Rush Limbaugh's," Raspberry wrote in his February 5 column. "Not because he's conservative. I don't care about that. But I do care about the demagoguery he has perfected to a science. I care about his gay-bashing, his racial put-downs, his merciless caricaturing of feminism or any other cause he disagrees with. It bothers me that he is so good at what I grew up in Mississippi watching racist politicians do—tossing the raw meat of bigotry to people who need desperately to feel superior to somebody." The bottom-line message was that: Raspberry could take the stance he took against gays in the military because he did it for the right reasons while Limbaugh could not.

The columnist soon found that Limbaugh was not the easy target he had anticipated. Howard Raymond, an insurance salesman from Alexandria, Virginia, was among the first to call. His message: "Rush Limbaugh is no bigot. He stands for all that is good and decent in this country," says Raymond. "That column was just too much for me. It couldn't go unchallenged. After I called, I wrote a letter to his office as well. Rush shouldn't have to stick up for himself all the time." As Raspberry quickly found out, Limbaugh didn't have to. More than two hundred letters supporting Limbaugh poured in.

Among them was one from Florida, that Raspberry published in his February 28 column: "You obviously do not listen to Rush enough to know that he is not a bigot. . . . Do you not think that the American public has enough intelligence to discern what is meritorious in your column and on Rush's show for themselves?" The letter hit home on two levels. First, it stated the truth. Raspberry did not listen to Limbaugh. And secondly, it clearly demonstrated what was now so painfully obvious: Raspberry had shown too little faith in his readers and had, instead, lowered the conversation to mudslinging.

The columnist needed to correct the deteriorating situation. "Raspberry is a thoughtful liberal," says media-watcher Bozell. "All his friends, who probably had never heard Limbaugh, told him all these awful things. Then after he received this overwhelming response, being a decent and honest fellow, he took a look."

Raspberry realized there was only one way to save face. It was clearly time to tuck his tail and make a public confession: mea culpa. Then maybe he could move on and forget this cold month of February.

"I've been doing penance," the columnist sheepishly wrote in his February 28 column. "I've listened to major portions of two Rush Limbaugh radio shows. I've done some heavy browsing of his new book, *The Way Things Ought to Be,* and now I'm ready to say it: Rush, I'm sorry. At the urging of some 60 zillion readers . . . I've taken another look at this phenomenon of the airwaves. I confess now that, apart from a couple of accidental listenings, I didn't know that much about Limbaugh. I still don't. My opinions about him had come largely from other people— mostly friends who think Rush is a four-letter word. They are certain he is a bigot. But is he? . . . Sure, he's taken digs at poor people and rioters and feminists and the NAACP, but why should any of these be immune?"

"Rush, I'm sorry?" From a prominent member of the liberal media? It was a watershed event. "The press has never been able to accept the fact that they lost the American people decades ago and that Rush has won their hearts," says *Boston Herald* columnist Don Feder. "They have deluded themselves into believing they are the will of the people. What really gets them is that Limbaugh contradicts the liberal media's self-image. The fascist stuff, the racist stuff, is the only way they know to attack him."

For Raspberry, the incident was one of rediscovering his audience. Concerning his characterization of Limbaugh, he concedes: "Some called and said, 'You had it right the first time.' Then again most of the responses— letters and phone calls—were along the lines of, 'I've got new respect for you. I've never heard a journalist say I might have had it wrong.' Frankly, that I didn't expect either."

Raspberry had ultimately done the right thing and emerged better for it. But others in the media were not so quick.

The New York Times addressed the subject of Rush Limbaugh's best-selling book, *The Way Things Ought to Be,* with thunderous silence until late February 1993. The book had reached Number One on the newspaper's prestigious Hardback Best-Seller List the previous September. For six months the book sat atop the list. For six months the *Times* ignored it in its review pages.

"When the book first came out, I was in Harvard Square and found it in no bookstore," says Feder. "The clerk told me there were no copies and she didn't know how to order them. I thought that odd. Then I heard that Erwin Glikes, then president of Free Press, had said he was told flat out at some big-city bookstores: 'We don't carry it because it is a fascist book.'"

"Rush was actually pleased in a way that the *Times* wouldn't review the book because it confirmed his view of how the media saw him. Besides, he didn't need a *Times* review—either for sales or for the credibility," explains John Fund, the *Wall Street Journal* editorial writer who collaborated with Limbaugh on the book.

Feder and others wrote columns about the shabby treatment the book was receiving. Limbaugh fans wrote letters to the *Times*. Once again the pressure drew results. A week before Raspberry's groundbreaking apology to Limbaugh, the *Times* finally recognized Limbaugh's book. The newspaper's TV reviewer, Walter Goodman, trashed the runaway best-seller. "This book, in part a recycling of radio monologues, is a rant of opinions, gags and insults with a few facts or near-facts sprinkled in like the meat in last week's stew," he wrote. "Some passages alternate between slobberings of sincerity and slaverings of invective. . . . Despite Bill Clinton's recent victory, right-wing populism, an American perennial, is in bloom, and at the moment Mr. Limbaugh is its gaudiest flower."

Limbaugh's fans weren't going to let the *Times* get away with such a scornful critique. "The review consisted of the same wearying condescension that should be expected from the religious Left," wrote Steven P. Sorenson of

Hinsdale, Illinois, to the *Book Review* letters page. "The contempt Mr. Goodman feels toward those who do not find solace in the superiority of indecision is best described as follows: What is the definition of a bigot? Anyone who is winning an argument with a liberal."

For some, the press's negativism actually attracted them to the maverick commentator. "I first decided to listen to Rush Limbaugh when all these bad things were written about him in the papers," reveals the humorist P. J. O'Rourke. "Talk radio is really all about filling airtime with quality. Rush does that better than anyone else. Those in the media who attack him haven't listened to him for the most part," says O'Rourke, who calls Limbaugh's dissection of Perot's book on NAFTA one of the most devastating things he has ever heard. "When I told a reporter about his review of Perot's book on the air, he said, 'Really? I thought he only made fun of blacks and gays.' "

That apparently was the impression that President Clinton had, too. In May 1993, just three months after Clinton's inauguration, Limbaugh attended the annual White House Correspondents' Dinner in Washington, D.C., at which President Clinton was the guest of honor. "At the dinner, the press and politicians come together to have fun at each other's expense," says *National Review* publisher Ed Capano. "After 12 years with Republicans in the White House, the press finally had one of their own in Bill Clinton. Surveys of journalists show that 80 percent vote Democratic. Clinton felt he was among friends. Many from his Administration and left-wing Hollywood were there too—Barbra Streisand and

Richard Dreyfuss, for instance. Rush of course was the bogeyman."

Earlier that week, Limbaugh had come to the defense of Clinton's attorney general, Janet Reno, after black Democratic Representative John Conyers had rebuked her handling of David Koresh and the Branch Davidians in Waco. "A few minutes into his routine," Capano says, "Clinton paused, then delivered this punch line: 'Limbaugh supported Janet Reno only because she was attacked by a black guy.'

"It didn't go over well at all," insists Capano. "There was a nervous rumbling in the audience and a smattering of applause. But no one laughed. I said to the others at my table: 'He just called Rush a racist.'

"Rush came over a few minutes later—he must have figured we were the only friendlies in the room," Capano adds. "He said, looking a bit exasperated, 'Was I mistaken or did Clinton call me a racist?'

" 'You weren't mistaken, Rush,' I told him. He was upset," recalls Capano. "It was really foolish of Clinton. First of all, anyone who listens to Rush knows that he's not racist. But I guess that's the point: the only ones who call him a racist are those who have never listened. Secondly, Limbaugh is quite a force. Why would the White House bother alienating 20 million people?"

While the liberal weekly *The New Republic* claimed not to be amused by the joke, it nonetheless defended the sentiment. "If you can't take a joke," the magazine wrote of Limbaugh, "then don't be one." But columnists, fans, and fellow conservatives rushed to the broadcaster's defense. Capano's *National Review* pointed out, "Mr.

Limbaugh was defending the attorney general even before Representative Conyers told her off."

The New York Times and *The Washington Post* didn't press the issue, but other newspapers did. "The charge makes sense only in a world where every white who disagrees with a black is automatically vulnerable to charges of racism," wrote *The New York Post.* "A special factor renders the 'joke' about Rush Limbaugh's alleged racism decidedly inappropriate: it was told by the President." And the editorial page of *The Orange County Register* jumped to the commentator's defense: "It only weakens President Clinton's image and strengthens Limbaugh's to make such a senseless attack. . . . Limbaugh's message appeals to the majority of blacks in this country."

"It's as if he couldn't resist taking a cheap shot at Rush even though he knew he would have to pay the price," assesses Capano. "I guess Clinton learned his lesson. George Stephanopoulos, his director of communications at the time, had to apologize for the President later that week."

But the battle was still being waged on all frontiers. In the spring of 1993, a new anti-Limbaugh vehicle from San Diego emerged, providing the national media with a new tool with which to bash Limbaugh. A newsletter with a catchy title *The Flush Rush Quarterly,* published by literary agent Brian Keliher, relied chiefly on negative personal attacks. In July, Mike Royko, of the *Chicago Tribune,* sized it up: *"Flush Rush* is subversive and un-American trash. Don't let your children see this contemptible 12-page newsletter. . . . After you read it, burn it. This is the least we owe to a wonderful man."

But for *The Washington Post, Flush Rush* was grade-A material, deserving of a grand introduction on the front page of the paper's hallowed Style section. "They have been wailing about it everywhere. Why in all of America is there not a visceral, red-blooded liberal who can stand up to the talk show bullying of the Rights' populist heavies?" wrote Ian Katz. "Why is there no streetwise political southpaw equipped . . . to go a few rounds with Rush Limbaugh? And all the while there he was, this avenger of the Left, this socially aware Rambo . . ." Later, the reporter seemed to chuckle when *Flush Rush* joked: "What's the difference between Rush Limbaugh and a whale? Fifty pounds and a sports jacket."

The Post's conservative counterpart, *The Washington Times,* responded, "Anyone like Mr. Keliher who seems to devote most of his waking life to trying to demolish Rush is bound to receive the liberal equivalent of the Congressional Medal of Honor, even when his rhetoric is cheap and his retorts are flaccid." Says *Washington Times* editor Sam Francis, "I looked at the barbs and criticisms that this newsletter had issued at Limbaugh and found them transparent, invalid and mean-spirited. It struck me as liberal hypocrisy. There were jokes about Limbaugh being fat. I'm on the hefty side myself. It struck me as tasteless and weak."

Francis feels *Flush Rush* and the liberal media, like most one-time listeners, completely miss Limbaugh's point. "Like me, he is often criticized for being mean-spirited toward the poor, homeless and handicapped," Francis explains. "When we make fun of poor people or handicapped people, we're not literally making fun of them. We're trying to break the icon the Left is trying to create around these types of people. Unless you attack that icon, it's difficult to answer liberal arguments."

In August, as Washington's two papers were jousting, Limbaugh fans were battling other adversaries in the press. "I get so irritated by what I read in the papers," declares Colin Bruner of Louisville, Kentucky. "Since listening to Rush, I've begun writing more letters to the editor. When I saw Nina Walfoort's column, I went right to my computer and pounded out a response." What had so raised Bruner's ire? Published in the *Louisville Courier-Journal,* Walfoort's column was a response to a fairly positive Limbaugh profile in *U.S. News & World Report:* "I wasn't impressed. I think he's conservative, fat, loud and definitely not for me," she wrote. "I had only a vague impression of what he looked like: Willard Scott, Ned Beatty, Rush Limbaugh—they're all the same."

"As Limbaugh always accuses the liberal and their bedfellow media of putting 'symbolism over substance,' " Bruner wrote in his letter, "I'm not surprised that superficiality was the thrust of her article. She failed to mention that he is the number-one talk-radio host in America, leaving the liberal Larry King a knave in the ratings." Bruner, a teacher for the deaf, remembers, "What motivated me to write that letter was the lack of substance in her critique. When a debate is based on attitude, there is nothing there. There's no running of the numbers in the argument. The shame of it is that most of the media vote Democratic, and all they can say is that he's fat. Rush meanwhile deals with the substance."

So egregious was Walfoort's liberal carping that even

neutral readers were motivated to write in Limbaugh's defense. "Actually, I'm not a Limbaugh fan myself," Gerald Griggs, also from Louisville, wrote in the paper's letters column. "But I do like the fact that he stands up for what he believes in at a time when other white males have resigned themselves to being the whipping boys of the entire nation. . . . What's fat got to do with it? If a male reporter wrote that a female contemporary was fat, he wouldn't be called mean-spirited, he would be called sexist. He would be accused of 'objectifying, victimizing and dehumanizing.' . . . Maybe Limbaugh is fat because he has more than the average supply of guts."

Paul Colford, *New York Newsday* media columnist and author of *The Rush Limbaugh Story,* noticed in critiques of Limbaugh that the more fiery the venom, the less serious the actual criticism. "I'm not a fan, but rather an observer," he explains. "What Limbaugh says to his uninitiated listeners is that you have to listen for a few days to really get the flavor. He has a great shtick with a great deal of intelligence to go along with it. The guy is compelling and provocative and only a journalist living in a cave would not see that.

"I really am appalled to read so many stories about him that are vitriolic and dismissive," says Colford. "There is something grotesque about the fact that people write at length about him without really ever having listened. It is going by hearsay, which is pathetic."

Molly Ivins provided evidence for Colford's observation. "Being attacked by Rush Limbaugh is like being gummed by a newt," Ivins wrote in her October 14 *Fort Worth Star-Telegram* column. "Do you think his fans are actually flattered by being called Dittohead?" she snidely wrote. She continued her tirade: "What I really hold against Limbaugh is that many of the people who listen to him seem so singularly unable to reason their way out of a paper bag."

The heat was turned up yet another notch when in November, Limbaugh proved a vocal and effective critic against Governor Jim Florio of New Jersey. More than ever before, it became obvious that Limbaugh's show was a vital platform for affecting elections. He routinely assailed Florio while acclaiming his opponent, Christine Whitman. Whitman, the underdog, won by a nose.

His growing authority in elections prompted a February 20, 1994, piece in the *Washington Post Outlook* section. *New Yorker* writer David Remnick conceded early on: "Attention must be paid. Limbaugh's last-minute scare campaign waged in the New Jersey gubernatorial campaign undoubtedly did more to elect Christine Whitman than any plot, real or imagined, by Ed Rollins."

Remnick suggested that Limbaugh was a storm on the horizon. "Just as Reagan talked of welfare queens in Cadillacs, Limbaugh seizes on the absurd detail, gives it an absurdist twist of his own, and sends it out into the world under the guise of analysis and principle . . . Like all demagogues, [Limbaugh must] scare his listeners, get them to believe in conspiracy, rumor. . . . Like Reagan, Limbaugh is neither curious nor brave; he would rather tell his audiences fairy tales than have them face the world."

Remnick scolded Limbaugh for among other things lacking irony. "All the good humor William F. Buckley was so intent on putting into the conservative movement, Limbaugh tries to replace with a smiley sort of malice." Remnick alluded to Father Coughlin, implicitly comparing Limbaugh and the anti-Semitic radio personality of the 1920s.

"Although I much admire David Remnick," Buckley responds, "Rush Limbaugh and Father Coughlin have in common exactly this: that both of them used, use, the radio. If you were to subtract everything Father Coughlin did that animadverted on the Jews, you would then have simply a right-wing, isolationist commentator. But people react to the name of Coughlin exclusively because of his racist message. Which is not the case with Rush. Merely to bring up his name in an examination of Rush Limbaugh is to suggest that there are similarities. One might as well say that there are similarities between Douglas MacArthur and Adolf Hitler: they both fought in World War II."

Both fan and foe bombarded *The Washington Post* with letters condemning Remnick's attack on Limbaugh. "Listen, my liberal friends," wrote Stephen Parks, of Derwood, Maryland, on *The Washington Post's* letters page in response to Remnick. "I am a regular Rush listener. Yes, I find Rush's comments on feminists a bit too snide. Yes, his statements on environmental issues are often poorly informed. . . . But these are not at the core of Rush's message, and the core is worth the wait. The core of Rush Limbaugh is iconoclasm, the breaking of liberal idols. . . . The fact that he is so popular should be a wake-up call to opinion-makers to reexamine their assumptions."

"I enjoy listening to him. It's a relief to hear the unspeakable spoken," says Parks, a physicist at a Maryland engineering firm. "He has a comic way of puncturing the haughtiness of the liberal intellectual establishment. There are portions of what Limbaugh says that I agree with, portions I don't, but all in all I really respect what he's all about."

Limbaugh devoted a portion of his March 4 radio program to the letters in that day's *Post,* offering his own defense against the Remnick piece. Dan DeGoricia, a Washington consultant, sitting in the Rush Room at Blackie's House of Beef, toasted Parks's letter as Limbaugh read it. "I love Rush," DeGoricia says. "He has just woken up a sleeping giant. Most conservatives are so involved with their jobs and their families that they haven't had time to do things politically. Essentially Rush is running the largest Poli-Sci 101 class in the country. He makes people pay attention."

The Post published a second letter in response to Remnick that day, which Limbaugh also read on the air. "We are all tired of being PC, as Washington demands of us at every turn," wrote Allison C. Guy of Bowie, Maryland. "We crave individual responsibility, morals, culture, values and, yes, family values, along with principles, compassion and spiritual guidance. . . . Instead, Washington and the present Administration tie our hands behind our backs and lead us over the brink of destruction. Rush Limbaugh unties these hands and gives us hope . . ."

"I read this typical sarcastic piece in *The Washington Post,* which ridicules everything it doesn't agree with," says Guy, an office manager for a doctor. "I wrote the letter to get these aggravations off my chest. I think Limbaugh is intelligent, well-informed and, unlike *The Post,* he listens to different viewpoints."

In an April issue of *Forbes,* editor James W. Michaels pointed out how, in contrast to liberal journalists who couldn't take the time to listen to Limbaugh before attacking him, the commentator doggedly pursued the facts. "Limbaugh . . . works very hard," wrote Michaels. "Every working day he wades through eight newspapers, hundreds of faxes, newswires, mail and magazines, seeking ammunition for his forays against the lily-liberal politicians and their sycophants in the press and on the tube." But it's not just the hard work, Michaels also declared, it's the message. "What's Limbaugh's secret? He doesn't sing, dance or probe the sex lives of celebrities. In economic terms Limbaugh helps the market clear. He supplies a product that is in great demand but short supply. . . . He tells people that it is okay to believe in family and hard work, okay to believe in traditional values, okay to get a little thrill when the flag flaps in the breeze. . . . In this way he speaks to and for a large part of America."

In addition to practicing poor journalism, the press was practicing unsound business, Michaels asserts. "The media are making a very bad mistake," he explains. "In most portions of America, the liberal media have been trying to sell a liberal product to a conservative audience. When you pick up a publication and it doesn't offer the world you recognize, you turn elsewhere." That elsewhere has become talk radio and, more specifically, Rush Limbaugh.

Limbaugh himself told the magazine *Cigar Aficio-*

nado: "Rather than being an agent of influence, I think I am someone who validates what millions of Americans think and just don't hear expressed in the media. In fact, they are treated to television shows and movies that make fun of what they believe."

This fact was beginning to dawn on the viewer-sensitive media. Suddenly Limbaugh, who had first appeared on *Nightline* in 1990, became a favorite television guest. In 1993, Jay Leno had joked about Limbaugh and his fans at Dan's Bake Sale: "The last time this many conservatives gathered in one place was Berlin in 1935." But, like Raspberry before him, Leno would rethink his criticism. Less than a year later, Leno invited Limbaugh to appear on *The Tonight Show*. Limbaugh was the first guest, and when he walked out, to what one might have expected to be a hostile crowd, an interesting thing happened—they roared with approval. Limbaugh's reception was much warmer than that of the aging redheaded flame Ann-Margret later in the show.

Leno was very solicitous at first. He led by asking Limbaugh about his love life. Limbaugh quickly steered the discussion to politics. There was a brief back and forth. "Leno said, 'There are some things I agree with you on and some things I don't,' " remembers Brent Bozell. "Rush challenged him by asking, 'What do you agree with me on?' Leno said he agreed with Rush on fiscal and regulatory issues but that on social issues he thought Limbaugh was a bit crazy.

"Rush raised the case of a six-year-old boy who was charged with sexual harassment for kissing a girl in his class on the back of her head. Leno wanted to know why

Rush was so against all the recent charges of sexual harassment. Rush went on to say that Leno was taken in by the PC crowd. What is wrong with a six-year-old boy innocently kissing a girl on the back of the head? he asked. Surely we don't want to encourage it, but should we really charge him with sexual harassment?"

Leno backed off. "Here's the point," Bozell says. "On Leno's own show, Rush took over. That's unprecedented."

"You know that you have made it," *Newsday*'s Colford says, "when Letterman and Leno begin making you the butt of their jokes and having you on their shows. Limbaugh was trotted out with regularity on the end-of-the-year Top Ten lists. His romantic life was covered at length by the major supermarket tabloids—*National Enquirer* and *Star*. The fact that the tabloids regarded Limbaugh's love life as akin to Ted Danson's meant he had arrived as a public figure."

That was reconfirmed by Limbaugh's April 1994 guest appearance on CBS's sitcom, *Hearts Afire*. Both the invitation to appear on the show—produced by Clinton pals Harry Thomason and Linda Bloodworth-Thomason—and the episode's subsequent ratings proved that Limbaugh had indeed reached prime time. "It was really important for him to do well," says Markie Post, the show's voluptuous and brainy star. "He was so excited. He went on about it for days on his radio show. He totally took responsibility for the ratings. I'm not sure that he is not correct. We beat *Murphy Brown*. No other show coming after *Murphy Brown* had ever beaten it, and we did. We give Rush a lot of credit for that."

A few days later, *Weekly World News* cashed in on Limbaugh's Hollywood romance: "Rush Limbaugh Meets with Space Aliens! Historic rendezvous takes place at secret New Orleans estate!" The dome-headed creatures apparently came to encourage the commentator to run for the presidency in 1996. Limbaugh had clearly become one of the nation's most popular public figures, whose appeal cut across all lines. Who else could speak to the cynical Letterman audience, sell tabloids, and argue policy with President Clinton's top advisors?

The steady recognition of Limbaugh as an articulate, well-reasoned commentator by such shows as *Nightline* and *Meet the Press* showed that the rating-conscious media had backed off its attempts to vilify him. Partly through the force and intelligence of his listeners, Limbaugh had moved from the fringes to the legitimate. In April 1994, *Nightline* held a special ninety-minute show: "Whitewater: Overcovered or Undercovered?" *Nightline* assembled media heavyweights—ABC's Brit Hume, *Wall Street Journal* editor Robert Bartley, *New York Times* executive editor Max Frankel—on the campus of Iowa's Drake University for the event. Included via satellite was Limbaugh, who by then had become the voice the media turned to for the views of the Right. Ted Koppel led the show, after a brief introduction, by engaging Limbaugh and Clinton advisor James Carville in debate. Limbaugh got the most airtime.

"Ted has Limbaugh on *Nightline* for two reasons," says Hume. "One, Limbaugh is sufficiently articulate so that he can represent a point of view effectively and he can stand up for what he articulates. Two, he helps attract an audience. Ted leads off with Rush, as he did in Des

Moines, to engage the viewer and keep people watching." Limbaugh had clearly come a long way from the night he had been perceived as an easy target for the butt of the President's ill-begotten joke.

But a year after Clinton's jab at Limbaugh at the Correspondents' Dinner, the President went after him again— this time with the fiery bitterness of a true adversary. By now, Clinton fully understood that Limbaugh was no longer a fringe jester. With Democrats looking weak in the polls six months before the November general election, Clinton blamed his party's sluggishness on the commentator: "In the rural South, where you've got Rush Limbaugh and all this right-wing extremist media just pouring venom at us every day and nothing to counter that, we need an election to get the facts out," Clinton told a CNN forum.

"They are really worried about Rush at Democratic headquarters and at the White House," says *The Wall Street Journal*'s John Fund, who wrote the paper's editorials on Whitewater. "Clinton gets a Rush report every day. Someone's job at DNC is to listen to Rush and report to various people what he is saying. He's really getting to them."

Because of his growing popularity and overt political message, Limbaugh will always be the focus of media attacks. But will legitimacy encourage the media to soften their blows? Not likely, believes William Rusher, author of *The Coming Battle for the Media*. "They will continue, and he will continue to prevail," assesses the former *National Review* publisher. "I am awed at his ability to stand on the high wire without falling off. He goes on for 15 hours a week, having to weigh every conceivable application of what he says. He's got to think how the critics will take what he says because the liberals will romp all over him any chance they get, no matter how popular he gets."

Meeting the Press

In April 1993, NBC Washington Bureau Chief Tim Russert invited Limbaugh on Meet the Press *as guest commentator for the end-of-show roundtable, normally the domain of such Washington sages as William Safire, Bob Novak, and David Broder.*

"I listen to Rush somewhat regularly. He is obviously very smart, and has an astute understanding of trends. He represents a philosophical strain in the body politic, and he vocalizes a real frustration among voters and among the American people in general. Limbaugh cannot be dismissed. You simply can't dismiss anyone who has the loyal listenership he does, particularly of the magnitude he has. These are not rabid conservatives, either. There are moderates and even closet liberals who have written to me to say what big fans they are. When it was announced Limbaugh was coming on *Meet the Press,* we received a fair amount of mail: many people complained that we shouldn't legitimize this guy. But we got a very strong positive response as well. I also got a very strong favorable response after I spoke with Limbaugh on his radio show. He is a lightning rod. But you have to give him credit—he works very hard at getting his facts right."

—Tim Russert, NBC Washington Bureau Chief, host, *Meet the Press*

A Toast and a Roast from Markie Post

"I met Rush at the White House Correspondents' Dinner. I saw him across the room and walked over and said, 'I really would like to have lunch with you sometime. I don't know why, other than the fact that you're so under my skin. I can't not listen to you and I can't agree with you, but you're just so intriguing.' That is what I felt, but all I really said was, 'I'd like to have lunch with you sometime.'

"He went, 'Sure! I'd love to.' So I didn't have to explain myself any further. Later—I had to go back to Los Angeles—we talked on the phone. I told him, 'I really don't know why I want to do this other than part of it is I would like to have—from you—a conservative education so that I really know what I'm talking about.' My grandfather, who grew up in Ohio on a farm, voted for Nixon and Goldwater. He was a wonderful man. I don't have a knee-jerk reaction to the word conservative. I'm a moderate liberal.

"We never had lunch, but we had better. The first time—he was in L.A. for a book party for his second book—I invited him to come to the show and then afterwards, we'd go out to dinner with John Ritter and Linda and Harry [Thomason]. They'd all get to know each other. And that's what we did. We went back to Harry's office, played Trivial Pursuit till 3:00 in the morning. Rush and I won. The thing is, on his show a couple days later, Rush said we were great people, we were a lot of fun, but he said, 'However, I did win at Trivial Pursuit. I beat the liberals, and I just want everyone to know that.' Well, I want to go on record as saying, *I carried him.*

"We didn't talk about politics a lot. It would have been a hot point. We talked about areas where we could agree. I can tell you where I do tend to agree. Welfare is not working at all. We need to give people a helping hand, but we can't baby them through life. And our justice system has become an excuse system. It has gotten ridiculous. I am appalled at the Menendez non-verdicts. We have become afraid to say what is right and what is wrong.

"On women's issues, we have talked about that. I said, 'How can you call everybody who even thinks about women's issues Femi-Nazis?' He said, 'Not true. Not true. There are only about seven in the world. Twelve at the most. I'm just talking about the ones with no sense of humor who hate men.' I said, 'Rush, I've never heard you say there are 12 Femi-Nazis. You leave the impression that every feminist is a Femi-Nazi.' The women who have no sense of humor who say that all sex is rape, of course, they're fringe people. They're dead wrong. So, to a certain extent, if he's talking about 12 Femi-Nazis in the world, I agree with him. But in terms of women's issues, I think he's being a little disingenuous. I don't think he believes that.

"I adore him. He's a doll. He's got a lot of bluster

about him, but I find that kind of endearing because I feel that underneath is a very sensitive young kid, who like all of us, wants to be liked. He's very smart, maybe too smart for his own good and awfully nice. He listens to you. It's the one thing you don't see or hear on his show, because unless somebody is calling in with a point of view that surprises him, which people few people do, or educates him, which very few people do, then basically it's a monologue. But in real life, he keys in to people and listens to what they say, which surprised me.

"I would love it if he came on the show again. We've had guest stars before who aren't actors, and you don't give them too many lines. Rush had to carry a huge load on that show, and he was wonderful. The romantic part was neat. That was out there. I'm a married woman on the show. He said, 'What am I doing? I can't do this. I don't stand for this.' With actors, you try to set up a reality. You really look people in the eye and say it. You pretend it's real. Some people get nervous. Rush was great. He really stuck in there. We didn't cover him with a lot of editing and line readings right before he went on. He took to it naturally. He just really aced it. And I'll tell you who really loves Rush Limbaugh: the crew members. The Hollywood writers, producers and actors are the elite and it's not politically correct to like Rush, but the crew just loved him.

"What Linda did, in my opinion, was quite remarkable, being good friends with the Clintons and giving Rush a format that was fair. Everybody got their licks in, and his were just as strong as anybody else's. But while you thought there was going to be this huge debate on the issues, it turned out to be this mutual attraction, where we just couldn't even argue with each other. It showed the human side of politics. Really it's just two people who come face to face, and like each other. That's what actually happened in real life, too."

Ten

Storming Congress:
The New Populism

Rush has made it significantly more expensive to be liberal and significantly easier to be conservative. He describes issues better than I do, and that is why he's doing what he's doing. He has a positive impact on Congress if you are conservative. But if you were to call Dick Gephardt [the majority leader], you would get a different answer. I think he creates the conditions in which people understand the cost of having Democrats in Congress and the costs of 40 years of one-party rule. In that context he raises the price of voting wrong. He does for conservatives what National Public Radio does for liberals.
—Georgia Congressman Newt Gingrich,
Republican whip

When first elected to Congress in 1986, Oklahoma Republican Jim Inhofe walked across the House floor to share some banter with his longtime nemesis Mike Synar, a Democrat whose district, like Inhofe's, includes parts of Tulsa.

"I said, 'All right Mike, we're both here now. You've been here 12 years, I'm new—we might as well try to get along,' " recalls Inhofe. " 'But I have to ask you something. You're in something like the top five percent most liberal members of Congress. I'm sure I'll be in the five percent most conservative. Yet we both represent the same city. How do you account for that?' " Before he could answer, Ed Markey from Massachusetts came up and said, "It's easy, Inhofe. All you have to do is vote liberal and press-release conservative."

This sad but truthful overt hypocrisy, so cavalierly delivered by a veteran of Congress but so little known by anyone else, stunned Inhofe. "Markey's comment just blew my mind," he recalls. "I thought, 'Even in liberal Massachusetts, they have to lie to people at home in order to vote the way they vote.' So I started figuring out what vehicle is in place to allow them to do that. It took me—I'm a slow learner—about a year to figure it out. It was what House Speaker John Nance Garner had done 63 years ago by putting the veil of secrecy over the discharge-petition process."

Little did Congressman Markey realize, his friendly statement to the rookie Republican had planted the seed for the most significant congressional reform in the post-Watergate period: the reinvigoration of the discharge petition, a key procedural tool for rescuing bills bottled up by obstructionist congressional leaders. Six years later, Inhofe would have to enlist the talk-radio cannons, primarily Rush Limbaugh, to blast away the bipartisan insider guile for good.

The issue was clearly an important one to Limbaugh and anyone interested in making Congress accountable. If a committee chairman was preventing a bill from being released to the full House for a vote, a majority of congressmen could sign a discharge petition to force the legislation to a vote. Since popular measures, such as term limits and the balanced-budget amendment, often disappeared into Democrat-dominated committees, the discharge petition had the potential to make Congress more responsive. But, thanks to Garner, for more than sixty years, its effectiveness had been thwarted because the names on petitions were kept secret. Anonymity made it easier for congressional leaders to press members into removing their names when a petition approached a majority and for members to profess support for legislation while withholding their names from its discharge petition and allowing it to be killed in committee. "It allowed a person to say one thing at home and come back and defeat the very thing he says he's for," says Inhofe.

In March 1993, the Oklahoma congressman set out to change that, proposing a bill to end the secrecy of those who have signed a petition. A discharge petition to free his bill from the clutches of Rules Chairman Joe Moakley was seven votes short of a majority going into the August 1993 recess. To win, and to stop House leaders from forcing some members to remove their names, he figured he would have to call in the big guns: "That's when it got around to Rush Limbaugh," explains Inhofe.

The congressman set up in his Capitol Hill office a

war room, complete with red pins indicating influential talk-radio shows on a map of the U.S. and flags for the districts of members who hadn't signed the petition. In August, Inhofe called Limbaugh to update him and to encourage the broadcaster to press the fight, and Limbaugh unsheathed his rhetorical sword. For him, the issue was easy to frame: "Secrecy versus the people," he told *Forbes Media Critic*. The telephones rang off the hook.

While Limbaugh beat the drum over the national airwaves, Congressman Inhofe appeared on seventy-five other key talk-radio shows targeted at the districts of non-signing members. The pressure hit home, literally. As soon as the August recess ended, Inhofe had enough signatures to disgorge his reform from Moakley's committee. But antagonistic House leaders weren't defeated yet. Now, they threatened to amend the Inhofe measure to make it meaningless. Limbaugh counterattacked, popularizing the slogan, "Hands Off Inhofe."

The Oklahoman's resolution finally passed, undiluted, on September 28, in a 384 to 40 rout. In one swift stroke, it became difficult for congressmen to safely shelve popular measures, like term limits and spending cuts, by publicly supporting a bill, yet not signing the petition that would release it from a hostile committee.

"We took this to the people through talk radio," pronounces Inhofe triumphantly. "We had some 23 organizations, United We Stand America, *The Wall Street Journal* and talk radio. Without any one of those ingredients, we probably couldn't have pulled it off. But the most significant one has to be talk radio. And the guy who gave talk radio the impetus that it has right now is good old Rush. There is no doubt, he is responsible for a lot of the members we got."

The victory provided another indication of Limbaugh's clout in a Washington that considered itself above the rough-hewn common sense of Middle America. Nothing had shaken up Congress quite so quickly and effectively as the invigorated audiences of his and other talk shows. "I think Rush has an impact in the sense that Washington insiders are all acutely aware of the fact that he's there," says Gary Bauer, president of the Family Research Council, a pro-family lobbying group in D.C. "It's tougher than it was a few years ago to get away with these inside-the-Beltway games that count on an ignorant electorate." Marlin Fitzwater, the former Bush Administration spokesman, agrees: "It's ironic that Rush is probably the least heard in the city where he has the most influence. Washington people are so snobbish we think we don't listen to the radio personalities of the world, but we're probably more sensitive to the pressure they create than anyone else."

This newfound influence of talk radio frightened the establishmentarians in Congress. "They're scared to death," says Congressman Inhofe. "Clinton and the Democrats don't run polls every day for nothing. They want to know what effect Rush is having on the American people on these issues. I really believe that most of the polling is to try to see 'How can we counteract that jerk up in New York?' Rush is driving them crazy, and I love it."

"The Democrats in Congress are apoplectic about talk radio," says Representative Bill Paxon, a New York Republican. "They don't have any problem with bias in the national media when it works in their favor. But when it comes to what works against them, what they perceive to be unfair, they want to silence it. They will continue to do what they can to silence the voice of opposition. That is what Rush is: the powerful and effective voice of the opposition. They hate to answer the Rush Limbaugh questions, so they just want to silence him."

In the summer of 1993, stunned by Limbaugh's growing influence, Representative Bill Hefner (D., N.C.), House Energy and Commerce Chairman John Dingell (D., Mich.), and Senator Ernest Hollings (D., S.C.) attempted to do just that by calling for the revival of the Fairness Doctrine. The doctrine, once used to ensure balanced political coverage by forcing broadcasters to air both sides of a political debate, was killed in 1987 when the Reagan Administration allowed it to lapse. For most broadcasters, it was good riddance. With so many voices in the media, it was hard to make a case that some points of view were being censored. In fact, the doctrine had only spooked broadcasters into a self-imposed blandness and served as a weapon with which politicians could harass their media enemies. The idea to renew it was clearly prompted by the inconvenient ferment Limbaugh sparked in the heartland.

Nearly a dozen mostly Democratic congressmen immediately jumped on the bandwagon, and promoters of the Fairness Doctrine were on a roll. But in the late summer of 1993, Limbaugh explained to listeners the efforts afoot in Congress to bring it back. "Rush himself started the opposition to the Fairness Doctrine," recalls *Wall Street Journal* editorial writer John Fund. "And then we at the *Journal* wrote an editorial just before Labor Day that drew out the honest liberals." Editorials soon appeared in *The Washington Post, The Los Angeles Times,* and *The Philadelphia Inquirer* admonishing the doctrine as anti-free speech. "We made it respectable to take the free speech position," says Fund. "If we hadn't given Rush cover, they would have acted like *The New York Times Book Review:* This man is beneath us. Congress was after him," adds Fund. "There really could have been a Hush Rush law if he hadn't stopped it."

Limbaugh fans, meanwhile, sent their message to Congress by writing letters to newspaper editors. The *Wall Street Journal* editorial, assisting Limbaugh in his efforts to knock down the Fairness Doctrine, generated dozens of letters from Limbaugh supporters, who criticized congressional attempts to try to balance the views of radio personalities.

"The Left's perspective comes across strong and clear in magazines, newspapers and TV sitcoms," wrote Justin Clifford of Denver in the September 30 *Wall Street Journal* letters page. "Conservatives are incessantly subjected to liberal propaganda hurled at them by the media. Now, a powerful, conservative voice from the political wilderness emerges. The 20 million listeners Rush Limbaugh has acquired so quickly represent the pent-up demand for fair representation of our political, social and moral perspectives."

Even those who didn't agree with Limbaugh's politics or count themselves among his fans rallied to his defense. "I am a lawyer, a Democrat, supporter of President Clinton and teacher of constitutional law at Santa Clara University," announced M. Dean Sutton, on the same day's letters page. "Rush Limbaugh is special. He is able to cause my relatives, work associates and the coffee shop waitress to think and argue openly and passionately. . . . May Rush Limbaugh continue to contribute to the marketplace of ideas without government restriction or political repression."

Similar sentiment was expressed in letters to op-ed pages in *The Los Angeles Times, The Orlando Sentinel* and other papers nationwide, who unlike *The Journal* were giving credence to the Fairness Doctrine. Even the offices of Congressmen Hefner and Dingell admit to having received hundreds of phone calls telling Congress to back off.

And at least one Limbaugh fan, Edd Hendee, the forthright owner of the Taste of Texas, one of Houston's busiest restaurants, delivered the message in person. "I was in Washington, D.C., lobbying for the National Restaurant Association on the health-care package, and I went by to see Representative Hefner, and to tell him, 'Listen, I appreciate that you guys are trying to make good law and not bad law, but I don't think this is a good law. And while I'm not in your state, I've got about 25,000 people in my customer base who are absolutely nuts about Rush Limbaugh. I intend to let them know who sponsored the bill if it gets to the floor for a vote.' And his aide said, 'Oh no, no, no, no, no. Please don't do it.' He said, 'We've already been contacted by more people than ever before. Our eyes are wide open. We're going to back off on it."

The idea of restoring the Fairness Doctrine was flattened before it took even its first steps toward passage.

Hendee concludes, "Rush, by the strength of his character and the folks who support him—the Dittoheads—had absolutely shut down the resolve of this congressman to ever mess again with Rush Limbaugh."

With such a clear mandate, Limbaugh found himself the loudest and most popular opposition voice in America. Along with the rest of talk radio, he was quickly becoming a new component in the balance of power. As former Education Secretary William Bennett told *National Review,* "He is larger than a leader of the political opposition. He represents a shift in the culture. Another 10 years of the political change he stands for will take us beyond Republicans and Democrats."

Limbaugh was the catalyst for a new politics that combined rapid-information technologies of the 1990s—fax machines and talk radio—with traditional grassroots organizing to create a well-informed, homespun, but high-tech, activism. He filled the airwaves with public policy talk traditionally relegated to a few slender columns at the back of newspapers. As a result, ordinary people became faster and better informed than ever before, and they knew how to hit the right buttons in Washington—usually by starting with the ones on their phones.

In early 1994, the phones were put to work again, and once more Limbaugh demonstrated his ability to change the way Congress voted. The legislation in question was not as significant as the discharge petition nor as threatening as the Fairness Doctrine, but the swiftness with which Limbaugh moved and mobilized activists was startling.

In February, California Democrat George Miller proposed an amendment to a House education bill, called HR6. The amendment would have required all teachers—including parents teaching their own children at home—to be certified by their state governments. "Since almost all home-schooling parents would not have met the certification requirement," explains home-schooling advocate Mike Farris, "it was basically the equivalent of a nuclear attack on home-schooling."

But the mainstream media weren't going to cover a provision in the huge education bill that affected such a small, usually silent group. So when Farris heard about the Miller language a scant eight days before the vote, the home-schooling advocate turned to the voices fighting government intrusion—mainly Limbaugh. "We knew Limbaugh would be appalled by another education establishment power grab and that his large audience would be, too. We sent a fax alert through our network, which is about 150 leaders of state and regional organizations," he recalls, "and said, 'Turn on the phone trees. It's time to go.' The following day we began to spread the word more widely through talk radio."

On the Friday before the vote—scheduled for the following Thursday—Farris appeared for two hours on the Marlin Maddoux radio show, which reaches several hundred stations. On Monday Limbaugh informed his listeners of the coming battle. "It had substantial impact," Farris says of Limbaugh's appeal. "When Rush mentioned it and agreed with the position we were taking, that was an important confirmation of our view that helped energize a lot of people."

Congress received more than a million calls assailing

the Miller language. "On Monday I was home, and my local talk-show host and Limbaugh were talking about it," recalls Congressman Bill Paxon, of New York. "I told my office that the next day, Tuesday, we would receive a lot of phone calls on HR6. Sure enough, we received a thousand calls—on just the provision on home-schoolers. In the past, only home-schoolers would have called, but people had heard about it on Limbaugh and were genuinely outraged. Limbaugh gave organization to that outrage, and they picked up the phone," Paxon emphasizes. "This is happening more regularly. People are finding out about pending congressional actions in real time. And they can impact the process. I couldn't even call in to my office. The Capitol switchboards were so overwhelmed that you would get locked out before they even got you into the system."

Less than two weeks before the vote on the Miller amendment, Democratic leaders in the House had expected easy passage. But after Limbaugh, Farris and others had spread the word, it was clear the tide had changed. The amendment was eventually scrapped. Republican Representative Dick Armey then proposed an alternative amendment that stated there can be no requirements for federal certification of private-school teachers and home-schoolers. It passed with the support of every Republican. Only fifty of the 259 Democrats opposed it.

It was a remarkable victory for home-schoolers and those wary of government intervention in Americans' lives, and it wouldn't have happened without talk radio and Limbaugh. "It's the only means that conservatives have for effective equalization of the media message," says Farris. "The bad news is they have all this other stuff. The good news is we're pretty good at talk radio."

The next month, a Republican congressman from Oklahoma would once again turn to Limbaugh for help. In 1992, it had been revealed that a number of congressmen had received stamps from the House Post Office, then exchanged those stamps for cash—in essence stealing money from Congress. The case had made big news, and Postmaster Robert Rota eventually had admitted to his involvement in the scheme. In his confession, he said there were "several" members of the House involved in the operation though no names were made public. "As far as we could tell, there was going to be no internal investigation," reports Brian Lopina, administrative assistant to Representative Ernest Istook, of Oklahoma. "The congressman thought there should be."

On March 2, 1994, the House was to vote on two resolutions concerning the investigation of the House Post Office scandal. Istook offered a House resolution that directed the Ethics Committee to investigate the matter immediately. Democratic Representative Dick Gephardt offered a resolution that said no House investigation was necessary—let the Justice Department look into it as it sees fit.

"We, of course, hoped to win," remembers Lopina. "But we wanted to be sure if we didn't, not to lose too many Republicans on the vote. Of course, we clearly were arguing from a strong position. It is as if a business executive embezzled money from a corporation, and the board of directors was failing even to look into the matter. But in order to get that message out, we needed help.

So the congressman decided to send Rush a letter to see what he could do."

On the morning of March 2, Limbaugh read Istook's handwritten letter on the air. "Rush, here's the deal," the letter read. "Today the House votes on two different ways to handle the House Post Office scandal (re: embezzlement by congressmen)." Descriptions of the two resolutions followed. "The Ethics Committee does not know, and has not tried to find out which members of Congress, and how many, stole from the taxpayers. . . . I hope you'll tell the country today."

Limbaugh did, of course, tell his listeners, and they responded. Congressman Istook's office received several hundred phone calls of support, beginning immediately after Limbaugh mentioned the impending vote on the air. "All were in favor of the Ethics Committee looking into the matter. This sort of thing really resonates out there," Lopina remarks.

The Gephardt measure won out, but with Limbaugh's help, fifteen Democrats voted for opening an investigation. "The Democratic leadership put a lot of work into keeping party members on board. We were fortunate only to lose two Republicans. Rush didn't win it for us, but he certainly made it an issue. He made the other side sweat, and I think if we had had more time, we could have pulled some more Democrats over," Lopina explains.

So how much effect do Limbaugh-generated phone calls have on Congress? "Congresspeople will generally ignore any phone call unless they start coming in by the dozens," observes Congressman Bob Dornan (R., Calif.), known as "B-1 Bob" when he guest-hosts Limbaugh's

radio show. "Just a mere dozen phone calls a day on the
same issue captures the total focus of a congressperson.
Hundreds dazzle the office."

"Rush rarely explicitly instructs people to call. In fact,
he did once, and that was just to prove a point," explains
former Bush aide Mary Matalin, who is the host of
CNBC's *Equal Time* and an occasional guest host on
Limbaugh's radio show. In July 1993, *U.S. News & World
Report*'s Steve Roberts had asked Limbaugh in an interview if he tells listeners to call Congress. "Rush insisted,
'You wouldn't be asking me if I did, if I had,' " explains
Matalin. To prove to Roberts what would happen if he
instructed listeners to call and protest Clinton's budget,
which was working its way through Congress at the time,
Limbaugh did so. "The switchboards were overwhelmed;
they jammed," discloses Matalin.

Organized activists are the linchpin of Limbaugh's influence on Congress, and he keeps them energized as no
other political or media figure can. "It is demoralizing to
people of a certain political bent if their views are not
widely shared," explains ABC News White House corre-
spondent Brit Hume. "Limbaugh has emboldened people.
Bill Buckley had that effect on conservatives in the Fifties
and the Sixties. Rush Limbaugh inspires many more people, certainly in a different way, today. He's a rallying point.
People take comfort and encouragement that there are like-
minded people out there. It contributes to their activism."

One such activist is Alyse O'Neil, who lives in Naples,
Florida, and has worked for thirty years on behalf of Phyllis Schlafly's Eagle Forum, an Illinois-based women's
group that lobbies against abortion and condom distribu-

tion and in favor of traditional family values. "We call Congress frequently," O'Neill says. "Whenever there's a bill coming up that we want them to vote on, we have a telephone tree.

"Rush Limbaugh is the most exciting thing that ever happened to me—besides my husband," exclaims O'Neil. "I've worked with and idolized Phyllis Schlafly, but I've felt sort of like a turtle, creeping, creeping with our message. When Rush came on the air, I just couldn't believe that this man was saying every single thing we believe in and making us laugh at the same time. I told Phyllis, 'You never made me laugh. Bill Buckley never made me laugh.' Rush gave us a shot of adrenaline. We were getting tired. We were getting weary."

O'Neill quickly realized that associating her organization with Limbaugh would be a great way to recruit and motivate volunteers. So she bought a Limbaugh video and threw a wine-and-cheese party. "I wrote a letter to the editor and called a radio station here to tell everybody what I was doing," she relates. "I rented out the Naples depot and a few hundred conservatives, who might have thought they were all alone, showed up and learned that they weren't."

Now all those Limbaugh fans are on O'Neill's phone list, providing a fresh infusion of manpower. "You could organize people before, get the activists to go out there— but not all those young people who come now," she says. O'Neill now has a formidable lobbying force of three-hundred people.

In addition to bolstering organized conservative groups, Limbaugh motivates individuals to get involved politically as well. They in turn impact Congress. Darrin Miller, a computer programmer, had voted only in presidential elections until he began listening to Limbaugh in 1991. "He really made me feel that I could make a difference," says Miller, who moved from Connecticut to Nashville for country music and a better-paying job. Not only did he volunteer for Bush/Quayle in 1992, but he has gone to rallies and helped pass out fliers for Republican Fred Thompson, the actor and lawyer running for the U.S. Senate in Tennessee. "I will continue being active" states Miller. "I can't see how I can listen to Rush and not act on the feelings I have politically."

The same is true for Matthew Harris, a Chicago-based marketing analyst for the Walgreen's chain, who spends a lot of time on the road, scouting out new store sites. "I have definitely become more politically active," affirms Harris, who considers Limbaugh "a home away from home" while he is in his car. Harris keeps a list in his planner of fifteen radio stations that carry Limbaugh so no matter where he travels, he can tune in. "I have stronger opinions, and I talk about them more at dinner with my family, at election time and at the office," Harris adds. "I called my representative and the White House constantly in favor of NAFTA. I called about the crime bill. I wouldn't have gotten active like this if I weren't listening to Rush. He focuses my political feeling in a way that paints a clear picture of what is wrong with a specific piece of legislation. Rather than something being wrong because the Democrats did it, he explains it's wrong because it's wrong."

It is not just that listeners have become more active;

they have also become more politically aware. "Rush informs, teaches and empowers," explains John Fund. "The attack on Congress begins with scholars and think tanks. It goes to editorial pages and magazines, then to talk-show hosts, then to barbershops and conversations on the street. Then it reaches mainstream media."

"Some say Rush is only preaching to the converted," emphasizes William Rusher, a senior fellow at the Claremont Institute. Sure, he's talking to the converted. But I'll tell you this: 20 million people who are converted are one thing if they are a diffused mass, but 20 million who are organized, informed, exhorted, disciplined and directed are quite another matter. And that is what Limbaugh does: he gives them ammunition, he gives them confidence, he gives them the future and the feeling that they are winning.

Indeed, politicians around the country notice the more-informed and invigorated constituents. "I hold about seven or eight town meetings a year and the turnouts have dramatically increased," says Congressman Paxon. "It used to be that when I would go to a town meeting for five or six hours on a Saturday, they would talk about general issues and not really have a clear idea of what they wanted. Now they don't talk about general issues, such as crime. They talk about specifics they have heard on Limbaugh or elsewhere. It is one of the most positive, forceful, dynamic factors impacting the process."

State Senator Bob Schaffer of Colorado also sees it at the state level. "Rush has instilled a sense of confidence in our constituents," he says. "Now constituents call and write. They're much smarter than before. They know the issues better."

"Every day he educates about six million people around the country who then become centers of communication," agrees Newt Gingrich, the House Republican who keeps in close touch with Limbaugh, faxing him regular briefings. "He allows you to take up specific issues. For instance, I briefed him on a provision of the crime bill that establishes quotas for murderers and quotas for the death penalty, and he spent 20 minutes on the air describing it. What was at first fairly obscure for millions of people, now became very real."

"Our phones started ringing after his show," recalls Tony Blankley, press secretary to Gingrich. "It happened in other offices, too. That many calls from people who have clear opinions on the issue have to make marginal congressmen think about their votes."

The ability of conservatives to turn phone calls into votes is a concern for some on Capitol Hill. "This is bothering the liberals," says Inhofe. "When I had my discharge-petition reform up there, they said, 'Well Inhofe, if you have your way, we're going to have government by talk radio.' And I said, 'Well, great! That's America talking right there."

A Congressman Stands In

If Limbaugh is hated by one side of the aisle in Washington and looked down upon by some inside-the-Beltway sophisticates, he has loyal friends among Republicans. He even has a congressman guest-host his show on occasion—the ebullient B-1 Bob Dornan. Back in 1970, Dornan was a talk-show host on a San Francisco AM station managed by Ed McLaughlin, the man who had the vision and broadcasting acumen to give Limbaugh a national show twenty years later. "Rush had been on the air a year and a half," remembers Dornan, "and he had not taken a vacation. Ed said, 'Rush, the sheer physical demands of this show—you must take a vacation.' Rush, being humble, said, 'What will happen to my ratings? No one can do what I can. But Ed said, 'Oh, yes. I was watching C-SPAN last night, and a host I had 20 years ago still has the fire in his belly.' So he forced Rush to take a vacation, and I stood in."

A Congressional Aide Discovers Limbaugh

"I first heard Rush Limbaugh in Houston, Texas, in 1989, just after Bush was elected. Rush had just shortly come on the air. I worked in Washington D.C., but I was down visiting for summer break. My brother said, 'Hey, have you heard this guy Rush Limbaugh?' And so I tuned in and thought the guy was just hilarious. He was dead on the money, too, on what he was talking about.

"Within the next six months or so, it came like a wave. I discovered that there were three stations here in the area that carried him. I went driving to New York City one afternoon in 1990, and I never lost Limbaugh. I just kept changing stations, and there he was. Live. I bought a radio and placed it on my desk here in Congressman Armey's office. It has an alarm that I set, and at exactly noon it would ring and remind me to turn on the program.

"When his television show went on the air, I got the bug bad. I kept wondering when were we going to get him in D.C.? When? When? When? I had to go again to Texas to see him on TV. Then I found out Baltimore was carrying him, and so I subscribed to Fairfax Media General so that I could get him. Shortly after that, they got rid of their Baltimore channels. So I wrote a letter to WDCA here in Washington and asked them to carry him. They never wrote back, but they did put him on.

"I thought the discussions he had were extremely timely. It wasn't, let's talk about something that happened 25 or 30 years ago. As soon as you saw an event take place, whether it was the Persian Gulf War or the 1990 tax hike, Limbaugh was there the next day with detailed information and insightful commentary. That was useful. As a matter of fact, I followed a lot of the election commentary through the Rush Limbaugh program. He helped me to understand how many millions of other Americans think the way I do and view events the way I do. It amazed me to watch something take place, a presidential debate, say, moments later to see the media spin the event and then the next day, tune into the Rush Limbaugh program and understand that what I originally perceived was what had actually taken place.

"He communicates complicated and sophisticated ideas with humor, lightheartedness, and makes it pleasant and fun. So much of public policy is dry and difficult to get a handle on. Limbaugh has made sophisticated and difficult terminology familiar to people. He's explained underlying theories and motivations behind the various types of public policies. His analyses are in-depth, and yet he does it in a manner that's very light-hearted. One of my favorite songs of his is 'Imagine': Imagine a world without liberals. The lyrics are just fantastic, especially when he gets to the refrain: 'Imagine a world when everyone paid their own way.' It's just right there, just right there."

—Horace Cooper, Texas Representative
Dick Armey's Legislative Director

Eleven

Project 21
Talks Black

*What makes a minority whiner or quota black call
a radio host a racist? I don't think there's a racist
bone in Limbaugh's body. But look at me—with my
dark skin, frizzy hair and Negroid features. They call
me a racist. What chance does a white guy like Limbaugh stand?*

—Ken Hamblin, KNUS talk-show host,
Denver, Colorado

"Things that you never, ever see on television," pro-
nounced Limbaugh, setting up a segment on a January
1994 show about Project 21, a group whose aim is to
revolutionize black leadership for the twenty-first century. "They had a meeting in Washington last week,
which was unreported anywhere except on C-SPAN, yet
the same old voices in the civil-rights movement—no
matter where they go, no matter how small or large the

audience—they are always displayed, and they always have the same old story to tell."

A videotape rolled of the Reverend Jesse Jackson dressed in ecclesiastical garb. From the pulpit at the National Cathedral, Jackson called for more government programs. "His way has failed for 30 years," Limbaugh intoned, with the smugness of a lawyer who knows he has a surprise witness in the courtroom that day. "Here's what you never see on television, but you should."

The videotape rolled again, but this time it showed a handsome young black man in a conservative but stylish business suit behind the podium at Washington, D.C.'s National Press Club. "Principles and morality. . . . If we don't have that, it doesn't matter," said Edmund Peterson, a former Bush Administration official, now a television host and senior adviser to Project 21. "We've spent $3 trillion on programs designed to help people, but the morality is gone, the principles are shot to you-know-what."

It was the first of four clips that Limbaugh showed that evening from the inaugural press conference held by Project 21 to present the group's report, "Black America 1994: Changing Direction." Limbaugh's TV audience enthusiastically applauded Peterson's words. Throughout the segment, Limbaugh stressed that he was both deeply impressed and dismayed—impressed by Project 21's beliefs, goals, and the accomplishments of its members; dismayed that this group, with such a positive message, was receiving so little attention from the mainstream media.

"I think these guys are brave and courageous in making these statements and calling a press conference,"

Limbaugh added. "They're going to be ostracized by the mainstream civil-rights leadership. They've got guts, and we're glad to show what they say to you." Then Limbaugh paid the group a most tangible compliment by doing what he does for few others. He displayed Project 21's phone number—in a red, white, and blue banner, no less—to his viewers.

"The response was tremendous," declares Project 21's media coordinator, Charles Kalina. "For days, it was impossible to get through to the office. We had to tell our regular callers to fax us, and we would call them. Even that was difficult because as soon as you put the phone down, it immediately rang again. Just for laughs, I actually started timing it, and the maximum we had was seven seconds between phone calls. The phone lines were just burned up."

All and all, the C-SPAN broadcast, the Limbaugh television show, and other media coverage generated some five-thousand telephone calls to Project 21. "Before the Limbaugh show, we had received, I'd say, around a thousand calls—and we thought that was a lot—but that was only a gradual trickle," relates Kalina. The Limbaugh torrent lasted several days, and Limbaugh's audience was willing to put its money where its mouth was.

"We rely on contributions from foundations that share our interest in promoting individual responsibility and reliance," says Horace Cooper, legislative director to Congressman Dick Armey and a founding member of Project 21. "After Rush Limbaugh ran our press conference on his program, we received all kinds of checks and money."

"We've gotten thousands of dollars in contributions,

completely unsolicited," observes Kalina, "from people who saw us on the Rush Limbaugh show and said, 'I think what you guys are doing is great. I'd like to support you.' It's amazing."

"The simple fact that we were talking about the subjects we were talking about, being the people we are, made us a media event," explains Kevin Pritchett, a deputy staff director for Senator Trent Lott of Mississippi and one of Project 21's founding members. "In a sense, I'm surprised because what we're talking about—being tough on crime, having a pro-growth agenda for the black community—is old hat to me. But to hear and see the response from the Rush Limbaugh audience, I'm just overwhelmed. People were asking how they could help, get involved, give money. Number one, it shows that he has a very enthusiastic audience. Two, it shows his reach. A lot of people believe in his message, and if he says something is good, they're going to try to support it."

A former *Wall Street Journal* reporter and editorial writer, Pritchett knows what it's like to be out on an editorial limb—in 1990 he was editor in chief of *The Dartmouth Review,* the often-castigated conservative newspaper—and he understands Limbaugh's appeal. "He is very funny, but he is different from other political pundits for the simple reason that he is factually based. The studies and some of the statistics he cites, I know as a journalist, are accurate. He doesn't rely on emotion or feeling. It isn't just rhetoric. He has this great knack for weaving facts from different sources together into a cohesive message. You feel good about hearing someone who agrees with you and who backs it up with fact."

It may surprise Limbaugh's detractors, whose opinions have been shaped by such statements as Larry King's ("There's a new organization being formed called Feminists, the Homeless and Blacks for Limbaugh. They are meeting in a phone booth in Wichita"), but many in the black community, like Pritchett, think Limbaugh's message is the right one for all people, regardless of color.

"The liberals without any basis always say Rush is racist," states Pritchett. "Having listened to and watched Rush, and having met him twice, I can tell you the guy doesn't have a racist bone in his body. He's not there to spread hate or divisiveness; he's just there to tell the facts. Some people want to shut him down by calling him a racist. The characterizations of his audience are unfair, basically painting them as a bunch of scared honkies hiding under their beds waiting for the black menace to overtake them.

"The Rush Limbaugh audience is made up of people like you and me: black, white, Asian, what-have-you," adds Pritchett. "I'm sure many more blacks listen to Limbaugh than people think. I suspect a lot just don't tell their friends. The guy doesn't wear a white sheet. He just tells it like it is, and he talks about values and ideas that are not just in white America but in black America as well."

In his own slyly defiant way, Limbaugh addressed this subject during the Project 21 segment and took a shot at his liberal detractors. A second video clip of the group's news conference featured Howard University senior Stuart De Veaux, who said, "I've seen the causes and effects of violence . . . [The solution] has to come from within the community, simply put. Once again, we're looking for solutions from the government, and that will not work." Limbaugh's studio audience erupted with applause, and Limbaugh responded, "You notice all these white people cheering a black guy, don't you? It's real racism, don't you think? Make a note of that."

"Anyone who's met him—I did at the Republican convention—has to acknowledge he's a genuinely compassionate, friendly person, very down-to-earth," attests Horace Cooper. "It's unfair to say he comes across in any way as bigoted or racist. Now, to people who measure their success and authority by how much power and how many resources they can command from the federal government, he is a threat. And if calling him a racist or a bigot helps diminish his effectiveness, there's an incentive for people to do that. But I watch his television program, and more and more I see black Americans sitting there," continues Cooper. "Those are people who say, 'I'm going to travel all over the country to get to New York City and call in advance to get myself a ticket so I can be in the audience.' "

A clip of Cooper's speech followed De Veaux's on the Limbaugh show: "We want to build on what's best and what's working in America, and that is the notion of individual initiative and responsibility," declared the young Texan. "If we're going to come up with solutions, what we need to start with is not government programs, not handouts. The problem with depending on the government is you can't depend on it. . . . We have to start recognizing that individuals are the best people to solve problems." In admiration, Limbaugh deemed his words "the original American ethic."

Cooper later elaborates, "The way we continue perpetuating the lack of success and the lack of prosperity is to tell people, 'Don't even try.' One of the reasons why so many black Americans supported Clarence Thomas's promotion to the Supreme Court is he embodied the idea that by hard work and effort, you can overcome adversity. That message has resonance within the black community. Rush Limbaugh speaks about that. What Limbaugh says to every American—and I hear more and more black Americans calling into the program, saying, 'You know, I think you're right'—is that there is opportunity in this country. Certainly there's adversity, certainly there's difficulty, but there's still opportunity, and if we work hard enough, we can be successful."

"Black liberals are not responding based on what has ____ the religious backbone of the black community," ____asons Emanuel McLittle, founding editor of the five-year-old Detroit-based *Destiny Magazine*, a publication for conservative blacks that Limbaugh has read from on TV. "They're responding to white liberalism. They're not thinking for themselves. But black conservatives are basically responding to the old, cultural, moral system that many of us feel has allowed us to survive to this point."

McLittle agrees with Pritchett and Cooper that Limbaugh, far from being racially divisive, actually raises the conversation above race and focuses on principle. "Rush Limbaugh has a black audience," claims McLittle. "He is probably the largest national figure for people who want to hear a point of view other than the one largely circulated in the black community, which teaches basically that white folks are racist devils and that it's not possible to succeed here. There are many people black and white but certainly black who are rather perplexed, tired of hearing that, who'd like to get on with life. They want to be in America's mainstream, and they see certain enemies to that. Whether you call it liberalism or the status quo or the establishment, Rush Limbaugh is definitely its antithesis.

"I am particularly in love with his focus on the wrongs of government," McLittle continues. "I am tickled to hear someone say what many of us believe in our hearts is the biggest problem in this country. We don't believe that the problems that plague this country are due to racism or that the problems that plague this country are economic. We believe there is a problem—liberalism—that is not only destroying what used to be a relatively decent and simple government but has infiltrated and become a part of the fabric of many major institutions in America.

"Most of what people learn in college and most of what you get in entertainment has a slant to it," observes McLittle. "Most of what we see and hear and read in newspapers and on radio has a slant to it, and it is the same slant. And whereas 40 years ago, you could have denied the slant, and you could have said it doesn't exist, or it isn't harmful, or it's acting in the best interests of most people, the data is in now, and a quarter of black men are in prison, young girls are pregnant at 15 years old, and the numbers of us who stay at the bottom rung of the economic ladder are struggling with the grease that we find on that rung. We've seen enough," insists

McLittle. "Even those of us who used to be liberals, we now clearly see what the problem is. It is undeniable, and Rush Limbaugh is doing something about it.

"You're starting to see black Americans break away from the group mentality that holds to the thoughts of some leader or some agenda. We're starting to become individualistic in our thinking, not held to some prescription for being black. We are starting to engage in political and social debate. There is an up and a down and a sideways and a good and a bad, and that is very healthy for blacks. Some people may have a problem with the fact that the first person to speak in an honest way about what is really wrong with us is white, but I don't," states McLittle. "I'm energized by the fact that it's being said."

In early April of 1994 while Limbaugh was on vacation, McLittle was interviewed on the Limbaugh radio show by regular guest host Walter Williams, a George Mason professor who is also on *Destiny Magazine*'s editorial board. That week, the episode featuring Project 21 was also rerun. "The situation was repeated," says Kalina, gleefully. "Of course, it was very gratifying to have that response again. It was just overwhelming. And again, most of the comments we got were people saying that it was very refreshing.

"Star Parker, one of our participants, was interviewed in the March *Limbaugh Letter*, and we got calls from that, too," notes Kalina. Parker, a former welfare mother turned publisher and lobbyist for urban policy reform, told Limbaugh, "You have a lot of Dittoheads here in L.A. . . . And I really appreciate your honesty because sometimes it seems hard, the things you say, especially when blacks are involved . . . somebody's got to say it. And because we dare not cross the silent code line, I'm glad somebody's crossing it and not afraid to be labeled a racist. They're going to call you that anyway. You need to know that you have friends out here. Everybody is not a Jesse [Jackson], a [Louis] Farrakhan or a [Benjamin] Chavis."

The exposure Limbaugh provided Project 21 was felt from coast to coast. "I've gotten so many calls, especially since you aired the Project 21 clip," Parker told *The Limbaugh Letter.* "I get white calls. I get black calls."

"I had a couple from Oregon come in one morning in April and say they saw me on the Rush Limbaugh program," says Horace Cooper. "They were going to be in Washington, so they looked me up. And they gave me a check for $100 for Project 21. These weren't rich people by any means. It was just impressive."

In Washington, Cooper felt Limbaugh's impact in other ways as well. "As a law student, when we discussed telecommunications issues and free speech in class, Rush Limbaugh was the example that immediately came to people's minds. It was, 'I don't like Limbaugh's views, but he's got a right to speak,' " says Cooper, who, while working for Congressman Armey, attended the evening program at George Mason University's law school. "You know, 10 or 15 years ago we would have been talking about draft dodging or burning a draft card or something like that in law school, but here, Limbaugh is the paradigm for discussing whether or not free speech ought to be protected and whether censorship should exist and under what circumstances. That's a pretty significant impact."

The final segment of the press conference that Limbaugh showed was from Council Nedd II, cohost of *Capitol Watch* on National Empowerment Television and a former legislative assistant to Maryland Representative Roscoe Bartlett. "I take issue with the NAACP giving that award to Tupac Shakur," Nedd emphasized. "We saw that again a couple of years ago, them giving the same award to Rodney King. We have to realize what sort of behavior we're paying homage to. Do we want to pay homage to people like Rodney King—who was in fact a criminal? People forget that he did break the law before he got beat up. Tupac Shakur—he did shoot someone. We can't make these people heroes. They're not giving a positive message, and it's just not healthy."

Nedd's point was clear. With an incredulous look on his face, Limbaugh followed up with another statement aimed at those in control of the mainstream press: "Once again, wouldn't you say that all this is uncommon, that this is uncommon to hear black people speaking this way? Why is this not news? Given what the news media themselves say makes news, this ought to be a lead story the day it happens, but it's buried."

Ultimately, Limbaugh's coverage of Project 21 has shortened the route to achieving its long-term goals. "I think we have the conversation going; now we have to put that conversation and those ideas into action," says Kevin Pritchett. "The first job of Project 21 was to write articles and to provide interview subjects for the media, which, as we know, is overwhelmingly liberal, but now with the media exposure and people excited, we need to move forward and do some positive things besides op-ed pieces and TV appearances.

"Many people, black and white, have asked to join Project 21," says Pritchett. "It's not just a black thing. It involves a whole bunch of people. Civil-rights leaders of the past, Martin Luther King and Malcolm X, wanted to create such a multiracial coalition to attack poverty and hopelessness in the inner cities and the rural areas around the country. These problems are human problems, not just black problems. I think Project 21 is possibly able to fulfill the dream of getting many different people from many different spectrums involved. That would be my vision."

Black Talk Radio

Riding Limbaugh's long coattails is a wave of conservative talk-show hosts, including a strong contingent of black personalities. From coast to coast, such AM-philosophers as Errol Smith, Larry Elder, Armstrong Williams, Earl Jackson, Ron Edwards and twelve-year veteran Ken Hamblin, who is also a columnist for The Denver Post, *spread the word: Free markets and personal responsibility are the only road to prosperity no matter what the race, religion, or the nationality of your ancestors. Here's what they have to say about Limbaugh:*

"Kevin Johnson of the Phoenix Suns supports St. Hope Academy, a school for young, disadvantaged black men. Rush was so impressed that he showed up as a guest unannounced at a fund-raising dinner for the academy. He just wanted to be a part of something great. He even spoke about it on his radio show the next day. When

Rush was in Houston for the playoffs against Phoenix, he came up to Johnson and only wanted to talk about Saint Hope. He said there ought to be more Kevin Johnsons in the black community.

"Rush will go down in history as the person who revolutionized talk radio, not only in this country, but globally. He's a radio, ratings and marketing genius. He's the maestro. He does talk radio like some people play the violin. Nobody does it better. He's a mini-empire that helps a lot of people. If he told his audience to go to war, they would because they believe in him. People are so dissatisfied with what's going on in Washington. They just want someone to be honest with them, and they see Rush as that guy. We need an alternative. We need more like him. I wish we could clone him."

—Armstrong Williams, *The Right Side,*
WOL, Washington, D.C.

"Rush Limbaugh has found a magical formula of mixing good conservative principles with humor and wit. As a black man, I find that some of the issues that affect the black community are conducted so seriously and solemnly. There's always talk about the legacy of Dr. King. Rush has opened the door to dealing with these issues with a light spin. Clearly some of his listeners are black, and certainly know of blacks who listen to Rush Limbaugh. He's reaching people who have held these beliefs and kept them pent-up until he came along."

—Errol Smith, *Head to Head with Errol Smith,*
KIEV, Los Angeles, California

"Rush's audience is America. I think the average American is conservative and has no sympathy whatsoever for the wacky liberal answers to the problems we have in this country. Rush encourages me to be myself. Ultimately, you succeed by being who you are. I listen to him rarely now only because I don't want to be influenced by what he does creatively. Rush is such a powerful talk-show host that one could be tempted to do what he does. I want to have my own show, my own brand of humor, pathos, cynicism and everything else I bring to it. I'm complimented often by people who say, 'You are the black Rush Limbaugh.' I take it as a compliment, but I don't want to be the black Rush Limbaugh. I want to be Earl Jackson."

—Earl Jackson, *Earl Jackson Across America,*
WSSH, Boston, Massachusetts, and
Talk America Radio Network

"I thoroughly enjoy his show. I think he's funny. He's witty. He has a great staff that feeds him good stuff. He's thoroughly entertaining. He certainly has changed radio in that somebody with a strong point of view can pound on the podium for three hours. He did not invent the format, but he took it to another level."

—Larry Elder, KABC, Los Angeles, California

"I remember when my wife came home from a trip to Chicago and said, 'I heard this guy Rush, and you have to listen to him.' I listened, and it took me about 15 minutes to realize he was good. He is the only radio host who I don't have to check for rough edges. I'm not embarrassed to say I'm a Dittohead. I've been called the black Rush Limbaugh. I don't know if it was always meant as a compliment, but I always took it that way.

"The phenomenon of Limbaugh is the accuracy associated with the statements he makes. The liberals can turn around and say what they want, but the fact remains that the die is cast. Wherever their policies are passed, mayhem, ruin, debauchery and crime result. All of these things that I discuss on a smaller scale, Limbaugh focuses on across the fruited plain. He is the key hanging from Benjamin Franklin's kite, and he disperses the electricity along that string, and it focuses back on Washington.

"Limbaugh is the Elmer's glue that makes some poor guy in Ohio, who gets beaten up because he's surrounded by liberals on the job, know that he is not the only guy who is fed up. Limbaugh allows him to know that there are people who, once pulled together, represent the majority, and that is the biggest threat to the socialist agenda in this country."

—Ken Hamblin, KNUS, Denver, Colorado

"I've never met Rush, but I've spoken to him by phone. I was lucky to catch him off the air. At the time, I was just being broadcast on one station here in Detroit, and the odds were against me. I just wanted to ask him, 'How did you do it?' My commentaries are more sarcastic than his. Among the things he told me was, 'Look, you've got to lighten up, Ron. You've got to have fun. If you have fun, everything else will come.' And since then, everything else has come. I have to really thank him for that advice.

"Dittoheads are great. They represent a cross section of America. You have the farmer out in Iowa and the Wall Street executive. I've met knowledgeable professors who admire him. My own doctor listens. Believe it or not, there are even people on welfare who like him. I see Rush as a revolutionary. He reinvented talk radio while bringing conservative thought to the front page, and he's succeeded by having fun battling liberals. And yet while people are laughing, they receive his message about how the liberal establishment is ruining this country. And that is making a lasting impression. Americans, especially today, have to be tantalized a little bit. I admire Rush for catching on to that and benefiting from it, not backing off and saying, 'Oh, well, I'll just be an average Joe Blow talk-show host.' No. He built on that reality and is making history, and I applaud him."

—Ron Edwards, *The Edwards Notebook,*
WMUZ, Detroit, Michigan

Emanuel McLittle, founder and editor of *Destiny Magazine,* on Limbaugh

"When my granddad decided to go off and find a house for his wife and kids, he just went and took five acres of his uncle's land, and one weekend, they built a house. In today's America, newlyweds enter into a very complicated proposition in buying a house; they will pay for it for the rest of their lives. And just that one aspect of life is a commentary on the complexity, the energy, that it takes merely to live. Americans are so busy merely living, merely paying the bills. It's so hard, and it's so expensive that much of what they think and feel is set aside. They merely watch, sometimes with great fear and consternation, what is going on in the country, what is going on with the government, what is going on in the media. Therefore, I theorize that there is a tremendous silence, a silence that gives way to nothing but an internal glow in the American consciousness that Rush Limbaugh detected and speaks to. And it doesn't have a color. I think that the world would be shocked to know how many blacks listen to Rush Limbaugh."

Twelve

NOW vs.
Florida's O.J.
Activists

*Keep wearing those Florida orange juice aware-
ness ribbons, and continue to support our consumer
buyouts. We are in phase three, and it's now Code
Orange. We've got to melt down the fax machines
of our representatives who oppose what we're doing.*
—Ron Calfee's Dittohead Hotline message

In February 1994 the Florida Citrus Commission made
what it thought was a shrewd business decision. Rush
Limbaugh had been a tremendous boon to Snapple, a
sleepy regional fruit drink company that burst onto the
national scene largely due to Limbaugh's persistent promotion. The commission, which also contracted radio
personalities Larry King and Dr. Dean Edell, would pay
Limbaugh's price to have him encourage the consump-
tion of Florida orange juice on his show.

In addition to Snapple, other evidence corroborated

the commission's reasoning. A survey conducted by Video Storyboard Tests revealed that seventy-two percent of those asked said that when Rush Limbaugh promotes a product, it is coming from his heart. In contrast, ninety-two percent said that when Howard Stern promotes a product, it is strictly for the money. "People don't take Limbaugh's advertising as advertising," Dave Vadhera, publisher of *Storyboard Test* newsletter, told *The New York Daily News*.

With Limbaugh pumping Florida O.J., the commission expected at the very least to attract more male buyers, one of its weaker markets. But what they didn't foresee when they announced the $1-million six-month contract with the conservative commentator was a national uproar.

While the hirings of King and Edell went virtually unnoticed, within a week after announcing the Limbaugh contract, the commission had received fifteen-hundred phone calls, letters, and faxes for and against the decision to use him.

The state chapters of the National Organization for Women (NOW), the NAACP and various gay and lesbian groups protested with angry press releases and letter-writing campaigns to the commission. "The decision to buy time on Limbaugh's show was insulting, offensive and unwise," argued Siobhan McLaughlin, president of the Miami-based state NOW chapter. "It would be very difficult for me to purchase Florida orange juice if Limbaugh is the spokesman." NOW called for a "girlcott" and began to mobilize its forces for a protest.

On the air, O.J. went with Limbaugh's persona like hot dogs go with ballparks. He savored glasses of juice and extolled the health benefits, citing both nutrition news from *The New York Times* and American moms. Limbaugh called his detractors' tactics childish and embarrassing. "Clean out the shelves," he urged his fans. "Keep chugging the stuff." When C-SPAN broadcast his February 18 radio show live, jugs of O.J. were front and center.

In mid-February, Mary Toothman, a columnist for *The Tampa Tribune,* wrote the first of a string of columns supporting the NOW boycotts and ridiculing the decision to hire Limbaugh. "Orange juice: it's not just for heterosexuals anymore," wrote Toothman, supporting protests by gay activists. "Rush Limbaugh has no business peddling fruit for the Florida Department of Citrus."

Meanwhile, the Florida Federation of Business and Professional Women's Clubs and the Gay & Lesbian Americans announced boycotts of Florida orange juice.

With these groups stirring up an ugly showdown, Florida Democratic Governor Lawton Chiles entered the fracas. He objected to the selection of Limbaugh to promote Florida orange juice, not because Rush Limbaugh was conservative, he claimed, but rather simply because he was a political figure.

By early March, the pressure from NOW and other groups influenced Coca-Cola, which owns Minute Maid, Five Alive, and other brand names that rely on Florida citrus products, to scold the commission. "We have to be sure that a procedure is set up to see that this doesn't happen again," says Chris Bozman, spokesman for Coca-Cola. "Hiring a controversial figure like Limbaugh is a bad marketing move."

Sensing mounting pressure against the commission

and Limbaugh, NOW announced a March protest rally outside Kash 'n' Karry, one of Tampa's largest supermarkets, which is in an exclusive section of town. Meanwhile, Rush Limbaugh loyals were not taking the Limbaugh bashing sitting down. They flooded *The Tampa Tribune* with mail after each of the Mary Toothman columns. They also wrote and telephoned the chastised Citrus Commissioners to tell them plenty of Floridians were on their side. In fact, over five-thousand correspondences urged the commission to continue having the broadcaster promote Florida citrus.

Among the letter writers was Ron Calfee, of Windermere, Florida, a Disney World pizza-delivery man who promised the commission he would not only buy and drink more O.J. himself but he would also take the fight to the streets. A longtime Limbaugh listener, Calfee knew a number of fellow employees listened to Rush. "I figured, why couldn't there be a Limbaugh fan club?" he says. "We needed a group to stand up for traditional family values. And who better represents those values than Rush Limbaugh? At a time when our nation is in moral decline, Rush is spreading a positive moral message." So Calfee founded Rush Disney.

In July 1993, he advertised the club in *Eyes and Ears,* Disney's employee publication, and set up a "Dittohead Hotline" with information about meetings and events. Two months later, fifty active members, led by Calfee, were meeting on Disney property monthly to discuss Limbaugh-inspired conservative ideas. When non-Disney people wanted to join, Calfee started the Unofficial Rush Limbaugh Appreciation Society (URLAS) and joined forces with the nearby La Piaza Restaurant, where the group eventually began holding meetings.

Calfee drafted by-laws, which among other things stated the group's intention to extol family values, to participate in activities that foster good government, and to honor hard work and free enterprise. URLAS meetings were kicked off with the Pledge of Allegiance and a prayer. Conservative lecturers and politicians, such as gubernatorial candidate Ken Connor, visited for a meal and to talk politics. The local CBS and NBC affiliates and various newspapers covered the group, which quickly grew to some two-hundred strong.

NOW's announcement to boycott Florida O.J. was a call to arms for URLAS members and Limbaugh supporters statewide, as Tampa's EIB affiliate helped beat the drum. "Rush had been great for our station and for the Florida citrus industry. We heard about the protest and figured people should know," says WFLA station manager Gabe Hobbs. "For a week, we told all who disagree with NOW to go to Kash 'n' Karry and to be sure to sport their 'Rush Is Right' bumper stickers," a hundred thousand of which WFLA had doled out during the past year in various promotions.

Meanwhile, NOW raised the stakes. Patricia Ireland, the group's Washington, D.C.-based executive director, joined the protest to attract protesters and press attention. On the morning of Thursday, March 10, WFLA's Mark Larson exhorted listeners to show up at Kash 'n' Karry: "Those who love O.J. and love Rush Limbaugh should go on out to say hello to these NOW women," Larson said. Among those who did was Jim Bucken, a Tampa businessman.

"Stand up for your O.J. rights," Bucken exuberantly urged friends and colleagues on their answering machines. "I enjoy listening to Rush, and I drink Florida orange juice. I didn't appreciate that people were trying to stop him from promoting it and trying to stop people from drinking it," remarked Bucken, who loaded eight friends into his blue Ford van and headed to the rally.

"I heard about it on the radio, and a friend also called and said I just had to go," recalls Jessica Bonine, a Tampa retiree. "He said, 'We'll buy all the Florida orange juice in the store to show our support for Rush.' " Late in the afternoon, as the winter sky began to darken, Bonine, equipped with an "I Love Rush & Florida O.J." placard, drove over to Kash 'n' Karry.

"We expected this boycott by NOW to be a big deal. Any counter protesters who showed up as a result of our announcements was terrific," explains Hobbs. "But, as it turned out, someone who didn't know better would have thought this was a pro-Rush rally and not one organized by NOW."

Four camera crews focused on Patricia Ireland, as she and five other women, their backs to the store, futilely tried to make a statement. But the din of some three-hundred to four-hundred shouting, sign-bearing Limbaugh and O.J. supporters prevented that. Many carried their signs inside the store to purchase orange juice. The supermarket, if not the NOW women, had shrewdly judged the prevailing sentiment and stocked up on juice. By one account they had quintupled their supply, and they sold every last drop.

"Go home. Rush is right! Go home. Rush is right!"

the crowd chanted as they guzzled O.J. from quart containers. "Whenever Patricia Ireland tried to speak, the crowd drowned her out," Hobbs remembers. "It was all very polite—no profanities or threats. Both sides were fairly vocal. I kind of felt sorry for the NOW women. They must have sensed defeat when they saw the accumulating crowd. It just kept growing, and there were only six of them."

"I was really amazed at how many people showed up and how organized we turned out to be without anyone really being in charge," explains Bonine, who bought eight gallons of orange juice.

"These feminists don't at all speak for me," says Ohioan Jessica Jones, who winters in Florida. "I bought two gallons to support Rush. He has a good message that is pertinent to men and women, blacks and whites. I was raised to love my country—to be the best I could be, to get an education and not to rely on handouts. NOW doesn't stand for that. Rush and his supporters do."

After an hour, the frustrated NOW gang was ready to call it quits. There was no way to save face, and they didn't even try. "It didn't help Patricia Ireland's cause much to leave in a chauffeur-driven limousine," gibes Hobbs. "One of the NOW women flipped the bird at us from inside the limo." But by then it didn't matter.

Energized by their success, Calfee and club members planned more demonstrations of support for Limbaugh and Florida orange juice in Orlando. Dutch Schafer, a talk host at Orlando's EIB affiliate, WDBO, pitched the pro-O.J. demonstrations on his show for days. During the week following the NOW protest, Calfee, Schafer, and

URLAS supporters showed up at restaurants, street intersections, and public gathering places to hand out fresh-squeezed orange juice from 6:00 to 8:30 A.M. They also handed out Florida O.J. awareness ribbons, which were pinned to lapels and flown from car antennas. Calfee encouraged anyone who would listen to buy O.J. " 'Descend on stores and buy out all of their Florida orange juice. Give it to charity or drink it yourselves,' I told them. We couldn't simply stand by and let these groups like the NAACP, NOW and the gays and lesbians heap condemnation on our hero. We hoped to do for Florida orange juice what Rush Limbaugh did for Snapple."

But the anti-Limbaugh forces weren't finished yet. Nadine Leach, owner of Nokomis Groves in Sarasota, announced at a February Citrus Commission meeting: "This man's middle name is controversy and ridicule, and he enjoys stirring up hate." In early March, Leach blasted Limbaugh again, "He's hurting my sales already. We've got to stop him from these promotions. We as growers can't associate with him. He is hurting our business."

To prove her wrong, on March 22, some fifty people showed up at Orange Blossom Indian River Citrus Market, a citrus-product outlet in South Orlando, for another buyout. "We carried placards along the highway to encourage passersby to come in and buy Florida O.J.," says Gloria Laird, a retired nurse from New York. "We had such a diverse group there—a couple in their eighties and a mother pushing her baby in her stroller, with a little carton of orange juice in the baby's hand. Then at a specified time we went in and made our purchases."

At day's end, the Limbaugh supporters had purchased

some 150 gallons. Among the buyers was Judy Rainey, who drove for an hour from Winter Park to Orlando to take part. "I now serve my kids orange juice instead of Coke, both to support Rush Limbaugh and Florida orange juice and because the people at Coca-Cola think it's such a bad idea," says Rainey, a housewife and mother of three. "We used to drink a gallon of O.J. a week. Now we drink at least three or four."

Unable to impact sales, NOW and the NAACP took their cause to the members of the Florida legislature. Their goal: to make sure new appointees to the commission would not renew Rush Limbaugh's contract. Failing to ignite the general public, finally, someone would listen. Senator William Turner, a black South Florida Democrat who chairs the committee responsible for confirming commission members, urged Governor Chiles to reconsider three appointments. "There were a bunch of all-white millionaires on that commission. It's no wonder they chose someone like Limbaugh. Just look at the tapestry of Florida. There are all different races and ethnicities," Senator Turner said. "Does this board depict that tapestry?"

On March 23, Democratic State Senator Pete Weinstein also blasted the commission's decision: "We're looking for people who will provide the best possible image for Florida citrus and not engender hate. I want to know why they chose Limbaugh," he told the Associated Press. Capitulating, Republican Senator Gary Siegel, also on the confirmation committee, told *The Tampa Tribune:* "Whoever they choose should be an apolitical person."

Once again the ball was in the people's court. A week after the Indian River buyout, Lakeland's WLKF radio talk-show host Lynn Breidenbach, whose show airs prior to Limbaugh's in Lakeland, began promoting another orange juice buyout. "These senators have to realize what side their bread is buttered on," reasons Breidenbach. "It's a business decision. It's not a political decision. If Patricia Ireland or someone with her views had the number of listeners Limbaugh has, then the commission would pay her to promote orange juice. If that were the case, we would be on the road to hell, but at least plenty of people would be drinking orange juice."

Breidenbach, who commands two and half hours on the air each day herself, is a Limbaugh fan. "Limbaugh espouses what Middle America has believed in for years," she remarks. "The press and legislators criticizing the commission are kowtowing to a small crowd. They know Limbaugh is good for sales, and they know the commission is using him as a promoter and not a spokesman. When push comes to shove and they make Limbaugh a political football, we will take action."

Breidenbach's buyout was sure to have an impact because Lakeland is the home of the Florida Citrus Commission. "It's the growers' money and the growers' decision to spend its money," she insists, reflecting the strong sentiments of her constituency. "Citrus products are an $8-billion business for the state. I'll be darned if I was going to let some loud-mouth women tell me what to drink."

Breidenbach promoted the buyout, which would coincide with the annual Senior Festival at the Lake Mirror

Civic Center, for three days on her show *Talk Back*. "The idea was to have people buy the Florida orange juice at their local stores and bring it to the civic center," she explains. "We would then donate the juice to seniors in the area."

On the air live for three hours during the buyout, Breidenbach urged people to pick up a gallon or two of juice and take it to the civic center. The response was overwhelming. "It was greater than we anticipated. We had elderly people and young families with children. We had teenagers. I even saw competing talk-show hosts who brought in orange juice because they support Limbaugh," recalls Breidenbach, whose exhortations produced a total of thirteen-hundred gallons of orange juice. "We had so much there was no place to put it all."

Florida orange juice and Rush Limbaugh were clearly receiving a windfall of support from the controversy. After the failed NOW rally and the escalation of the debate, Mary Toothman, who had earlier lambasted the Citrus Commission's decision to hire Limbaugh in her *Tampa Tribune* column, now reflected on the backlash to her columns. She even quoted a letter to her from Joan Roberts of Lakeland: "I guess I shouldn't expect you to write a fair, unbiased article since you are a liberal, as you have previously described yourself," wrote Roberts. "In your article, why did you conveniently fail to mention Larry King, the liberal talk-show host hired as the other orange juice spokesperson? You would rather ostracize Rush Limbaugh because he represents the conservative movement in this country. As I see it, these two men balance each other out. Rush has many followers, and not just among the silent majority! I have contacted the Florida Citrus Commission to stand firm and not back down to pressure from the liberal media." Toothman, who mentioned being overwhelmed with the responses, offered no defense of her previous columns. She concluded: "Toothman: 0; Rush Fans: 7."

The Limbaugh backlash was felt in other parts of the nation, too. In March, *The Boston Globe*'s Derrick Z. Jackson had joined the anti-Rush crusade: "Two, four, six, eight, no more Florida concentrate. . . . A day without orange juice," Jackson remarked, "is a day with sunshine on my conscience. No justice, no juice."

He, too, was besieged with angry mail. Jackson returned to the subject in an April *Globe* column: "I wrote that I would not buy Florida orange juice during the Florida Citrus Commission's six-month advertising campaign on the Rush Limbaugh show. Judging from my mailbox, the commission will be happy to know that orange juice has just replaced apple pie as our most patriotic fruit product." He also printed portions of fifteen letters from people who wrote to berate him. "Milan Knor of Plantation, Florida, vowed to purchase twice the amount of O.J. the columnist stopped buying," Jackson noted. Other comments ranged from "Go suck a lemon" to "Let the screwdrivers flow."

Even New York City's former mayor Ed Koch, a democrat, stood up for Limbaugh in his *New York Daily News* column. "Limbaugh's philosophy," Koch wrote, "is within the large tent of acceptable political points of view held by members of both major parties."

Ron Calfee, for one, claimed victory. "We showed up

all across the state in huge numbers, and outnumbered our opponents," he declared. "We alerted Dittoheads across the fruited plains to our cause. We sent the message that we are mainstream. When they attack Rush, they attack us and people around the country like us."

Part Three

Now and Tomorrow

Thirteen

Days, Dinners, and Downtime

> *I have gone to restaurants with a lot of famous people. I've gone to restaurants with Dan Rather when he was number one, right? I've gone to restaurants with George Bush when he was running for president. And I have never, ever seen anybody get the response Rush Limbaugh does.*
> — Peggy Noonan as quoted in *Vanity Fair*

When Limbaugh moved from the relatively small town of Sacramento to New York City in the summer of 1988, it was a leap of faith like none he had ever taken. Both his career and his life-style were going national, and the brash commentator had no idea what to expect. Starting out in the Big Apple, Limbaugh toiled in relative obscurity—no special treatment at restaurants, no recognition walking down the street.

One evening, John Fund, an editorial writer at *The Wall Street Journal,* took Limbaugh to Vile Body, the monthly cocktail party for Manhattan's conservative young guns.

This soiree, put together by Terry Teachout, an editorial writer at *The New York Daily News,* took place at the Manhattan Institute's plush Park Avenue town house, a setting producer Whit Stillman later used for his film *Metropolitan,* about New York's teen debutantes.

"Rush was already pretty well known nationally," says Fund. "But it was sad because these bright and earnest young writers, who Rush had read and respected, ignored him. He was just a guy on the radio to them. They probably don't even remember his being there."

With plenty to accomplish, Limbaugh steered clear of the bright lights in the big city. Instead, he worked tirelessly, poring over eight newspapers, and clipping key stories with a razor knife to prepare for his daily radio broadcast. When his television show began, his broadcasting day would stretch until eight P.M. and was often followed by business chores and a business dinner. He usually returned to his Upper West Side apartment around midnight.

On weekends, Limbaugh set about galvanizing his audience, which, it was all too apparent, did not live in New York City. Jetting from the Big Apple to the heartland for stops on his Rush to Excellence Tour and other promotions became the norm. When Los Angeles's KFI radio picked up his show, Limbaugh scheduled an event in L.A. Mike Venema, his publicist at the time, greeted the showman at the airport in a stretch limo. "I had never met him in person," recalls Venema. "I saw him get off the plane, by himself, carrying his own suitcase. Even in 1989, he was already the biggest thing in radio. He was shy and nervous. He kept tugging at his tie, like

Rodney Dangerfield. He wouldn't let me take his suit-case. He was very uncomfortable with protocol and all the attention."

Limbaugh was taken aback when he heard the station had gotten him a limo. "For me?" he asked. "Then, I told him a reporter from the *L.A. Times* was going to interview him," says Venema. " 'Interview me? Why do they want to interview me?' He was nervous and excited, but he performed. His magic was his wholesomeness. He could disarm the most rabid reporter."

"What surprised me most about Rush was the strength of his success." points out Claudia Puig, the *Los Angeles Times* reporter who interviewed Limbaugh. "We were backstage, and the fans in the auditorium were frenzied. It was like seeing a rock star. They got up on their chairs and chanted his name. I had never seen anything like that for a radio guy."

Limbaugh and Puig rode from her office at *The Times* to Orange County, an hour and a half away, stopping to eat at an Italian restaurant in Newport Beach. Puig, four months pregnant, was writing a profile of Limbaugh. "I had some preconceived notions. I didn't expect him to be charming, articulate and pleasant company," admits Puig. "I expected rhetoric and policy. We did talk about abortion of all things, my being pregnant." Puig told Limbaugh about her recent trip to a medical clinic for a preg-nancy test. The nurses were surprised to hear that she was going to keep the child. "I was shocked. When I said, 'Of course, I am,' they responded, 'Well, we have a place across the street if you decide not to.' "

"Rush used the story as part of his show," recalls Puig.

"It made me a bit nervous, but he didn't use my name. It was a great experience. We have stayed in touch ever since then. When I was pregnant with my second child a few years later, he called and said on my message machine, 'You little baby-maker, Claudia.' He teases me because I am not a conservative, but he contends that I really am. He might be somewhat right, I guess," she concedes. "I worry more about crime and schools now."

The next day, Limbaugh and Venema drove through Hancock Park, an exclusive section of Los Angeles. "He looked at the houses and wondered what people did to be so successful," says Venema. "He wanted to walk up to their doors and ask. I could tell then that he would make it some day."

"His pomposity is a fraud. He may be brash on the show, but personally he's cute and likable," declares deal maker Michael London, who called Limbaugh early in his second year in New York to pitch the idea of a Caribbean theme cruise. "Essentially Limbaugh was the theme," says London. "He would conduct discussions and give a talk. I called him and got right through with no screening. I sent him a proposal. Then I flew to New York, and we worked out a deal."

London enrolled a thousand people in three weeks. "The most you can usually hope for on these deals is 200 berths," he notes. "The guy is so entertaining and politically appealing. The success was unprecedented in the cruise industry." Seizing the opportunity to get closer to his shipmate devotees, Limbaugh went out of his way to make the trip memorable. As the cruise ship sailed by

Cuba, he gathered a crew on deck to hurl insults at Fidel Castro.

While people nationwide were lining up to hear Limbaugh speak and paying thousands of dollars to join him in taunting Castro, New York remained typically blasé. The best Limbaugh could do at *National Review* was a dinner with the editor of the letters page. But quietly Limbaugh continued to make and nurture valuable friends—Bill Bennett, Brent Bozell, John Fund, and other prominent conservatives. "I was doing a roast of Ollie North, and the sponsor was looking for an emcee," remembers Bozell, president of the Media Research Center. "Someone recommended Rush Limbaugh, who I'd never heard of. Rush flew down on his own nickel, and he was a huge success. Ollie and the crowd loved him. From that, we struck up a friendship.

"He is a private man, and he had a hard time understanding his success," says Bozell, who began to inform Limbaugh about media trends and coverage. "A few years ago he was selling ads for the Kansas City Royals. Now he is so popular he can't go out in public. He's extraordinarily personable, down-to-earth and generous to a fault."

In the fall of 1990, a few months after the second anniversary of Limbaugh's national radio show, *National Review* was to celebrate its thirty-fifth anniversary at the Waldorf-Astoria. Among the toast-makers were George Will, Tom Wolfe, Jack Kemp, Tom Selleck, and, of course, the magazine's founder, William F. Buckley, who would announce his retirement as editor that night. *NR* associate editor Allen Randolph invited Limbaugh to the event. "A few days after he received the invitation," Randolph remembers, "he called and said how sorry he was he couldn't come. 'One of the main reasons I came to New York was so I could go to things like this,' he told me. It was really too bad. It would have been nice to have him there." But even then he would have gone through the receiving line relatively unknown to America's top conservatives.

That was changing rapidly. In the summer of 1991, *National Review* published a short article about talk radio, focusing on Limbaugh and his great success. Shortly thereafter, Bill Buckley invited the broadcaster to his New York apartment for a dinner with the editorial board.

"I don't remember who specifically told me about him," reflects Buckley. "As often happens, a name creeps into one's consciousness. I am very backward on pop culture, and if I were captured by the Resistance and questioned to ascertain whether I was really an American or a spy, I would flunk such questions as 'Who won the World Series last year?' and would probably be executed. So, I admit, I was late in discovering Rush. But at some point I made a conscious effort to tune in, en route to the barbershop out in Stamford where I live, if memory serves. I am delighted that I did."

When Limbaugh arrived at Buckley's Park Avenue duplex, he was ushered into the Red Room, a small study overlooked by an imposing portrait of Pat Buckley and her three dogs. Limbaugh requested a Diet Coke. "Diet Coke?" Buckley exclaimed. "Don't you want a scotch or wine?" Buckley served him the Diet Coke.

At first, Limbaugh seemed awed by the salon atmosphere. But the conservative chatter made him feel at home, and he quickly warmed to the group. By dinner, he was on a roll. The editors, used to Buckley's razor-edge, if demure, humor, sensed the antic commentator's emergence and egged him on. Soon, Limbaugh held the floor, acting out his routines. He performed a rendition of "The Philanderer," a parody of Ted Kennedy sung to Dions' 1960s tune "The Wanderer." The editors guffawed in their seats.

Later, after cigars and brandy in the music room, Limbaugh thanked the editors and the Buckleys in particular. As he walked outside, Buckley's driver, Jerry Garvey, got out of his car to tell Limbaugh how much he enjoys his show.

"Was that a test of my intellectual ability?" Limbaugh asked one of the editors as they walked down the street, referring to the literary discussion that had accompanied the cigars. "Were they trying to see how smart I was?" He was reassured that it was just another typical conversation with Bill Buckley and his editors.

"He really enjoyed that dinner, and he went on about it on the air the next day," an editor says. "Of course we enjoyed it immensely, too. We all gathered around the radio to hear what he had to say." Limbaugh extolled the meal—cold salmon with mayonnaise—and the fine wine. "And you could take all you wanted," he concluded, lest anyone might think he was cowed by the setting.

While Limbaugh's New York contacts and friendships continued to grow, one of his closest comrades remained John Fund of *The Wall Street Journal*. The two had first met in Sacramento, when Fund was a staffer in the California state legislature and both traveled in conservative circles. They kept in touch regularly. So when Simon & Schuster editor Judith Regan, a former *National Enquirer* staffer who had picked up a good sense for Middle America, suggested Limbaugh write a book, the busy commentator turned to Fund. "Regan felt a book by Limbaugh would be a tremendous success," Fund remembers. "Many others were telling Limbaugh otherwise: 'Stay in radio. Don't cheapen yourself.' " Regan won. "Then Rush talked me into working on it. It didn't take much."

The book and the successful launch of Limbaugh's lucrative TV show would crown his rise to legitimacy. But already his immense popularity was undeniable, even in New York City. No longer a social pariah in liberal Gotham, Limbaugh could pretty much select the dinner date of his choosing. One evening, he dined with best-selling author and former Reagan speechwriter Peggy Noonan at the "21" Club. As *Vanity Fair*'s Peter Boyer describes it: "She and her escort were greeted by the maitre d', the captain and two waiters, all of whom followed the couple to their booth." As Noonan and Limbaugh were seated and ordered a drink, a crowd hovered around the table. "The next thing Noonan knew, she was standing in the restaurant's anteroom with a camera in her hand, snapping souvenir pictures of her date for a crowd of beaming strangers, one of whom commanded, 'Take one more, honey?' " Boyer wrote.

"I have gone to restaurants with a lot of famous people," Noonan told *Vanity Fair*. "I've gone to restaurants with Dan Rather when he was number one, right? I've gone to restaurants with George Bush when he was running for president. And I have never, ever seen anybody get the response Rush Limbaugh does."

Limbaugh could perform at the table, too. Marjabelle Young Stewart, the etiquette author dubbed the "Queen of Couth," named him to her list of the nation's top ten most polite people. She didn't hesitate to add that before he remarried he was a top catch as far as bachelors went, too. "Women are very attracted to beautifully mannered men." she explains. And then with Limbaughesque flair, Stewart, a strong Illinois Republican who even sports a Limbaugh/Kemp sticker on her car bumper, adds, "This is the only country in the world where it is your unalienable right to be well-bred, and Rush Limbaugh represents that. He looks like a great king. He's so joyous. Women just light up when they hear his name. He's beautifully groomed and great fun and so charming. And his table manners are impeccable."

Specifically? Stewart rattles off a list: "He keeps the fork in the left hand, strokes the meat, rotates the wrist, keeps his lips closed when he chews." According to Stewart, Limbaugh gets the nod from maitre d's, too. "They say he's a gentleman. He's quiet when he tips, and according to one, 'He takes care of those that take care of him.'

"But it is the art of conversation that lands Limbaugh on the top 10 list," she reasons, "not what you might expect from a man of such strong opinions. When he's doing his job, he really goes for it. But socially, he listens. He questions people. He leans in. One woman said, 'I thought he was looking at the color of my eyes. He was so intently listening. I was saying the most interesting things I've said in years.' That was because she had an audience. He never starts squirming. He's there. He's yours. It takes more energy to listen than it does to talk, and he has it. I say to his mother, 'Take a bow, Mrs. Limbaugh.' "

Limbaugh's good manners and other attributes did pay off. It was 1992—a presidential election year—and President Bush invited Limbaugh to the Republican Convention in Houston in the hopes that some of the commentator's populist appeal would transfer to his campaign. There, the once-failing Missouri DJ sat in the president's box with Barbara Bush and Marilyn Quayle. He had arrived. At *National Review*'s convention-hall party, at the top of the Sheraton Astrodome Hotel, Limbaugh was the star. "We had a lot of the big names at that party," remembers publisher Ed Capano, naming Jack Kemp, Bill Bennett, and numerous congressmen and senators. "Everyone wanted to talk to Rush. He couldn't move. He was surrounded by autograph seekers. Rush is the first rock star of the conservative movement," adds Capano, chuckling.

The social invitations culminated in the highest honor when President Bush invited him for a stay at the White House. As he entered the president's home, Bush greeted him with a hearty handshake, grabbed his bag, and headed for the Lincoln Bedroom. "Rush was mortified," wrote Washington pundit Ken Bode, of the President carrying his bags.

"I got to know Rush during the campaign. I was sending out a daily fax attack—exposing a lie a day from Bill Clinton," says Mary Matalin, political director in the Bush campaign. One day her fax attack mentioned that

Clinton campaign aide Betsey Wright had confessed that the campaign spent $28,000 trying to keep track of all the "bimbo eruptions": the accusations about Bill Clinton's extramarital affairs. "I got a lot of flak in the press about it. But Rush called and introduced himself—as if I didn't know who he was. He asked me to explain what happened. Then he did a long monologue on his show explaining the situation. Afterwards, I got a lot of supportive phone calls, defending my fax attack.

"After that we remained pretty close pals over the telephone," relates Matalin. She kept Limbaugh informed about the campaign, and he offered her assessments of the public pulse on issues and attitudes toward the Bush campaign, "There was a huge Rush presence in the campaign." Matalin recalls. "People absorb his right thinking and vocalize it. He empowers them with the art of communicating, gives them confidence that they are not backward or unsophisticated in the questions they raise. At events for the President, Rush signs poked up in every crowd: 'Megadittos,' or 'Dittoheads for Bush,' " she remembers. "That cheered me up when things got really depressing."

Finally on the eve of the election, Matalin, who would later guest-host Limbaugh's radio show when he was on vacation, met Limbaugh face-to-face. "Junior [George Bush, Jr.] and Roger Ailes, who was in on several campaign events, were big Rush fans," says Matalin. "The fact that Junior was so high on him told the President that it would be good to have him along." So Limbaugh was invited.

"He chatted with Bush in the holding room," Matalin

recalls. Special Prosecutor Lawrence Walsh had announced just three days before that there might be evidence that Bush knew of the plans to trade arms for hostages with the Iranians. The news took a great deal of steam from the Republican campaign. "Things were pretty low," says Matalin, "but Rush was great for the morale of the staff—and the President."

After Bush's disappointing loss, Matalin and Clinton adviser James Carville married in New Orleans on Thanksgiving Day. Limbaugh was traveling to the Caribbean with Roger Ailes and Robert and Georgette Mosbacher to vacation on the Mosbachers' yacht. In a last-minute decision by Limbaugh, their plane stopped off in New Orleans for the Matalin-Carville extravaganza before continuing on to the Caribbean. "It was really a great surprise," declares Matalin, now cohost of the CNBC-TV political talk show, *Equal Time*. "They came to the cocktail party before the ceremony and stayed for dinner. Rush got mobbed. My family and all five of Carville's sisters are Dittoheads. In fact, his sisters turned me on to Rush in the first place. They were crazy to talk to him and have pictures taken with him. My father—the biggest Rush fan in the country—said, 'This is the most exciting thing that has ever happened in my life.' "

After the celebration, the Mosbachers, Ailes, and Limbaugh spent four days adrift in the sunny Caribbean. Limbaugh typically kept his nose to the grindstone, but like the others, also lounged around on the boat. "They ate nice meals and had long conversations about politics and business deals," says Laura Cordovano, a New York realtor and friend of Ailes. But in one sense the big guys kept their feet on the ground. "Georgette cooked a lot of hot dogs for Rush and Roger," laughs Cordovano.

By early 1993, Limbaugh had reached celebrity status. Back in New York, Maureen Dowd, the *New York Times* columnist, took him to dinner to see what she could discover. In the playful prose that resulted, Dowd maintained her requisite cool detachment while revealing that she enjoyed Limbaugh despite herself: "He also asks if the reporter would care to switch seats, from the red leather banquette to the straight chair opposite, observing: 'I note that by virtue of where you're sitting, there appears to be a power imbalance. You're sitting lower than I am.' " The column continues: ". . . Some rapport finally develops when the menu arrives and the spokesman for the Fruited Plain, as he refers to America, asks the starving reporterette, 'You like caviar?'

"It is a relief, somehow, to discover that Mr. Limbaugh's culinary tastes are more Alexis Carrington than Archie Bunker," she quipped.

" 'Are you going to write about what we eat here?' he demands, offering a dramatic rendition for an amused waiter of the possible story that would result: 'And Limbaugh claims to be just an average guy and then orders $70-an-ounce beluga and forces it on a reporter."

Dowd wryly responds, "The reporter promises that there will be full disclosure that she never needs to be forced to eat caviar."

She does abandon her amusing superciliousness long enough to make a serious insight: ". . . Oddly enough, beneath the bombast, there beats the heart of a romantic, the shy high-school guy who rarely went out on dates, the child of the 60s who has never owned a pair of blue jeans and the insecure college dropout and couch potato who has survived two bad marriages and some lonely stretches in the wonderful world of New York dating.

" 'I love what I do,' " she quotes him. " 'It's the other stuff that bores me. I don't live for weekends. I have a vacation coming up the first week in April, and I haven't the slightest idea what I'm going to do. There's nowhere I want to go.' "

During the $505.96 meal, Dowd also discovered that Limbaugh has seven VCRs at home, and he buys videos instead of renting so he doesn't have to return them; he orders his food from the grocery store, using his computer; and he gets his clothes from Rochester Big and Tall, which delivers a selection and takes back what he doesn't want.

Around the same time, Bill Buckley again invited Limbaugh to dinner. This time the other guests were not the conservative intellectual set, but rather the New York social crowd, slow to take in outsiders, especially conservative ones. "Some of my liberal friends have asked me if I like Rush Limbaugh," Buckley says. "I respond by recalling an intellectual approached at a cafe in Madrid by a journalist during the high days of Francisco Franco. The journalist leaned over and whispered, 'What do you think of Franco?' The intellectual raised his finger and beckoned to the journalist to accompany him.

"They walked silently through the maze of urban Madrid, across grand avenues, down the length of the huge park to a canoe at the playground," recounts Buckley. "The intellectual rowed silently to the center of the lake, raised his paddle, and said, 'I like him.' Well, I like Rush Limbaugh, I tell them."

Also among the guests at Buckley's was novelist Keith Mano, who had been talking with the editors at *Playboy* about an interview with Limbaugh. "Being simultaneously on the mastheads of *Playboy* and *National Review,* I was probably the only person qualified. *Playboy* agreed, but I wasn't sure if Rush would. To my surprise, I ran into him at Bill Buckley's, at a dinner at which Rosalyn Tureck performed a piano recital." During cocktails and before dinner, the guests—among them novelist Louis Auchincloss, British media mogul Conrad Black and his wife, journalist Barbara Amiel, PBS talk-show host Charlie Rose, and others—gathered in the living room for a performance of Tureck playing on the Buckleys' Bosendorfer grand piano.

"Rush got along well with everyone. He seemed really to have enjoyed himself," says Mano. "I approached him about it, and he was very reluctant to do the *Playboy* interview. But after some months, he finally agreed."

In the summer of 1993, Mano held three long interviews with Limbaugh—two in the offices of his radio studio, the other behind the set of the television show. "Rush was awfully defensive. He seemed a bit confused. He didn't want to be there, that's for sure," observes Mano. "He knew I was conservative from previous conversations, but he kept saying 'you liberals' during the interviews. Wisely so, because it was *Playboy*'s interview. It was *Playboy*'s tape recorder. He felt that his TV producer, Roger Ailes, had roped him into it, so he was genuinely angry."

After the first interview, Mano, Limbaugh and Limbaugh's right-hand man, Kit Carson, had dinner at Patsy's, a restaurant near the TV studio. "When we went to Patsy's, he was so nice to all the waitresses. They loved having him there," Mano recalls. "He was much more relaxed. He likes to listen when he's not on the air. Kit was very grateful to come along. I don't think he gets to hang out with Rush very often."

But when Mano arrived for the third interview, Limbaugh was in no mood for idle chitchat, the kind that produces the whimsical pronouncements a magazine like *Playboy* likes to exploit. As if his stern expression and terse answers weren't enough, Limbaugh told Mano, "I don't know who asked you to come back, but they're probably not satisfied because it doesn't make me look bad enough in some idiot's eyes at the editorial board."

"What I wanted to learn from him was how much he is controlled by the audience he has created," says Mano. "I wondered if he was open to changing his opinions, or if satisfying that audience, which expects him to be the way he is, was the end-all. I'm not sure that I found that out.

"To him I was *Playboy*, even though often when I would ask one of the questions that *Playboy* insisted I ask—'Have you ever seen a porno movie?' for instance—I would do this," he says, grasping his neck and mock gagging to show disapproval. "Or I'd write a note on a pad: '*Playboy* made me ask it.' *Playboy*, of course, got the tapes, so I couldn't say, 'This is a stupid question, but I have to ask it.' We did have some fun though." To that porno question, Limbaugh said yes: "I had to be 28 or 29. I saw this X-rated movie at the home of a major-league baseball player who shall remain nameless."

He was, at times, his normally boastful self: "I can think of no better place to have views such as mine— which are the epitome of morality and virtue--published than in a magazine such as *Playboy*. It is as that great man Jesus Christ said: 'You go to where the sinners are.' "

On the whole, Mano says, Limbaugh spoke in full paragraphs, with few breaks in thought. "With the porno-movie question, there were lots of errs and ahhs, because he was very uncomfortable," Mano explains. "It was exhausting. The best stuff was about his childhood and love or no love and how he can't be coy. He had a good line in response to one of these questions: 'Nice guys never get laid.'

"But what impressed me most was that he is a very meticulous notetaker. All through the interview, he wrote little notes. He answered questions very carefully. He is a detail man beyond belief," says Mano. "But Rush states conservative positions so that a layman can understand them. And he doesn't let liberals get away with what he calls 'compassion fascism.' Liberals feel insecure about Rush because he is challenging their language, honing in on their rules of debate. Norman Lear would hesitate, Ed Asner would hesitate to go after Rush."

But like the publicist Venema, Mano also describes Limbaugh as being very disarming: "He has a cherubic face. He's a kid who doesn't understand why he can't say what he feels. He's a sentimentalist. He's chivalrous. He's a good person."

Rush told Mano: "I could probably get anybody on the phone I wanted. And I could probably get anybody to go to lunch with me one time, or have a drink." And, indeed, by late 1993, that was likely the case. Limbaugh no longer had to fly to California and spend a few hours with a newspaper reporter in a limousine to get his name in print. But making time for social lunches was another matter. Limbaugh was so busy that he scored his ultimate social coup—meeting Marta Fitzgerald, of Jacksonville, Florida, the woman who would become his wife—on CompuServe, the on-line computer service he uses and promotes. For the most part, Limbaugh successfully kept that part of his private life out of the spotlight.

Meanwhile, *The Way Things Ought to Be* became a huge success. It surpassed *Iacocca* as the best-selling nonfiction book in American history. Regan wanted another. Limbaugh again turned to his friend John Fund, but Fund was busy working on his own book *Cleaning House: America's Campaign for Term Limits*. So Limbaugh called Joseph Farah, the former *Sacramento Union* editor who had once induced Limbaugh to write a column for the paper.

"In 1990 when I was hired to revive this dying paper, we needed a miracle, someone who could capture the imaginations of the American people. He was the obvious choice," says Farah. "After a number of discussions, he said that he wanted to make it happen. Frankly he did it out of the goodness of his heart. We couldn't possibly pay him for his trouble, but we did develop a nice daily column. Essentially, it dealt with what he did on the air the day before. In fact, some days we would take a transcript of his radio show and pick a certain passage and edit it into a column. Other days he would sit down at a computer and send us a near-perfect draft."

Farah left the *Union* in 1991 but stayed in touch with Limbaugh and continued to discuss the possibility of starting a syndicated column. Both were busy, however, and nothing materialized. "Then one day, he called me up out of the blue and asked if I would help with this book," recalls Farah. "I said, 'Sure, of course.' " He flew to New York and spent a brief time with Limbaugh. "He wanted me to move to New York for a few months, but I felt I could accomplish more from Sacramento. It was tempting to hang out with Rush," Farah confesses. "But to get the book done, I had to squirrel myself away.

"He gave me chapter outlines, and I filled in the blanks," says Farah. "He had a very clear idea of what he wanted, and he was easy to work with, accessible. He has an extremely busy schedule, but I could reach him anywhere—at airports, at home, in his car. One day I was listening to the show, and just as I heard that little tune before a commercial, my phone rang. It was Rush. I thought to myself, 'My God, how can he do this? He's not thinking about what he's going to say in 60 seconds.' We chatted briefly, then he said, 'I got to go.' Without missing a breath, he was back on the air.' " Their book, *See I Told You So,* was another home run for Limbaugh.

"Rush is so much a celebrity now," observes John Fund, "that he can't even go shopping. He just can't do it." To relax, Limbaugh goes to places where he can have privacy—such as the "21" Club or to Roger Ailes's country house. Occasionally on business dinners he goes to his other favorite restaurants in New York, like when he and Brent Bozell went to Ruth Chris's Steak House in early 1994.

"There were four of us, and we really ran up the bill, lots of wine, the best steaks and after-dinner drinks," recalls Bozell, who takes credit for introducing Limbaugh to the restaurant chain in Washington, D.C., several years earlier. "At the end of the meal, of course, Rush won the fight as to who was going to pay the bill. When he asked the waiter for the check, the maitre d' came over and said the meal was on the house."

Limbaugh wouldn't accept that. He fought for five minutes, stubbornly refusing the free meal. "Finally," says Bozell, "the maitre d' looked Rush straight in the eye and said: 'If only you knew how much business you have brought this restaurant, Mr. Limbaugh, you would consider it immoral to pay for this dinner.'"

Dinner was on the house.

Women on Rush on Women

"I think he has received a bad rap from women. The women's groups have really done a number on him. As a woman, I don't find him offensive. I would rather have Rush speak for me as a woman than NOW. NOW doesn't speak for me. They don't speak for the majority of women. I am an intelligent human being, and Rush talks to me like an intelligent human being."

—Joyce Adams, Bellaire, Florida

"Living here in California, I'm surrounded by liberals, and Rush has given me a voice to speak what I believe without fear. Even though I still don't tell most of my friends I listen to Rush Limbaugh, I feel stronger and more confident as a conservative than I used to. I didn't like him at first. I thought he was negative towards women, but once I started hearing his political views, then everything else changed. It seemed like his concern for the country was more important. There are times I disagree with him. I don't watch TV very often—but sometimes I'll sit and watch Oprah, and she's had some very good shows. I ordered a transcript from one, and I was going to send it to Rush. It was about how people could get off welfare, and it was perfect. In that case, his lumping all daytime people together is too narrow. I'm not a women's libber at all, but it seems like for him there are two kinds of women: the Femi-Nazis and the stay-at-homes. There's a whole middle-of-the-road woman who's the working mother, who doesn't fit either of those categories. I think he's missing that, yet I do believe he respects women."

—Barbara Naylor, Los Altos, California

"When I was living in Lake Elsinore, California, I started listening to him, and at first I hated him. I thought he was pompous, and I thought he was a jerk. But the more I listened, the more I liked what he had to say. I fell in love with him. The feminists give women a bad name. They don't want to be treated like women, but they don't want to be treated like men, either. If I felt as if I didn't have an equal chance, I would move on. I believe that you do for yourself. Nobody can make me become equal with anybody except for myself. My firm belief is that women, if they work hard, will get where they want to be."

—Paula Pjeza, Huntsville, Alabama

Fourteen

New York, New York!
One Evening on the Air

My husband has everything. When I gave him the tickets to the show, he was so excited. Between Christmas and March 17, he told everyone who would listen that he was going to the Rush Limbaugh show in New York. I haven't seen him that giddy in years.

—Marsha Cothren, Nashville, Tennessee

Mechanical cyclopes spit powerful beams of light. Speakers erupt with the sounds of Limbaugh's spoofs: "Friends don't let friends vote Democratic," "National Bungee Condoms," "Dolphin-free tuna," "Shalala!" The rough edges of the wood-paneled faux studio keep catching your eye.

Suddenly the technicians, who scamper about so calmly in their preparation for national broadcast, making you feel that much more self-conscious, part, and someone recognizes the tall, thin Kit Carson. The electric buzz of the audience—your ninety giddy new friends, well-dressed, of course—comes to a sudden halt. Try as you might, you can't concentrate on looking composed. You are clapping very hard. The moment you have been waiting for is about to arrive.

For all the Rush Rooms and supper clubs, the bake sales and on-line conferences, and the long hours of listening, watching, and reading Limbaugh, only one experience puts the fan in the same room as the man: the filming of his TV show. That accounts for the months-long wait for tickets and the many hours of travel guests are willing to undertake to see one, possibly two, half-hour shows filmed.

"My husband asked me where I wanted to go, anywhere I wanted," says Joyce Adams of Bellaire, Florida, a former White House receptionist to Mrs. Nixon and Mrs. Ford. "I said I wanted to go see the Rush Limbaugh show in New York. It has been so long since the conservatives have had a voice."

"It's rough getting tickets," declares Sue Hollar, an audiologist and mother of two from Saugerties, New York. "You have to catch them at the right time, and you have to have the money to make a lot of long-distance phone calls. You have to keep on trying the ticket line. In February, there was a recording saying after March 17 you could call and get tickets, and I couldn't get through at all."

"This was the second time I had been," says Sue's husband Dave, a thirty-one-year-old computer programmer and church deacon. "The crowd's pretty pumped up. It's like your first at bat in the World Series." Hollar recalls the first time he heard Limbaugh: "I just happened to pick him up on the radio while on vacation in Kansas City. We were driving back to New York in the summer of '91. Rush's humor and ego are done playfully, but it does take a little getting used to. Well, he's in love with himself, but we should all be. I view it in good fun."

In the waiting room before the show, a Kay Bailey Hutchison supporter from Texas chats with some Christine Whitman boosters from New Jersey. Students in University of Alabama-Birmingham and University of Mississippi sweatshirts mingle, and other audience members readily strike up conversations with their new like-minded acquaintances. "Yeah, we love Rush down in Mississippi," says Cody Waters, one of the Old Miss students. "He really motivates us politically. Me and my buddies traveled all the way up here to spend the weekend but mostly to see Rush. I hope we get to meet him. I heard he signs autographs at the end."

At last, it is time to go to the set, which requires a walk down the studio's twisting gray corridors. The cluttered hallways look like a path to some forgotten back entrance and serve as a good reminder to the audience that this is serious business with many parts labor per each part glamour.

Wide-eyed, the audience fills the closely packed seats and takes in the set. The studio is a monument to Limbaugh: bookshelves containing nothing but his books, walls bearing posters of the magazine covers he has graced. An unabashedly un-PC alcove features a leather couch, a bearskin rug, and a mounted deer head given to Limbaugh by Ted Nugent and now wearing a copy of

See, I Told You So around its neck. Production crews zip around preparing for showtime.

Chief of Staff Kit Carson welcomes the crowd and—listing the successes of the Limbaugh phenomenon: "the most listened-to radio show in the world"—begins to pump up the already lively fans. He delivers the requisite instructions and explains the procedures with practiced efficiency: two shows because Friday's is also taped on Thursday; Limbaugh will say hello briefly and then return backstage to be introduced for the camera; no questions or photographs while the cameras are rolling.

Before introducing James Golden, better known as Bo Snerdly, Carson takes questions and comments. Sue Hollar tells the audience that for her, being on the show is a celebration. "I was just involved in a campaign to return Rush to the air in my area," she explains. "Nobody was told he was being taken off. We all either sat down to watch him or were set to tape him, and he wasn't on. Later, the station issued a statement on TV, hoping to get people to stop calling. We were told they couldn't get the rights to air the show anymore. Well, people just kept calling, and petitions were sent around. We badgered them and badgered them, and we won. The next thing we know, he's on the air twice. He was on originally only at 11 o'clock, and now he's on at a decent time, 9:00 and 11:00."

Golden, famous for his off-the-air interruptions of the radio show, which are voiced by Rush—"What's that Mr. Snerdly? You disagree?"—does a short comic routine. A handsome black man with a thin mustache and beard, Golden resembles anything but a "Mr. Snerdly." In fact,

Golden has his own New York talk-radio show, and he's a natural on stage. Now, the audience starts to loosen up, and Golden rolls into a test of the crowd's cheering power. With his encouragement, the volume rises from a sickly nervous din on try one to an unself-conscious roar.

The last warm-up act is CNBC president and Limbaugh TV producer Roger Ailes. The grand old man behind the scenes, Ailes—whose tie is loose, collar open and whose glasses hang from a shirt pocket in stark contrast to the prime-time slickness of Carson and Golden—steals the show. An Old Miss student asks him why Rush's name isn't outside on the awning, like Sally Jessy Raphael's. "To keep crazy liberals from rolling grenades down the hall," he replies. Ailes shoots a few comic arrows at Clinton and then ducks a prescient question concerning rumors that Limbaugh might be getting married, before disappearing behind the set.

The path has been cleared. Limbaugh appears, and the audience rises to its feet, like grade-school students standing for their teacher, only much more enthusiastic. As always, Limbaugh appears thrilled by the exuberant greeting. Then he raises his hands for silence. As if to reinforce the entertainment nature of the show—lest the seriously partisan crowd start thinking too deeply—Limbaugh has a couple of irreverent jokes to tell himself: "A man comes home to find his wife packing her bags," says Limbaugh. " 'Where are you going?' the man asks.

" 'I heard you can make $400 a night for sex in Las Vegas, so I'm going,' she says.

"The man says, '$400 for sex? Wow,' and he too starts packing his bag.

"The wife looks over at him and asks, 'Why are you going? *You* can't make $400 a night.'

" 'I know that.' he says. 'I just want to see you live off $800 a year.' "

The second joke is political: "Bob Packwood, Dan Quayle and Ted Kennedy are in a spelling bee together. Who wins? . . . Dan Quayle. He's the only one who knows *harass* is one word." There is a brief pause while the tumblers click, and then the deep, almost reluctant, hum from the audience. Limbaugh produces a sheepish grin, taking great delight in his un-PC innuendo. He compliments the audience on its fine appearance and behavior and contrasts them to Sally Jessy Raphael's audience: "To get people to go to Sally Jessy's show, they have to find street people who are wearing nothing but a raincoat. As you leave, you will probably see some of her audience asking you for money—so be careful."

When Limbaugh reemerges, this time it is for real. As usual, he basks in the applause and has to ask the crowd to stop. Congress and health care are the primary topics of his St. Patrick's Day show. The clips this evening show Democrat Pete Stark poorly defending the Clinton health-care plan in the Oxford-style debates on the House floor. Stark talks himself into a corner with contradiction while Republicans Bill Thomas and Newt Gingrich clearly relish the situation. During another segment, Limbaugh shows a shot of a sign in Atlanta: "Limbaugh for President in '96." The crowd roars.

Before a commercial break, little animated leprechauns, with the faces of Hillary and Bill Clinton and Leon Panetta, dance across the White House lawn, as Irish music plays. But it is during the commercials that Limbaugh amazes the audience. Instead of poring over notes for his next segment, he tells a lengthy joke that has Hillary and him facing off in an elevator. During another break, he calmly untangles a confusing question about the economy posed by a mortgage broker and then launches into a complex answer. Limbaugh is still answering the question when the producer notifies him that the commercial break is nearly over: seven, six, five, four, three. . . . At two, Limbaugh concludes the answer and turns to face the camera. Never missing a beat, he glides into his next monologue.

"Whenever there was a commercial break, someone blurted out a question," recalls David Hollar. "While the countdown is ticking, Rush is able, first off, to try and figure out what the person's asking because sometimes it's unclear and then to answer the question in a thorough way. And he never loses sight of what's coming up next on the show. It's amazing how Rush is able to multiplex so well."

Joyce Adams agrees. "I have to concentrate on what I am going to say next. Rush stays on top of things. He answered detailed questions from the audience and then went right into the show."

"I'm so used to his TV personality," says Sue Hollar. "I really didn't think he would interact with the audience or be so friendly. He is open and willing to talk. We were impressed that he could suddenly stop and then return to the task. He has a gift. The man is focused and intelligent. If people would give him credit for that, I don't think they'd call us mindless robots either.

"I have to laugh when they call us that," adds Hollar. "Mindless robots aren't able to agree or disagree with other people. It cracks me up, the childlike jokes thrown at the people who watch Rush Limbaugh. If you're going to attack somebody or point out somebody's contradictions or how they've not kept a promise, what's the best way to do it? You back it up with actual videotape of their words. That gives Rush credibility. He doesn't just say, 'Gee, two months ago, so-and-so said this.' He provides evidence and facts. I think it's the honest approach. The point is, he's out there to talk about what's going on in politics, to help people start to think for themselves, which is something we often don't do. We normally just sit back and say, 'Oh, let government do what they want.' To watch Rush, you have to think for yourself."

Before the Friday show is filmed, the audience changes seats to create the illusion of being different. Meanwhile, Limbaugh slips backstage and emerges with a new red, white and blue tie. During the first show, the audience was pumped up, and so was Limbaugh. For the second, the producers ask the audience to act as if they have not already greeted the host and to provide the same level of enthusiasm as the first time. They respond with another boisterous round of applause. But Limbaugh has changed his tone.

He approaches a table behind his desk, and the camera focuses on a replica of a statue created to commemorate the 150th anniversary of the Oregon Trail—a rifle-carrying white settler, his son, holding a Bible, and his wife.

The Portland Art Board has recently rejected the sculpture for not being politically correct. Limbaugh launches into a serious monologue: "This is a microcosm, ladies and gentleman, of exactly what's wrong in America today, our inability to respond and understand, to respect and learn, to treat honestly history. America is a great nation. America is a nation that was founded by great individuals, rugged individuals who were willing to give up their lives for freedom. And what has America become now?"

Limbaugh states that he is amazed at the public's reaction to the Whitewater affair. For every poll showing some Americans think something is being hidden from them and that President and Mrs. Clinton might have done something wrong, he says, you find stories that say the average American doesn't care, it doesn't matter to them. People don't seem to care, he reasons, because they expect something from the Clinton Administration, and as long as that promise is met or people believe it will be met, they don't care about anything else--not even the integrity of the office of the *President* of the United States of America.

"We have evolved into a society of producers and takers," expounds the commentator. "We have too many people in this country who don't care about the integrity, character, honesty of their leaders. We have people who think that America owes them something, and there are more of these people than you think . . . I'm talking about people born in this country who have not been educated properly to understand just what this country is all about, how it came to be and how it is in the process of losing its greatness."

At the end of the intense monologue, the audience, sensing it has just heard one of Limbaugh's most heartfelt and powerful addresses, cheers him spontaneously. During the break, the audience is silent, and Limbaugh looks over at the producers and says, "Sorry, Dick, I just felt compelled to do that." Then he asks one of the production assistants, "How many minutes do we have left?" The answer is a little more than six.

"The Friday show was great," declares Mercedes Jones, a twenty-five-year-old paralegal who flew up from Birmingham, Alabama, for the show. "It was just Rush and something that impassioned him. He's one of the few who really talks about what impassions him. We're so used to the Joe Six-Pack mentality, electing people who are later indicted, doing things without thinking first. Now you've got someone who makes you think, and at times you might get mad at him, like you got angry at your hardest college professor, who made you work and think. Then you realize he's the one who taught you the most, and you're very grateful.

"He's very down-to-earth, no matter what you hear about him," adds Jones. "His media persona is bulldogish. He turns people on or off; that's his job. Rush is not arrogant around the people that he works with. He has a good personality, and he seems to have good relationships. People respect him and work hard for him."

"There is a different attitude on the Rush Limbaugh show than there is on most TV sets," concurs Al Hacker, who attended the show with Jones. "His staff is very kind and courteous and helpful, and it's a great crowd."

After the second show, Limbaugh approaches the audience. The crowd starts forming a line before Carson can announce that Limbaugh only has time to sign books, his books: "No arms, legs or other body parts. No shirts, shoes, children or other paraphernalia."

While he signs away, Limbaugh chats with the audience. "I got to meet Rush," says High Point, North Carolina, native Jerry Highfill, who had planned an antiques shopping trip to Manhattan with his wife, Jenny, after scoring Limbaugh and Letterman tickets. "That was more of a thrill than just being in the Letterman audience. We've listened to Rush for about two years. The people who run Christian radio were bitter about the election, whereas Rush wasn't happy that Clinton won, but he wasn't bad-mouthing him, per se. He had a more Christian attitude. Like most people who call in, I agree with Rush 98.9 percent of the time."

"I told him a joke," relates Jenny Highfill, who is confined to a wheelchair. "I told him that if he was ever going to get married again, that he should marry a woman in a wheelchair because he wants a very strong woman, and women in wheelchairs are the strongest because of all the stuff we have to put up with. Plus, when you go to bed at night, you don't have to worry. We won't be heading to the kitchen and getting a knife. He loved it. He laughed and said that was very funny. We were the last ones there," says Highfill. "It was very exciting."

Fifteen

Run, Rush, Run!

The day he got the fax [telling him about the formation of the National Presidential Committee to Draft Rush in '96], I was watching the show to see if there was any difference, and I could detect an increased excitement and energy in Rush. The next day I think it really started to sink in that there was a potential grassroots movement underway. And for the next three or four days, Rush was pumped up. He hammered Clinton. And then he looked at the TV—and I think he was looking right at us—and he said, 'But I'm not a candidate.' I'll tell you what: he looked, acted and sounded like he was.

—Larry Deraps, president, NPCDR '96

Although Rush Limbaugh has stated in no uncertain terms that he is uninterested in running for elected office, there are some who believe that will change; among them are Larry Deraps and Don Fortmeyer, two TWA ramp workers at St. Louis's Lambert Field Airport, who don't seem to be able to take no for an answer—not even from Limbaugh himself.

For Deraps and Fortmeyer, whose daily work begins at 6:15 A.M., the political crusade started in the spring of 1993 during a work break. As Deraps tells it, his work buddy and political soul mate Don Fortmeyer, whom Deraps had introduced to Limbaugh's show a year earlier, suggested they form a committee to draft the broadcaster to run for president.

"The media wants to peg Rush as an entertainer not as a political figure," says Fortmeyer. "I don't think that's correct. I think his political ideas and his straightforward thinking are better suited for leading this country than what we now have."

Deraps, age forty-three, and the forty-year-old Fortmeyer became buddies in 1982, when they met while working for Ozark Airlines. Both had graduated from St. Louis's Florissant Community College, and both signed on with TWA when it bought Ozark in 1986. But what made the two members of I.A.M. (International Association of Machinists and Aerospace Workers) stand together virtually alone was their politics.

"They're blue-collar Democrats," states Deraps, referring to his fellow I.A.M. members. "Probably 70 percent vote straight union recommendation," he says. "We get into some heated arguments at work when subjects like entrepreneurialism and capitalism come up. Larry and I normally end up surrounded by 10 or 12 people who don't see eye to eye with us. They blame everything that has ever happened bad in the workplace—and the airline industry has really taken a hit—on Republicans and big business."

Although Deraps and Fortmeyer have limited political experience, they could clearly see that the Republican Party was floundering in the wake of the Clinton victory and that it needed fresh leadership. "Who knows where the party sits right now?" questions Deraps, who has also recently helped organize and lead Missouri chapters of the Christian Coalition. "They're wrestling with where they want to be. Do they want to be wishy-washy and try to appeal to everybody like Bush did? Or are they going to restart the Reagan Revolution, reuniting the coalition of evangelicals, Republicans and conservative Democrats?

"In Missouri after the November election, the political landscape changed dramatically," recalls Deraps. "All our conservative friends were swept out of office, and we decided we had to get busy and do something. So I got in touch with the Christian Coalition and started a chapter in St. Charles County." But that was just the beginning.

Deraps and Fortmeyer saw only one person who could get the job done on a national level, one person who they believed had both popular appeal and unwavering conservative principles: Rush Limbaugh. Quite simply, he was the man they wanted to make the next president of the United States.

Although they had never been politically active at a national level, Deraps and Fortmeyer were inspired by Limbaugh's rapid rise in popularity. "It was growing in leaps and bounds, and we realized we weren't the only ones that listened to Rush," says Fortmeyer, a deer hunter whose previous political work had been primarily for the Second Amendment Coalition of Missouri. "His popularity was such that if somebody organized, similar to Ross Perot, people would jump on the bandwagon. We figured it might as well be us."

So they called the Federal Election Commission (FEC) in Washington and found out that, despite the numerous "Rush for President" bumper stickers to be seen across the country, no one had officially started the process to elect Limbaugh to the office. Deraps requested the necessary forms, which he filled out and submitted by mail. But, when he called to follow up, the forms had been mysteriously misplaced.

"They couldn't find a record of the application, so I sent them a copy," says an incredulous Deraps. "They still couldn't find it." A determined man—and an airline worker—Deraps knew just what to do. He and his ten-year-old adopted son Jonathan hopped on the next TWA flight to D.C. for a day of patriotic sight-seeing. While they were there, they hand-delivered the application.

Deraps and Fortmeyer received good news from Washington postmarked June 26, 1993. Their "unauthorized political committee supporting only Rush Limbaugh III," as their press release would call it, had received FEC recognition, Federal ID number: C00281774. Enthusiastically, Deraps became the official treasurer and Fortmeyer the assistant treasurer of the National Presidential Committee to Draft Rush in '96 (NPCDR '96). The two wasted no time in producing a press release to coincide with the Fourth of July weekend.

Meanwhile, Deraps faxed Rush, telling him that the

FEC had recognized their committee and that they were going to announce its formation. The letter asked for any suggestions the Limbaugh camp might have on the wording of the announcement.

"The day he got the fax, I was watching the show to see if there was any difference," remembers Deraps, suddenly becoming inspired, "and I could detect an increased excitement and energy in Rush. The next day I think it really started to sink in that there was a potential grassroots movement underway. And for the next three or four days, Rush was pumped up. He hammered Clinton. And then he looked at the TV—and I think he was looking right at us—and he said, 'But I'm not a candidate.' I'll tell you what: he looked, acted and sounded like he was."

Officially, however, the fax to Limbaugh went unanswered. "I think it took them by surprise," admits Deraps. "This was only six months into the Clinton Administration. It was a little early to be discussing presidential candidates."

In an August 16, 1993, interview with *U.S. News & World Report,* however, Limbaugh responded to the question of whether or not he might enter politics with a witty—if somewhat disingenuous—dose of reality: "The countryside is strewn with the carcasses of many media types who thought they could get elected. Ten percent makes you No. 1 in the media, [but] 10 percent and you're a laughingstock in politics."

The Limbaugh organization wasn't the only one to turn a cold shoulder to the Rush for President committee. Deraps and Fortmeyer sent out 150 press releases to TV, radio, and print media announcing the committee and the "Gold Rush to 1996" essay contest, which called for entrants to write a short essay on why Rush would be a good president. In the release, Deraps and Fortmeyer clearly stated the committee's raison d'être: "Our goal is to notify Rush's 20 million fans of the exciting prospect of him being a front-running presidential contender. . . . Although Rush has stated he does not want to be President (for the time being), I believe he really does and is planning his possible entry into politics even now! He cannot do it alone, he needs our help. . . . That is why we formed the NPCDR '96."

Borrowing the tone of their champion's sometimes antic pronouncements, they concluded the letter with a call for donations to the committee and proudly declared: "Contributions are not tax-deductible for federal income-tax purposes but are considered highly patriotic and vital for the national security of the United States."

Unfortunately for them, the announcement did not get wide play. At the time, most of the world still wanted to give the new Administration a chance, and Clinton was in the process of making his first overseas venture, an important trip to Japan. The press release was almost universally shunned, although *National Review* editor Rich Lowry gave them a brief mention in a piece he wrote about Limbaugh for the voluminous *Washington Times* periodical *The World and I.* Lowry added credibility to the prospect when he wrote, "At first Limbaugh for President seems absurd—a man who has made a career of providing ammunition for opposition researchers and who has no political experience. But after watching

Buchanan—who has a similar résumé—and Ross Perot shake up American politics last year, who knows?" In a caption, Lowry wonders: "Rush, the VIP, sat next to Marilyn Quayle during the 1992 Republican Convention, but will he be standing behind the podium in '96?"

Although the reception was less than encouraging, Deraps and Fortmeyer remained undaunted. When the S & P Oyster Co. in the town of St. Charles opened Missouri's first Rush Room in November, they attended the opening-day ceremonies in "Rush for President" T-shirts (their slogan: "A Good American, a Great President, Rush Limbaugh in '96") and handed out their literature to the receptive crowd of close to one hundred. James Keough, a local businessman who helped organize and promote the Rush Room and who doled out Limbaugh T-shirts, mugs, and caps that day, met Deraps and Fortmeyer but remained skeptical. "The best place Rush can be right now is on the radio educating," he insists. "Maybe later when he has done his job, and there is a wave of spin-offs, 10 or 15 other Rush's out there, and Rush is in his late 50s, let's put him in control then."

Having only personal funds to work with, Deraps and Fortmeyer postponed plans to start a newsletter. Instead, they began to plan a spring fund-raiser. Fortmeyer wrote to Jack Jolley, the outdoor sign promoter who had helped publicize Dan's Bake Sale, to see if he might donate advertising space. With the help of Limbaugh's radio announcements and these signs, Dan's Bake Sale had attracted a huge crowd, proving the phenomenal impact Limbaugh was having. Ever optimistic, Fortmeyer and Deraps figured that, being located in the more populous

St. Louis area, they could double that turnout—especially if Limbaugh were to make an appearance.

But instead of responding positively to their request, Jolley passed the letter on to Limbaugh, according to Deraps, and Kit Carson, Limbaugh's right-hand man, promptly called Fortmeyer.

"He was very zealous in protecting his boss," remarks Deraps. "It kind of intimidated Don. It took him by surprise, a phone call out of the blue and here Kit Carson was jumping down his throat. 'Who are you guys and what are you trying to do?' "

"I would have thought he'd be a little more cordial," Fortmeyer relates. "I felt like it was the FBI with hot lights. He grilled me: 'Why are you doing it? Are you in it just for personal gain? Haven't you heard that Rush said he doesn't ever want to run for a political office?' It was a pretty one-sided conversation," confesses Fortmeyer with a wry laugh, obviously still bruised from the bullying. "As soon as I got one answer out, he was on to the next question."

At the end of the exchange, Carson suggested that Fortmeyer halt the effort. "I think the reason is we're kind of outside of Rush's realm of control," speculates Deraps. "We're a wild card. And I think that probably made him uncomfortable with what we are trying to do."

"I don't see a political career in it for myself," reasons Fortmeyer, having mulled over the conversation for more than a month. "That never crossed my mind. We just thought we would get some things going. A draft movement is to get people stirred up and excited."

After some careful reflection, however, Deraps and Fortmeyer decided not to be offended. "Larry and I sat down and talked about it and figured, well, what are they up to? Maybe they're just worried we're up to no good or something," says Fortmeyer. "I guess Carson's got to protect Rush," he concedes. "There are a lot of people out there who might try to take advantage of Rush's popularity. That had never crossed my mind until he called."

"We've been at this too long. We're not ready to fold up and go away," says Deraps, now with a defiant tone devoid of any echoes of hero worship. "Whenever anyone presses Rush about running for president, he says, 'Ah, I can't afford to take the pay cut.' But anyone who has made $32 million in the past two years can afford to take a pay cut. To people looking for strong conservative leadership, that's not a serious statement. He talks like a leader, but he hasn't taken that step. We want Rush, who says he is a man of principles, to establish these firmly in the upcoming presidential election, to help shape policies and platforms."

Now Deraps, goading the would-not-be politician Limbaugh, pushes home his point: "Right now people would just dismiss him as being a comedian—a fat, funny guy with a TV show—and would not take him seriously in the political arena. If he is a presidential candidate, well, then the man has been elevated somewhat. We're just trying to do that."

"We are not discouraged," insists Fortmeyer. "We still think that Rush would make an excellent candidate and president. No one else in the Republican Party is stepping forward and taking the lead."

So what's the next step for this committee to draft a reluctant—and, yes, necessarily circumspect—leader?

For one thing, Deraps and Fortmeyer would like to revive their "Gold Rush to 1996" essay contest, so named because the prizes are several lots of California mining acreage donated by Fortmeyer, who claimed the land himself using an obscure 1872 federal mining law. Originally from California's Simi Valley (home of the Reagan library), Fortmeyer staked out thirteen-hundred acres of San Bernardino County property in 1991 after studying government maps for six months. According to the law, he had to find minerals on the property, survey it, and research county records to make sure no other claims existed. He succeeded. With the fledgling Draft Rush campaign in need of assets, Fortmeyer, who supports his family on a salary of less than $35,000 a year, donated 1,000 acres, all accessible to an interstate, in what he describes as horse-and-ski country.

In addition to the contest, Deraps and Fortmeyer still plan to sponsor a fund-raising event. While organizing such an event is new territory for the two political novices, their end goals remain simple and clear. "We want to collect signatures across the country that will show Rush there are 20 million people that will vote for him," states Fortmeyer. "Once we get going, we hope to attract experienced handlers to help us along." Or, if Limbaugh then files himself, they would consider their work done. "Once there is an official committee by the candidate, then there can be no other official draft committees," says Fortmeyer. Of course, Fortmeyer and Deraps see that as a win-win situation.

"We haven't been very noticeable yet. If anything, we've just been a blip on the radar screen," says Deraps, who believes that if the Draft Rush committee could go directly to Limbaugh supporters, it would ignite a grass-roots movement that would empower the broadcaster and his conservative principles. "What we are lacking is finances to buy time on the radio."

Of course, easy access to the crucial airwaves lies in the hands of Limbaugh and his advisors. And before they consider giving air time to the Draft Rush committee, Limbaugh must make the fateful decision to seek office, or at least to strongly consider seeking office should the ground swell mount. A *yes* to that would both jeopardize his lucrative broadcasting business and expose him to all the scrutiny and vituperation his liberal enemies can bring to bear.

But Deraps counters: "He knows he has a lot of people out here who will work for him if he decides to run. He has to decide if it's time. Is the populace really yearning for someone who has his qualities and principles? This is what he has to wrestle with. We are hoping that he will decide that it is. He is the type of person who can be a great leader if he chooses to be."

For now, Deraps rationalizes Limbaugh's rejection of the committee as a matter of political necessity. "When the discussion gets around to presidential aspirations, he backs off. He is leaving his options open," notes Deraps. "If this thing really starts to gain momentum and he decides to opt out, he can still say, 'Listen, I don't know these folks. And I didn't put them up to it.' And that's the fact."

It is true that Limbaugh is cagey on the subject. When asked by James Bowman, reporting for *National Review,* "Are there *any* circumstances in which he would be a candidate?" Limbaugh responded, "Maybe, but I don't know what they are. . . . I have said never to this—never, ever, I don't want to do it. And I don't. . . . Primarily because, to do it, to be elected to anything, you have to walk around like this—with your hand out. And you have to beg people to put something in it. Somebody always does, and they want repayment. And not with dollars. It's going to be with your soul. . . . I don't look at it as fun."

To Deraps the operative word in all of that was the first: "maybe." He reads between the lines and sees the cards already falling into place. "There has been a national spokesperson for conservatives as far back as I can remember," he observes. "When I was young, I knew that Barry Goldwater was Mr. Conservative. And then it was Ronald Reagan. And he passed the torch over to Rush. There are a lot of similarities between Reagan and Rush. Reagan got his start in radio. Rush got his start in radio. Reagan went on to do movies. Rush has graduated to TV. Both have Roger Ailes as a close friend, confidant and adviser. It's no coincidence, in my opinion, that he has Ailes sitting in his back room guiding and shaping his career, his political thought, his political philosophy. I think Rush is being groomed for presidential politics."

Deraps may be right. Ailes, himself, when asked by Lowry whether he thought Limbaugh would make a good president, responded, "Absolutely. He's a great communicator and a great thinker." And on a May 1994 television show, two weeks after a tabloid had reported that extraterrestrials were urging Limbaugh to run for president, the commentator spotted a sign in the crowd: "Get a shot of that sign," he told the camera crew. "Keep holding it up. It says, 'Now is the time for all Dittoheads to unite in order to nominate Rush Limbaugh as candidate for president in 1996.' . . . Are you guys affiliated with *The Weekly World News* and the aliens I met with?" Limbaugh joked. "That I thought were Sally Jessy Raphael at first and insulted 'em when we first got together?

"Anyway, it's very kind of you," said Limbaugh. "I knew this was going to happen—there were going to be all kinds of draft Rush movements out there. Can't stop 'em. Don't intend to. These are good, decent American citizens making this movement come alive."

In the meantime, two good, decent American citizens, two blue-collar conservatives from Limbaugh's home state, will try to groom America for President Rush Limbaugh.

If there is one thing Deraps and Fortmeyer do understand about politics, it's that you can't win the game if you don't play. They remain deeply committed to Limbaugh and his ideals—so committed, in fact, that they're willing to take the heat to provide a mandate. That mandate, if they have their way, will mean that Limbaugh retransforms the Republican Party and leads it unflinchingly into the next presidential race.

His fans simply demand it.

Would You Vote for Limbaugh for President?

"It's entertaining to have turmoil on radio. The disagreement adds a spark to the program, but that's hard to do in politics. In some cases, it's better to sit back and do a little more listening and not be so judgmental immediately. He sets himself up for an argument every time. Would I support him? Well, I probably would."
— Michael Bernache, Mishawaka, Indiana

"I support Rush in anything he would do, and I think he would be tremendous if he ran. But in order to run for office, you have to make a lot of compromises, and I don't know if Rush could bring himself to play that game. It sounds funny for somebody who agrees with most everything Rush says to say that, but I just don't see the political process as holding the answers for this world. I think the answer is in Jesus Christ. I'm honestly not that political. I agree with Rush in that people's hearts have to be changed. If you change people's hearts, you almost don't need political systems, but that doesn't seem to be the way the wind is blowing these days."
— Paul Westphal, coach, Phoenix Suns, Arizona

"In my mind—I guess I look at it from a very strict standard—a viable candidate is somebody who can be a viable office holder, and I don't believe he can be. I think he'd go nuts. Being an office holder takes a different or additional set of skills than being a spokesperson. George Will and William F. Buckley are very good commentators on issues of the day. They help articulate and define those issues, but that doesn't mean they'd be good in office or good at running for office. Running for office is a lot of chicken dinners and a lot of grunt work, and I don't see Rush Limbaugh doing that. Nor do I happen to think that's where the best use of his talent lies."

—John Hiler, former Indiana Republican congressman
      and Deputy Administrator of the General Services
      Administration under George Bush

"He has said that he has no interest whatsoever in being in the political arena, so I believe what he says to be true. If it changed, then I would have an opinion. Right now I don't because he said he's never going to be involved. He's a radio commentator, and that's his job, and that's what we base our opinions on—what he's doing now."

—Barbara Wells, National Director,
      Teenage Republicans,
      Manassas, Virginia

"Certainly I would consider it. If he were in a primary with Jack Kemp, I don't know. A lot of me says, 'Absolutely,' but another part of me says, 'The entertainment side of Rush does not lend itself to his being very presidential.' Although when he was at Fort Collins, he spoke so eloquently. He is extremely intelligent. You can tell by his vocabulary. I hate to beat around the bush. I guess my answer would have to be, I would not rule it out."

—Richard Hood, Monroe, Louisiana

"I would support Rush if he ran for office. However, I think that he has other plans. He believes he is more powerful right now being on the radio promoting the conservative agenda than actually being in office. If he does run for office, I will be his first supporter."

—Jesse Binnall, Rancho Cucamonga, California

"There are so many people out there who have misguided skulls full of mush. They still watch Sally Jessy and Oprah, Geraldo and Donahue, and the rest of these idiots who are brainwashing them. And the president, no matter who he is, all he gets is a sound bite here and there. Rush knows how to maximize his effect on the American people. When he is ready to run for president, I will be for him. Until then, I am for whatever he thinks he should do. I tell you the one thing I am for, and that's a one-hour television show."

—James Keough, St. Charles, Missouri

"They say that after great wealth, there is only power. Rush has more power than a president of the United States could ever hope to have. The only thing that Rush doesn't have the power to do that a chief executive does is to turn out the militia. Rush can do everything else. Talk radio in the '90s is the most powerful political tool ever invented, in my opinion. But if Rush ran for president, you bet I'd vote for him."

—Jay Murrell, Shreveport, Louisiana

"He's so effective as an entertainer and political pundit. His message and his impact would be much diminished if he went out and gladhanded for votes. I admire him because he tells it like it is. He's not afraid of liberals; he's not afraid of anybody. That fearlessness is something thoroughly lacking, at the very least, in the Republican Party. What he does now has made him powerful and prominent. To trade that for the pain, the trouble and the lower income of campaigning for office would be the wrong career path for him."

—Kevin Pritchett, Washington, D.C.

"Oh, I'd hate to see him do that. He's above it. I just think it'd spoil it all. I'd rather see him advising in a cabinet post or something like that. I think he's too fine a person."

—Jean Smith, Boise, Idaho

Afterword

The American People Care

by Charlton Heston

Astute astronomers of all political persuasions have tracked in awe and anger the blazing course of the comet Limbaugh across the skies. In his tumultuous passage, he's illuminated conservative issues and shriveled liberal icons to blackened cinders. Friends and foes alike seem able to agree only on the undeniable: Rush Limbaugh's overwhelming success.

His radio show, which he broadcasts singlehandedly to (at last count) 640 stations for fifteen hours a week, reaches more than twenty-million listeners from Moscow to Tierra del Fuego, many of whom tape his airborne wisdom when they can't savor it live.

His nightly television show is carried by some 250 stations across the country, in some areas outrating David Letterman, Jay Leno, and Ted Koppel.

His monthly newsletter, *The Limbaugh Letter,* has more than 450,000 subscribers, making it the best-selling political newsletter in the country. Princess Diana he is not, but his face on any magazine cover, from *National Review* to *U.S. News & World Report*, usually makes that issue the magazine's all-time best-seller.

In the midst of all this, he's written two books. The first, *The Way Things Ought to Be*, struck a national nerve, becoming the biggest-selling nonfiction book in the history of American publishing, eclipsing the memoirs of presidents, generals, and those rock stars who can write. The second book is fittingly titled *See, I Told You So;* together, the two have sold more than seven-million copies—so far.

All this, of course, merely defines the phenomenon, not the man. Certainly others have tried to do more, with uncertain success. The leading conservative voices of our time—Bill Buckley, Bill Rusher, Bill Bennett (Why are so many conservatives called Bill?) and Bob Tyrrell—have pontificated with their usual fluency on both Limbaugh's function and future, without throwing a lot of light on their subject.

The dominant liberal media's response to Rush Limbaugh's tsunami of popularity has been largely an exercise in damage control. They try to marginalize Limbaugh by defining him as a sort of maverick pop phenomenon, like Madonna or Michael Jackson, denying him any significance in the real world.

Elected officeholders of both parties have been even more circumspect. Democrats are afraid of his popularity and generally just grumble the occasional platitude: "He shouldn't be allowed to speak of the First Lady like that."

The President, his instincts honed in his previous persona as "Slick Willy," has largely avoided comment.

President Reagan, on the other hand, with no need to prove anything further, has graciously passed his mantle as the "Great Communicator" to Limbaugh, though I suspect his own laurels still gleam undimmed in his study—and the hearts of his countrymen.

The elected GOP giants have applauded generously, but their comments are careful, perhaps because nobody really knows what's going on. Who is Rush Limbaugh, and what does he want?

I don't pretend any insight into "the real Rush," but I think I can understand something of what he's going through. I don't think he wants to be president, or indeed hold any public office. I think he's content just where he is. Overriding a hostile media, he has established for himself a "bully pulpit" reaching far deeper into the national consciousness than the one Teddy Roosevelt defined before the electronic age could put a man's opinions into every household, every commuter's car.

In passing, Rush has also picked up a large segment of the Geraldo/Oprah/Donahue audience, but while they're talking about cross-dressing and the prevalence of witches, he's addressing the national agenda—a profound difference. These shows, and dozens of wanna-bes, deal essentially in psycho popcorn; Rush is talking about the country, what it was in the beginning, what it should be as the century turns. To the amazement of culture mavens and decision-makers on both coasts, the American people care about this.

I believe Rush Limbaugh is firmly rooted in the bedrock

of American populism. One of those wise old dead white guys who invented this country, Thomas Jefferson, the only genius ever to occupy the White House, defined it: "The government governs best that governs least." You can't put it better than that. Weighed against that simple dictum, the 1,342 pages of Mrs. Clinton's health plan, for example, sink like a stone.

The instinct of those who govern is always for more power. It brought down republican Rome; it threatens our democracy. That's the basis of Mr. Jefferson's maxim. Andrew Jackson understood it, so did Lincoln and Reagan; yet none of them was able to prevail against it, surrounded as they were by a growing army of bureaucrats intent on a government that controls everything and everyone. Now, a decade after the events of George Orwell's prescient novel *1984,* we live in a society where many things are already unsayable, many distortions of justice mandated. Having destroyed communism, we are about to be swallowed by socialism. That's the clarion call Rush Limbaugh is sounding.

He speaks, as Reagan and Lincoln did before him, to the solid core of the American people. As did both of them, Limbaugh uses humor. The liberal has no time for humor; restructuring the economy, while saving the salamander and the spotted owl, funding the aberrant artist and destroying the philistine is serious work, certainly nothing to laugh about. Making America laugh at the liberals is no mean achievement.

One man has done it before him; he also won national popularity and, I think, is Rush Limbaugh's role model, conscious or otherwise: Will Rogers. He sprang from the same middle-class Midwestern roots and has the same down-home appeal and common sense. When Will Rogers said, "I never have belonged to an organized political party—I've been a Democrat all my life," he got the same kind of rueful laugh Rush gets with his gibes. Laughter is a powerful tool in public debate. I nominate Rush Limbaugh as the Will Rogers for our time. I can think of no better analogy, nor finer compliment.

About the Authors

D. Howard King is the founding editor of *Bubba Magazine* and the former director of book publishing at *National Review.* He is the author of two other books and his articles have appeared in *Forbes Media Critic, Men's Journal,* and *The New York Times.*

Currently an editor at *Reader's Digest,* **Geoffrey Morris** is the former executive editor of *National Review.*

INFORMATIVE –
COMPELLING –
SCINTILLATING –
NON-FICTION FROM PINNACLE TELLS THE TRUTH!

BORN TOO SOON   (751, $4.50)
by Elizabeth Mehren
This is the poignant story of Elizabeth's daughter Emily's pre-
mature birth. As the parents of one of the 275,000 babies born pre-
maturely each year in this country, she and her husband were
plunged into the world of the Neonatal Intensive Care unit. With
stunning candor, Elizabeth Mehren relates her gripping story of
unshakable faith and hope – and of courage that comes in tiny
little packages.

THE PROSTATE PROBLEM   (745, $4.50)
by Chet Cunningham
An essential, easy-to-use guide to the treatment and prevention of
the illness that's in the headlines. This book explains in clear, prac-
tical terms all the facts. Complete with a glossary of medical terms,
and a comprehensive list of health organizations and support
groups, this illustrated handbook will help men combat prostate
disorder and lead longer, healthier lives.

THE ACADEMY AWARDS HANDBOOK   (887, $4.50)
An interesting and easy-to-use guide for movie fans everywhere,
the book features a year-to-year listing of all the Oscar nomina-
tions in every category, all the winners, an expert analysis of who
wins and why, a complete index to get information quickly, and
even a 99% foolproof method to pick this year's winners!

WHAT WAS HOT   (894, $4.50)
by Julian Biddle
Journey through 40 years of the trends and fads, famous and infa-
mous figures, and momentous milestones in American history.
From hoola hoops to rap music, greasers to yuppies, Elvis to Madonna – it's all here, trivia for all ages. An entertaining and evoca-
tive overview of the milestones in America from the 1950's to the
1990's!

*Available wherever paperbacks are sold, or order direct from the
Publisher. Send cover price plus 50¢ per copy for mailing and handling to Penguin USA, P.O. Box 999, c/o Dept. 17109, Bergenfield, NJ 07621. Residents of New York and Tennessee must
include sales tax. DO NOT SEND CASH.*

PINNACLE BOOKS HAS
SOMETHING FOR EVERYONE—

MAGICIANS, EXPLORERS, WITCHES AND CATS

THE HANDYMAN   (377-3, $3.95/$4.95)
He is a magician who likes hands. He likes their comfortable shape and weight and size. He likes the portability of the hands once they are severed from the rest of the ponderous body. Detective Lanark must discover who The Handyman is before more handless bodies appear.

PASSAGE TO EDEN   (538-5, $4.95/$5.95)
Set in a world of prehistoric beauty, here is the epic story of a courageous seafarer whose wanderings lead him to the ends of the old world—and to the discovery of a new world in the rugged, untamed wilderness of northwestern America.

BLACK BODY   (505-9, $5.95/$6.95)
An extraordinary chronicle, this is the diary of a witch, a journal of the secrets of her race kept in return for not being burned for her "sin." It is the story of Alba, that rarest of creatures, a white witch: beautiful and able to walk in the human world undetected.

THE WHITE PUMA   (532-6, $4.95/NCR)
The white puma has recognized the men who deprived him of his family. Now, like other predators before him, he has become a man-hater. This story is a fitting tribute to this magnificent animal that stands for all living creatures that have become, through man's carelessness, close to disappearing forever from the face of the earth.

Available wherever paperbacks are sold, or order direct from the Publisher. Send cover price plus 50¢ per copy for mailing and handling to Penguin USA, P.O. Box 999, c/o Dept. 17109, Bergenfield, NJ 07621.Residents of New York and Tennessee must include sales tax. DO NOT SEND CASH.

FUN AND LOVE!

THE DUMBEST DUMB BLONDE JOKE BOOK   (889, $4.50)
by Joey West
They say that blondes have more fun . . . but we can all have a hoot
with THE DUMBEST DUMB BLONDE JOKE BOOK. Here's a
hilarious collection of hundreds of dumb blonde jokes — including
dumb blonde GUY jokes — that are certain to send you over the
edge!

THE I HATE MADONNA JOKE BOOK   (798, $4.50)
by Joey West
She's Hollywood's most controversial star. Her raunchy reputation's brought her fame and fortune. Now here is a sensational collection of hilarious material on America's most talked about
MATERIAL GIRL!

LOVE'S LITTLE INSTRUCTION BOOK   (774, $4.99)
by Annie Pigeon
Filled from cover to cover with romantic hints — one for every day
of the year — this delightful book will liven up your life and make
you and your lover smile. Discover these amusing tips for making
your lover happy . . . tips like — ask her mother to dance — have his
car washed — take turns being irrational . . . and many, many
more!

MOM'S LITTLE INSTRUCTION BOOK   (0009, $4.99)
by Annie Pigeon
Mom needs as much help as she can get, what with chaotic sched-
ules, wedding fiascos, Barneymania and all. Now, here comes the
best mother's helper yet. Filled with funny comforting advice for
moms of all ages. What better way to show mother how very much
you love her by giving her a gift guaranteed to make her smile
everyday of the year.

*Available wherever paperbacks are sold, or order direct from the
Publisher. Send cover price plus 50¢ per copy for mailing and handling to Penguin USA, P.O. Box 999, c/o Dept. 17109, Bergenfield, NJ 07621. Residents of New York and Tennessee must
include sales tax. DO NOT SEND CASH.*